AMERICAN SPORT

A DOCUMENTARY HISTORY

Peter Levine

History Department
Michigan State University

PRENTICE HALL
Englewood Cliffs, New Jersey 07632

Library of Congress Cataloging-in-Publication Data

Levine, Peter.
   American sport : a documentary history / Peter Levine.
      p.   cm.
   Bibliography: p.
   Includes index.
   ISBN 0-13-031378-5
   1. Sports--United States--History--Sources.   I. Title.
GV583.L478 1988
796'.0973--dc19   88-28988
                                                              CIP

Editorial/production supervision and
   interior design: Teresa Carriero
Cover design: 20/20 Services, Inc.
Manufacturing buyer: Ed O'Dougherty

 © 1989 by Prentice-Hall, Inc.
A Division of Simon & Schuster
Englewood Cliffs, New Jersey 07632

Printed in the United States of America

10 9 8 7 6 5 4 3 2 1

ISBN 0-13-031378-5

Prentice-Hall International (UK) Limited, *London*
Prentice-Hall of Australia Pty. Limited, *Sydney*
Prentice-Hall Canada Inc., *Toronto*
Prentice-Hall Hispanoamericana, S.A., *Mexico*
Prentice-Hall of India Private Limited, *New Delhi*
Prentice-Hall of Japan, Inc., *Tokyo*
Simon & Schuster Asia Pte. Ltd., *Singapore*
Editora Prentice-Hall do Brasil, Ltda., *Rio de Janeiro*

Acknowledgment is gratefully made for permission to use material from the following
sources:

The excerpt from *Virginia Magazine of History and Biography* is reprinted by permission of
Virginia Magazine of History and Biography.

"Journal and Letters of Philip Vickers Fithian, 1773-74" is reprinted by permission of *Colonial
Williamsburg*.

These acknowledgments are continued on page (200), which constitutes an extension of the copyright page.

FOR RUTHIE

CONTENTS

PREFACE

On Friday morning, April 15, 1804, as they had for over 100 years, the people of St. Peter's Parish met their neighbors of All Saints parish at the town square in East Mousley, England, to welcome Good Friday with a traditional game of football. Dressed in their everyday clothes, hundreds of men, women, and children filled up on cider and ale, devoured local treats, and shared gossip as part of the celebration of this annual Christian holiday.

Eventually the "game" began. Residents of each parish, joined by holidayers from the countryside, gathered on either side of a large cow bladder stuffed with cork shavings placed at the center of the square. The object of the game was to see which group could push the bladder, by any means possible, past the other parish's "goal". For the pride of St. Peter's, this meant moving the slippery object some two miles east to the mill pond that defined the boundary line of All Saints parish. For the stalwarts of All Saints, the goal was to push the bladder two miles to the west to the St. Peter's parish church. Without benefit of formal rules, uniforms, spectators, or a predetermined time limit, the game raged for two days and two nights—intermittently stopped by the vissicitudes of weather, nature's call, and the drunken state of the "players." At times the number of people of both sexes and all ages on each side went as high as 300, although no one kept count nor demanded that each parish contest with equal numbers. On Friday night, desperate that the Peter's team was gaining the upper hand, a creative "member" of All Saints delayed the game by removing the shavings from the bladder and hiding the pigskin under the petticoats of a compatriot. He gave up the deception when a band of St. Peter's players beat the truth out of him. By early Sunday morning when St. Peter's finally managed to plant what was left of the bladder in the middle of the All Saint's millpond, only a handful of drunken adolescents on either side were still involved. No one was around at 4 A.M. to applaud the victory or record it for posterity.

It takes little imagination to enumerate the vast differences between this early version of football with what passes for the sport in the United States today. Whether played on the sandlots of small towns or in massive concrete stadiums before thousands of paying spectators and millions of television viewers, football is distinguished as a game in which players and spectators are clearly defined, rules formally established, specialization of roles encouraged, records kept, and victory all important. From Pop Warner organizations to the National Football League, bureaucracies regulate competition and ensure compliance. How different from Good Friday in nineteenth century England! There, the purpose of the game was less victory than communal celebration of a religious holiday. Rules, time limits, uniforms, or specialized roles were unheard of and participation was open to all. No one kept track of the game nor recorded its results.

In less than two centuries, sport in the western world has undergone dramatic change. Today, in the United States, sport is an organized, distinct activity in a segmented and highly complex society. For most people, it is part and parcel of their everyday life. When and why modern sport appeared in this country, how this transformation came about, the dimensions and functions of sport and what it can tell us about ourselves and our society defines the purpose of this book.

American Sport: A Documentary History illustrates the development of modern, organized sport as a primary institution of life in the United States. Ranging chronologically from the early seventeenth century to the present day, it offers a collection of primary documents from a wide variety of sources that collectively illustrates the changing nature of sporting activity in America and its growing significance and role. From the speculations of Cotton Mather about the dangers of amusements in seventeenth century New England to Jackie Robinson's moving account of signing with the Brooklyn Dodgers in 1946, each document offers the reflections, views, and experiences of participants and observers of the American sporting scene.

The book contains four parts. "The Colonial Experience, 1609-1776," traces the beginnings of sport in America, at a time when it was, for the most part, an unorganized activity limited to very few people. "The Promise of Sport, 1776-1865," illustrates the beginnings of modern organized sport in the United States and suggests connections between that development and the transformation of the American economy and social values in the first half of the nineteenth century. "The Emergence of Modern Sport, 1865-1910" focuses on that critical period that witnessed the acceptance of modern, organized sport as an integral social and economic institution of American life. "Twentieth Century American Sport" carries the significance of that fact down to the present by grouping documents under four headings, each of which deals with significant aspects of the relationship between sport and society: "The Business of Sport," "Race and Sport," "The Politics of Sport," and "Women and Sport."

Although this collection does cover the sweep of American history, like any venture of this sort it is not complete. Not every sport is covered with equal attention, indeed many receive no attention at all. Although every effort has been made to provide material that is entertaining, readers will look in vain for descriptions of the achievements of Knute Rockne or the contributions of Arnold Palmer to the game of golf. To be sure, many of the documents do come from familiar voices and focus on well-known events. Ultimately, however, inclusion depended on their ability to provide focal points for discussing and analyzing the development of sport and its relationship to larger social, cultural, political, or economic issues. Each section of the book begins with a brief introduction that outlines its major themes. And each document is introduced with a note that sets it in historical context and provides suggestions about how to consider and analyze its significance.

Sport is a fact of our lives today. For some people it is a cause of celebration—an incubator of American individualism and an example of the opportunity, equality, and mobility that all Americans enjoy. Less sanguine observers of the American scene see sport as a reflection of the worst tendencies in American society. For them, political manipulation, greed, racism, and sexism abound there as they do in the larger world. Still others view sport as an escape from the realities of everyday life—totally divorced either as a reflector of a larger social reality or as a shaper of it. *American Sport: A Documentary History* provides the opportunity and the means to evaluate all of these views in ways that will enrich your own understanding of American sport and its place in our world.

ACKNOWLEDGMENTS

Ten years of teaching a course in the history of sport in America at Michigan State University has been critical to the completion of this book. Without the help and suggestions of my students, who, through trial and error, have shown me which documents work well and which are best forgotten, I would not have been able to finish it. Special thanks go to Don Mrozek, who first convinced me to offer a course in sport history, to Larry Gerlach, who has been a good friend, consistent supporter and an invaluable critic, and to Linda Werbish who helped me put this book together. Judy Skea also assisted in typing the manuscript. I also want to thank Steve Dalphin and Teri Carriero of Prentice Hall for their help.

As always, the love and friendship of my wife, Gale, and my daughter, Ruth, have enriched my life and my work. This book is especially for Ruthie, an accomplished "athlete" in the world of dance, sometime follower of the Detroit Tigers, and a person with more than enough love to understand my own passions for "spaldeens," egg creams, and the New York Knickerbockers. I'm proud to be her father.

Peter Levine
East Lansing, Michigan

CHAPTER ONE
THE COLONIAL EXPERIENCE

1609–1776

Whether focusing on patterns of settlement or reasons for supporting the American Revolution, the history of colonial America offers a rich and varied tapestry of people and beliefs that defy simple summary or explanation. The Puritans who came to Massachusetts Bay in 1620, the English aristocrats who settled the Virginia tidewater and the Carolina coast, the Dutch merchants and patroons who populated the Hudson River Valley in New York, and the Quakers who established themselves in Pennsylvania came to the New World for different reasons, were of different religious persuasions, and adapted their beliefs and their culture to the American environment in different ways.

As European immigrants and New World settlers, however, they did share some ideas that shaped early American attitudes towards sport and physical activity. One was acceptance of a society based on deference, class, and inequality that separated people by wealth and distinction and that prescribed different roles and lifestyles depending on one's social status. An additional variation to this pattern added by those whites who came to America was slavery for blacks—by 1700, an established fact in every American colony with a disproportionate number of slaves in the South.

Another shared characteristic was the cultural baggage of sport that the colonists brought to America. Both aristocrats and common people had in their collective memories knowledge of a rich variety of sporting activities that they and their ancestors had engaged in since the fifteenth century. From horseracing and cock fighting to tennis and "kicking camp," a European sporting heritage came over to the New World as assuredly as did religious beliefs.

Even more fundamental than shared ideas about social structure and an historical memory of sport, however, was the colonists' understanding that the initial tasks of settlement and survival and the ongoing battle to establish and maintain a successful economy and ultimately an independent nation left little opportunity, regardless of class, race, sex, or religious persuasion, to participate actively in sport or to view it as a separate, distinct, and acceptable activity. In simplest terms, the most significant point that can be made about sport in colonial America is how insignificant it was to the lives of most colonists.

Still, although modern notions of organized participatory or spectator sport were nonexistent and activity was limited, there were occasions when colonial Americans engaged in sporting activities. The examples that follow, while hardly covering the experience of every colony or detailing every sport that colonists engaged in, do reflect both the class distinctions and the European sporting heritage common to colonial America. They suggest how an understanding of a people's involvement in sport can illuminate the nature of a society's values and culture. The documents also offer a portrait of sport in colonial America that serves as a benchmark for marking the development of organized modern sport in the United States.

The Puritans

William Bradford arrived in America aboard the Mayflower in 1620 intent, as were the Puritans who accompanied him, on establishing a corporate, religious community that would be a "city upon a hill" for the rest of the Protestant world to emulate. The goal of the Puritans was to live life on earth in ways that did not detract from the possibility of ultimate salvation with God. Firm believers in predestination, the Puritans nevertheless argued that how one lived on earth indicated one's chances for salvation. Acceptance of one's place in society and rigorous, unrelenting pursuit of one's "calling" and of God's love offered the possibility of grace. Anything less were sins against God and sure signs of eternal damnation for both the individual and the community.

Although the Puritans allowed recreational diversions that did not detract from fulfilling one's calling or from their love of God, they did condemn any activity that turned them away from these saintly pursuits. English folk sports like "kicking camp", a crude and savage version of football that were cause for drunken brawls, or ball games like "stool-ball", a precursor of cricket, had no place in their world.

The following section from King James I's *Book of Sport* (1618), a declaration to his subjects "Concerning Lawful Sports To Be Used," illustrates how sport and recreation caused conflict between the Anglican majority and a Puritan minority that precipitated the Puritan exodus to the New World. Aside from providing information on the nature of this disagreement, what does the document reveal about athletic activity in seventeenth century England? According to James, what positive social purposes were served by active participation in sport? Do his arguments sound familiar?

BY THE KING

Whereas upon Our return the last year out of Scotland, we did publish Our pleasure touching the recreations of Our people in those parts under Our hand: For some causes Us thereunto moving, We have thought good to command these Our directions then given in Lancashire with a few words thereunto added, and most appliable to these parts of Our Realms, to be published to all Our Subjects.

Whereas We did instantly in Our progress through Lancashire, rebuke Some Puritans and precise people, and took order that the like unlawful carriage should not be used by any of them hereafter, in the prohibiting and unlawful punishing of Our good people for using their lawful Recreations, and honest exercises upon Sundays and other Holy days, after the afternoon Sermon or Service: We now find that two sorts of people wherewith that Country is much infested, (We mean Papists and Puritans) have maliciously traduced and caluminated those Our just and honourable proceedings. And therefore lest Our reputation might upon the one side (though innocently) have some aspersion layed upon it, and that upon the other part Our good people in that Country be misled by the mistaking and misinterpretation of Our meaning: We have therefore thought good hereby to clear and make Our pleasure to be manifested to all Our good People in those parts.

It is true that at Our first entry to this Crown, and Kingdom, We were informed, and that too truly, that Our County of Lancashire abounded more in Popish Recusants than any County of England, and thus hath still continued since to Our great regret, with little amendment, save that now of late, in Our last riding through Our said County, We find both by the report of the Judges, and of the Bishop of that diocese that there is some amendment now daily beginning, which is no small contentment to Us.

The report of this growing amendment amongst them, made Us the more sorry, when with Our own ears We heard the general complaint of Our people, that they were barred from all lawful Recreation, and exercise upon the Sunday afternoon, after the ending of all Divine Service, which cannot but produce two evils: The one, the hindering of the conversion of many, whom their Priests will take occasion hereby to vex, persuading them that no honest mirth or recreation is lawfully or tollerable in Our Religion, which cannot but breed a great discontentment in Our peoples hearts, especially of such as are peradventure upon the point of turning; The other inconvenience is, that this prohibition barreth the common and meaner sort of people from using such exercises as may make their bodies more able for War, when We or Our Successors shall have occasion to use them. And in place thereof sets up filthy tiplings and drunkenness, and breeds a number of idle and discontented speeches in their Ale-houses. For when shall the common people have leave to exercise, if not upon the Sundays and Holidays, seeing they must apply their labour, and win their living in all working days?

Our express pleasure therefore is, that the Laws of Our Kingdom, and Canons of Our Church be as well observed in that County, as in all other places of this Our Kingdom. And on the other part, that no lawful Recreation shall be barred to Our good People, which shall not tend to breach of Our aforesaid Laws, and Canons of our Church: which to express more particularly, Our pleasure is That the Bishop, and all other inferior Churchmen, as Churchwardens, shall for their parts be careful and diligent, both to instruct the ignorant, and convince and reform them that are misled in religion, presenting them that will not conform themselves, but obstinately stand out to Our Judges and Justices: Whom We likewise command to put the Law in due execution against them.

Our pleasure likewise is, That the Bishop of that Diocese take the like straight order with all the Puritans and Precisians within the same, either constraining them to conform themselves, or to leave the Country according to the Laws of Our Kingdom, and Canons of Our Church, and so to strike equally on both hands, against the contemners of Our Authority, and adversaries of Our Church. And as for Our good peoples lawful Recreation, Our pleasure likewise is, That after the end of Divine Service, Our good people be not disturbed, letted, or discouraged from any lawful Recreation; Such as dancing, either men or women, Archery for men, leaping, vaulting, or any other such harmless Recreation, nor from having of May-Games, Whitson Ales, and Morris-dances, and the setting up of May-poles and other sports therewith used, so as the same be had in due and convenient time, without impediment or neglect of divine Service: And that women shall have leave to carry rushes to the Church for the decoring of it, according to their old custom. But withall We do here accompt still as prohibited all unlawful games to be used upon Sundays only, as Bear and

Bull-baiting, Interludes, and at all times in the meaner sort of People by Law prohibited, Bowling.

And likewise We bar from this benefit and liberty, all such known Recusants, either men or Women, as will abstain from coming to Church or divine Service, being therefore unworthy of any lawful recreation after the said Service, that will not first come to the Church and serve God: Prohibiting in like sort the said Recreations to any that, though conform in Religion, are not present in the Church at the Service of God, before their going to the said recreations. Our pleasure likewise is, That they whom it belongeth in Office, shall present and sharply punish all such as in abuse of this Our liberty, will use these exercises before the ends of all divine Services for that day. And We likewise straightly command, that every person shall resort to his own Parish Church to hear divine Service, and each Parish by itself to use the said recreation after divine Service. Prohibiting likewise any Offensive weapons to be carried or used in the said times of recreations, And Our pleasure is, That this Our Declaration shall be published by order from the bishop of the Diocese, through all the Parish Churches, and that both Our Judges of Our Circuit, and Our Justices of Our Peace be informed thereof.

> Given at our Manor of Grenwich the
> four and twentieth day of May, in
> the sixteenth year of Our Reign of
> England, France and Ireland, and
> of Scotland the one and fiftieth.
> God save the King.

Plymouth Colony

The following selection from William Bradford's *History of Plimmoth Plantation*, completed in 1651, suggests that Puritan migration to the New World hardly guaranteed the success of their religious experiment. Between 1621 and 1656, with the exception of five years, Bradford served as governor of Plymouth colony, the first Puritan settlement in America. His *History* includes remembrances of his tenure and discussions of the problems of maintaining Puritan values in a society increasingly filled with new immigrants who were not Puritans. In this excerpt from 1621, Bradford notes that some residents of Plymouth are at play in the streets. What games are they playing? Why was Bradford upset? Does his concern suggest anything about the social structure or values of Puritans in Plymouth? Does his use of the word "sports" correspond to contemporary uses of the term?

THE PERILS OF BALL-PLAYING

Herewith I shall end this year. Only I shall remember one passage more, rather of mirth then of waight. One y'day called Chrismas-day, y' Gov' caled them out to works, (as was used,) but y' most of this new-company excused them selves and said it wente against their consciences to work on y'day. So y' Gov' tould them that if they made it mater of conscience, he would spare them till they were better informed. So he led-away y' rest and left them; but when they came home at noon from their worke, he found them in y' streete at play, openly; some pitching y'barr, & some at stooleball, and shuch like sports. So he went to them, and tooke away their implements and tould them that was against his conscience, that they should play & others worke. If they made y' keeping of it mater of devotion, let them kepe their houses, but ther should be no gameing or ravelling in y' streets. Since which time nothing hath been atempted that way, at least openly.

The Puritans at Massachusetts Bay

By the end of his tenure as governor of Plymouth, William Bradford had real reason to be pessimistic about the possibility of establishing and maintaining his ideal religious community. The enticement of an abundant wilderness and the promise of secular economic success coupled with the variety of people who were settling the colonies increasingly denied the Puritans the isolation necessary for their experiment to succeed. But they continued to try. They made changes in their religious doctrine, including the half-way convenant of the 1660s intended to keep the children of church members in the fold. Continual efforts to maintain the religious zeal of their members also fueled the attempts of Puritan leaders to carry out the mission of the original settlers. One example of these efforts that also indicates how certain recreations were tolerated comes from the pen of Increase Mather, one of Massachusetts Bay's leading Puritan ministers in the late seventeenth century. The following excerpt from Mather's thirty page essay, *An Arrow against Profane and Promiscuous Dancing, Drawn Out of a Quiver of the Scriptures* (1684), sets out both the positive and evil effects of this form of recreation. What kinds of dancing did Mather find acceptable? According to this Puritan minister, what were the dangers of "promiscuous dancing?"

AN ARROW AGAINST PROFANE AND PROMISCUOUS DANCING

Concerning the Controversy about *Dancing*, the Question is not, whether all *Dancing* be in it self sinful. It is granted, that *Pyrrhical* or *Polemical Saltation*: i.e. when men vault in their Armour, to shew their strength and activity, may be of use. Nor is the question, whether a sober and grave *Dancing* of Men with Men, or of Women with Women, be not allowable; we make no doubt of that, where it may be done without offence, in due season, and with moderation. The Prince of Philosophers has observed truly, that *Dancing* or *Leaping*, is a natural expression of joy: So that there is no more Sin in it, than in laughter, or any outward expression of inward Rejoycing.

But our question is concerning *Gynecandrical Dancing*, or that which is commonly called *Mixt* or *Promiscuous Dancing, viz.* of Men and Women (be they elder or younger persons) together: Now this we affirm to be utterly unlawful, and that it cannot be tollerated in such a place as *New-England* without great Sin. And that it may appear, that we are not transported by Affection without Judgment, let the following Arguments be weighed in the Ballance of the Sanctuary.

Arg.1 *That which the Scripture condemns is sinful.* None but Atheists will deny this *Proposition*: But the Scripture condemns *Promiscuous Dancing.* This *Assumption* is proved, I. *From the Seventh Commandment.* It is an Eternal Truth to be observed in expounding the Commandments, that whenever any sin is forbidden, not only the highest acts of that sin, but all degrees thereof, and all occasions leading thereto are prohibited. Now we cannot find one Orthodox and Judicious Divine, that writeth on the Commandments, but mentions *Promiscuous Dancing*, as a breach of the seventh Commandment, as being an occasion, and an incentive to that which is evil in the sight of God. Yea, this is so manifest as that the *Assembly* in the *larger Catechism,* do expresly take notice of *Dancings*, as a violation of the Commandments. It is sad, that when in times of Reformation, Children have been taught in the C[a]techism, that such *Dancing* is against the Commandment of God, that now in *New-England* they should practically be learned the contrary. The unchast Touches and Gesticulations used by *Dancers*, have a palpable tendency to that which is evil. Whereas some object, that they are not sensible of any ill motions occasioned in them, by being Spectators or Actors in such *Saltations;* we are not bound to believe all which some pretend concerning their own Mortification. . . .

Now they that frequent Promiscuous Dancings, or that send their Children thereunto, walk disorderly, and contrary to the Apostles Doctrine. It has been proved that such a practice is a *Scandalous Immorality*, and therefore to be removed out of Churches by Discipline, which is the Broom of Christ, whereby he keeps his Churches clean. . . .

And shall Churches in *N[ew] E[ngland]* who have had a Name to be stricter and purer than other Churches, suffer such a scandalous evil amongst them? if all that are under Discipline be made sensible of this matter, we shall not be much or long infested with a *Choreutical Dæmon*. . . .

The Catechism which Wicked men teach their Children is to Dance and to Sing. Not that Dancing, or Musick, or Singing are in themselves sinful: but if the Dancing Master be wicked they are commonly abused to lasciviousness, and that makes them to become abominable. But will you that are Professors of Religion have your Children to be thus taught? the Lord expects that you should give the Children who are Baptized into his Name another kind of Education, that you should bring them up in the nurture and admonition of the Lord: And do you not hear the Lord Expostulating the case with you, and saying, you have taken my Children, the Children that were given unto me; the Children that were solemnly engaged to renounce the Pomps of Satan; but is this a light matter that you have taken these my Children, and initiated them in the Pomps and Vanities of the Wicked one, contrary to your Covenant? What will you say in the day of the Lords pleading with you? we have that charity for you as to believe that you have erred through Ignorance, and not wickedly: and we have therefore accounted it our Duty to inform you in the Truth. If you resolve not on Reformation, you will be left inexcusable. However it shall be, we have not given our Testimony and delivered our own Souls. *Consider what we say, and the Lord give you understanding in all things.*

Horse Racing in Virginia

Unlike the Puritans, the English who settled Virginia in the seventeenth and eighteenth centuries did not view their coming as a religious mission but rather as an opportunity for fame and fortune. Although they did not find gold in the streets as some had hoped, they did find tobacco. Over time, a class of wealthy aristocrats, who, by the 1660s, had substituted black slavery for white indentured labor and who made their fortunes by exporting the golden leaves, came to dominate Virginia society. Anxious to emulate their British counterparts and to distance themselves from the common Virginia farmer, many of these people embraced participation in certain sporting activities as a means to those ends.

Horse racing for high stakes was a very popular sport among wealthy Virginians—an activity that involved personal honor, large sums of money, and a well-defined place as a member of the aristocratic class. Race distances varied between quarter-mile sprints and rides of several miles through the countryside.

Although there were no formal schedules, racecourses, or grandstands, gambling was always present and contests often the occasion for social gatherings of the elite.

The following selection, taken from the proceedings of the county court in Henrico County, Virginia, during the late seventeenth century, provides insight into the seriousness with which wealthy Virginians viewed sport. Although court records might seem an unlikely source of evidence about a society's interest in sport, what kind of information about the specifics of horse racing in Virginia can be obtained from them? What information do the records offer about the relations between social classes or about colonial economy?

VIRGINIA COURT RECORDS

"William Randolph, aged about 38 years, Deposeth: That about Saturday last was a fortnight this depon't was at a race at Mawvern hills [Malvern Hills] at w'ch time Mr. Wm. Epes and Mr. Stephen Cocke came to this depon't and desired him to take notice of ye agreem't: w'ch was That ye horse of ye s'd Epes and the horse of Mr. Wm. Sutton was to run that Race for ten Shillings on each side, and each horse was to keep his path, they not being to crosse unlesse Stephen Cocke could gett the other Riders Path at ye start at two or three Jumps (to ye best of this dep'ts knowledge) and also that they were not to touch neither man nor horse, and they further desired this dep't to start the Horses, w'ch this dep't did and to ye best of this dep'ts Judgm't they had a fair start, & Mr. Cocke endeavored to gett the other rider's path as afores'd according to ye agreem't, but to ye best of this dept's Judgm't he did not gett it at two or three Jumps nor many more, upon w'ch they Josselled upon Mr. Epes horses's path all most part of the race.

And further saith not,

Wm. Randolph."

"August 1st, 1689."

Other testimony was given by Godfrey Spruill, William Lewis, and Joshua Wynne, who stated that they had been present at the race at Malvern Hills, that they saw the horses as they were coming in "Josselling for the path," and that Mr. Wm. Sutton's horse, on which Stephen Cocke laid, won. Mr. Wynne stated that he started them "and as soon as they were off Wm. Cocke closed in w'th ye boy and bore upon the boy's path, going about sixty yards in that manner."

Wm. Randolph, who appears to have been an ardent supporter of the turf, was again a witness in August, 1690. Captain Soane had made an agreement to run his horse against one belonging to Mr. Littleberry Epes, which was backed by Mr. Robert Napier, 10 a side. Mr. Napier did not produce his horse at the appointed time, and the suit was for the amount of the stake, as an agreement had been made that the horse which did not appear should forfeit the whole amount. . . .

HENRICO RECORDS, 1677–99

"At a Court held at Varina, Ap'l lst, 1689, Richard Ward complains against John Stewart, Jun'r, in a plea of debt for that, that is to say the s'd plaintiff & defendant did on the 12th day of June Last, covenant and agree in the following words:

"It is Covenanted and agreed this 12th day of June, 1697, Between Mr. Richard Ward of the one part, in Hen'co Co'ty, & John Steward, Jun'r, of ye other part in ye same Co'ty" Witnesseth, that the aforesaid Mr. Richard Ward doth hereby convenant, promise & agree to run a mare named Bony, belonging to Thomas Jefferson, Jun'r [Grandfather of the President], af'st a horse now belonging to Mr. John Hardiman, named Watt, the said horse & mare to Run at the race-place commonly called ye Ware, to run one quarter of a mile. And ye said John Steward, Jun'r, doth hereby Coven't & agree to Run a horse now belonging to Mr. Jno. Hardiman, of Cha: City Co'ty, the said horse named Watt to Run ag'st a mare belonging to Thomas Jefferson, Jun'r named Bony. The s'd horse to give the s'd mare five horse Lengths, Vizt: that is to say ten yards. And it is further agreed upon by the parties above s'd, that the s'd horse & mare are to Run on the first day of Jly next Ensuing the date hereof. And it is further agreed upon by the parties above s'd that if the s'd mare dothe come within five Lengths of the fores'd Horse, the fores'd John Steward to pay unto Mr. Rich'd Ward the sum of five pounds Sterling on Demand, & the s'd Richard Ward doth oblige himself that if the afores'd horse doth come before s'd mare five Lengths, then to pay unto the afores'd John Steward Jun'r, the sum of six pounds Sterling on Demand. It is further agreed by the p'ties aforesaid, that there be fair Riding & the Riders to weigh about one hundred & thirty Weight, to the true p'formance of all & singular the p'misses, the p'ties above s'd have hereunto set their hands the day and year above written."

"And the plaintiff in fact saith, That pursuant to the afores'd agreement, The s'd horse & mare, to-wit: The horse named Watt, belonging to Mr. John Hardiman & the mare named Bony, belonging to Mr. Tho. Jefferson, Jun'r, were by the s'd pl't'f & Def'd't brought upon the afores'd Ground to Run upon the first day of July, and the word being given by the person who was appointed to start the s'd horse & mare, The afores'd mare, with her Rider who weighed about one hundred & thirty weight, Did Leap off, and out running the afores'd horse came in first between the poles which were placed at the comeing in of the s'd Race, commonly called the Ware, one quarter of a mile distance from the starting place appointed; and was by the s'd mare, with her Rider of about one hund'd & thirty weight as afores'd, fairly Run.

"Wherefore the afores'd pl't'f saith that the afores'd Mare, Bony with fair Running & Rideing, according to agreement, Did beat the s'd horse Watt, and that according to the true meaning of the s'd agreem't he, the s'd plaintiff, hath Woon the wager, to-witt: the sum of five pounds sterling of the afores'd John Steward. And thereupon he brings suit ag'st the afores'd John Steward, Jun'r, & demands Judgem't for the afores'd sum of five p'ds Sterl., with Co'ts, &c. To which the Defend't, by Mr. Bartholomew Fowler, his attorney, appears and upon oyer of the plaintiff declaracon pleads that he oweth nothing by the covenants, &c., and thereof puts himself upon ye country & ye pl't'f likewise.

"Whereupon, it is ordered that a Jury be impanelled & sworn to try the issue, To-witt: Thomas Edwards, Wm. Ballard, Phill Childers, John Watson, Edward Bowman, Will Hatcher, Amos Ladd, John Wilson, Phill. Jones, Edw'd Good, John Bowman.

"Who Returned this Verdict: We find for the plaintiff. Upon the motion of the plaintiffs' attorney the s'd Verdict is Recorded, & Judgment is awarded the s'd pl't'f against the Def'd't for the sum of five pounds Sterling, to be p'd with Costs, als Ex'o."

Plantation Sport

Horse racing was not the only activity engaged in by Virginia aristocrats. On the eve of the American Revolution a young New Englander, Philip Fithian, traveled south to tutor the children of Robert "King" Carter, a slave-holding tobacco planter who presided over Nomini Hall, his huge Virginia estate along the banks of the James River. In these selections from his diary, Fithian inadvertently offers information about both Virginia sport and society. What kinds of sporting activity does he describe? Who is participating? What can we learn about slavery and about social and sexual relations among the white Virginia aristocracy? What purpose does sport seem to play in the society that Fithian describes?

PLANTATION SPORT

Tuesday, August 2, 1774:

Ben & I drest ourselves pretty early with an intention to Breakfast with Colonel Tayloe, but the Servant who went with us was so slow in preparing that we breakfasted before we set out—We arrived at Colonel Tayloe's however by half after nine—The young Ladies we found in the Hall playing the Harpsichord—The morning cool with a fine Breeze from the North for I forgot to mention that about Midnight last Night a violent Gust of Blackness, Rain, & Thunder came on & gave us present Relief from the scorching Sun; there was no Dust & the riding was pleasant—The Colonel, his Lady, Miss Polly, Miss Kitty, Miss Sally, rode in their Great Coach to the Ferry—Distance about 4 miles—Ben & I on Horseback— From Colonel Tayloe's to this Ferry opposite to Hobbs's Hole the Land is level & extremely good; Corn here looks very rank is set thick with Ears, & they are high & large, three commonly on a Stalk—Here I saw about an Acre & a half of Flax, which the people were just pulling, exceedingly out of Season—This is the only Flax I have seen since I have been in the Colony; I am told they raise much in the upper Counties—Here too is a great Marsh covered with thick high Reed—The face of this part of the Country looks fertile, but I apprehend it is far from being healthy—We came to the Bank of the Rappahannock; it is here about 2 Miles over the Shipping on the other Side near the Town lying at Anchor look fine; no large Vessels can haul along the Wharves on account of shoal Water— There were six Ships riding in the Harbour, and a number of Schooners & smaller Vessels—Indeed, says Mrs Tayloe, Captain Dobby has forgot us. Here we have been waiting for a full half hour, shall we take the Ferry Boat Colonel & cross over, & not stand any longer in the burning heat?—I was pleased not a little with the proposal tho' at the same time, I laughed with myself at Mrs. Tayloe's truely Womanish impatience!—At last they are coming—The long-Boat came, well furnished with a large Awning, and rowed with four Oars—We entered the Ship about half after twelve where we were received by Captain Dobby, with every possible token of welcome—Since I have been in Virginia, my inclination, & my fixed purpose before I left home, both of which were very much assisted by a strict Attention to the instructing my little Charge, these have kept me pretty constantly, almost wholly, indeed out of that kind of Company where dissipation & Pleasure have no restraint—This entertainment of Captain Dobby's, elegant indeed, & exceeding agreeable, I consider as one among a prodigeous throng of more powerful similar Causes, of the fevers & other Disorders which are common in this Colony, & generally attributed to the Climate which is thought to be noxious & unhealthy. The Weather here indeed is remarkably variable. But taking away & changing the usual &

necessary Time of Rest; Violent Exercise of the Body & Spirits; with drinking great quantities of variety of Liquors, these bring on Virginia Fevers—The Beaufort is a Stately Ship; Captain Dobby had an Awning from the Stern over the Quarter quite to the Mizen-Mast, which made great Room, kept off the Sun, & yet was open on each Side to give the Air a free passage. At three we had on Board about 45 Ladies, and about 60 Gentlemen besides the Ships Crew, & Waiters Servants &c. We were not throng'd at all, & dined all at twice—I was not able to inform myself, because it seemed improper to interrupt the General pleasure, with making circumstantial inquiries concerning Individuals, & saying pray, Sir, what young Lady is that yonder in a Lute-String Gown? She seems genteel; where does her Father live? Is she a Girl of Family & Breeding? Has She any Suitors? This when one could not be out of the Inspection of the Company, would have seemed impertinent so that I did not much enlarge my Acquaintance with the Ladies, which commonly seems pleasing & desirable to me; But I took Notice of Several, & shall record my remarks—The Boats were to Start, to use the Language of Jockeys, immediately after Dinner; A Boat was anchored down the River at a Mile Distance—Captain Dobby and Captain Benson steer'd the Boats in the Race—Captain Benson had 5 Oarsmen; Captain Dobby had 6—It was Ebb-Tide—The Betts were small—& chiefly given to the Negroes who rowed—Captain Benson won the first Race—Captain Purchace offered to bett ten Dollars that with the same Boat & same Hands, only having Liberty to put a small Weight in the Stern, he would beat Captain Benson—He was taken, & came out best only half the Boats Length—About Sunset we left the Ship, & went all to Hobbs's Hole, where a Ball was agreed on—This is a small Village, with only a few Stores, & Shops, it is on a beautiful River, & as I am told commonly six, eight, & ten Ships loading before it the Crews of which enliven the Town—Mr. Ritche Merchant; he has great influence over the People, he has great Wealth; which in these scurvy Times gives Sanction to Power; nay it seems to give countenance to Tyranny—The Ball Room—25 Ladies—40 Gentlemen—The Room very long, well-finished, airy & cool, & well-seated—two Fidlers—Mr. Ritche stalk'd about the Room—He was Director, & appointed a sturdy two fisted Gentleman to open the Ball with Mrs Tayloe—He danced midling tho'. There were about six or eight married Ladies--At last Miss Ritche danced a Minuet with—She is tall slim Girl, dances nimble & graceful—She was Ben Carters partner—Poor Girl She has had the third Day Ague for twelve months past, and has it yet She appeared in a blue Silk Gown; her Hair was done up neat, without powder, it is very Black & Set her to good Advantage—Soon after danced Miss Dolly Edmundson—A Short pretty Stump of a Girl; She danced well, sung a Song with great applause, seemed to enter into the Spirit of the entertainment—A young Spark seemed to be fond of her; She seemed to be fond of him; they were both fond, & the Company saw it—He was Mr Ritche's

Clerk, a limber, well dress 'd, pretty-handsome chap he was—The insinuating Rogue waited on her home, in close Hugg too, the Moment he left the Ball-Room—Miss Aphia Fantleroy danced next. the best Dancer of the whole absolutely—And the finest Girl—Her head tho' was powdered white as Snow, & crap'd in the newest Taste—She is the Copy of the goddess of Modesty—Very handsome; she seemed to be loved by all her Acquaintances, and admir'd by every Stranger, Miss McCall—Miss Ford—Miss Brokenberry—Ball—Two of the younger Miss Ritche's—Miss Wade—They danced till half after two. Captain Ritche invited Ben & I, Colonel Tayloe & his Family with him—We got to Bed by three after a Day spent in constant Violent exercise, & drinking an unusual Quantity of Liquor; for my part with Fatigue, Heat, Liquor, Noise, Want of sleep, And the exertion of my Animal spirits, I was almost brought to believe several times that I felt a Fever fixing upon me, attended with every Symptom of the Fall Disorders—

Thursday, September 8, 1774:

Cloudy & cool. I rise now by half after six—I found it necessary to flogg Bob & Harry on account of lying in bed, after I come into School—At twelve Mr & Mrs Carter, with all the Family except Ben, Harry & Myself; Ben staid of choice, & Harry I kept at Home on account of a sullen Impudence when I dismiss'd them—I told them that they both had my leave to go but at the same time it was my advice that they should stay—Harry then answered D– –n my Soul but i'll go!" At this I informed him that he had at once dismiss'd himself from my authority. & without singular signs of Submission I should never take him under my direction more—And therefore that he had general & unbounded Liberty to go not only to the Horse Race, but where & when he chose—He seem'd startled, & began to moderate his answer: I ordered him out of the Room, & told him to use his liberty. Mrs Carter took with her all the young Ladies, & all her children— Ben & I with great satisfaction dined alone. Nelson, to Day, kill'd another Rattle Snake; near the place where he kill'd the other, which had twelve Rattles—Harry grew sick and refused to go to the Race, he came soon to my room & with every Sign of Sorrow for his conduct begg'd me to forgive him, at first I refused, but at length I took him in, yet informed him that I shall pass over no other instance of what may be called rudeness only.— The Colonel on his return, in the evening informed us that the Race was curious, & that the Horses were almost an even match—That the Betts were Drawn & no Money paid—That the Rider of one of the Horses weighed only forty Seven pound—Strange that so little substance in a human Creature can have strength & skill sufficient to manage a Horse in a March of Importance—Something alarming happened a few nights ago in the Nieghbourhood at Mr Sorrels a House in sight—It is supposed that his Negres had appointed to murder him, several were found in his bed chamber in the middle of the night—his Wife waked—She heard a whispering, one perswading the other to go—On this She waked her Husband, who run to his Gun; but they escaped in the dark—Presumption is sto strong together with a small confession of the Fellows, that three are now in Prison—The ill Treatment which this unhappy part of mankind receives here, would almost justify them in any desperate attempt for gaining that Civility, & Planty wich tho' denied them, is here, commonly bestowed on Horses!—Now, Laura, I sleep in fear too, though my Doors & Windows are all secured!—

CHAPTER TWO
THE PROMISE OF SPORT
1776–1865

It is not surprising that Washington Irving's fictional character, Rip Van Winkle, hardly recognized anything about his old New York village when he fell asleep in the 1770s and awoke twenty years later. America's Declaration of Independence not only marked the end of the colonial period but also the onset of economic and social change that had a significant impact on the development of sport in the United States. Between 1750 and 1860, the population of the country increased from 1.5 million to 32 million, fueled in part by a constant and growing stream of European immigrants. Population growth coincided with territorial expansion and urbanization. While still predominately a nation of farmers, an increasing number of people, especially in the Northeast, lived and worked in cities, finding employment in a manufacturing economy undergoing transformation from a craft to an industrial society. In 1790, less than four percent of the nation's population lived in towns or cities with populations over 8,000. By 1860, over seventeen percent resided in such settings. Another critical factor in population growth was the increase of the black slave population of the United States from some 500,000 in 1776 to nearly 4 million by 1860, with virtually all slaves living in the southern states by the 1820s. The significance of slavery in the South and its absence in the North was to be the critical factor that propelled the nation to Civil War by mid-century.

These new patterns of work, living, and population distribution dramatically affected the development of sport between 1800 and 1865. The beginnings of industrial capitalism in the Northeast, especially after 1820, produced a new white middle-class with increased leisure time and a willingness to accept participation in a wide variety of sporting activities as a legitimate way to spend it. The popularity of horse racing, pedestrianism, and even baseball accompanied the expression of positive attitudes about physical activity far different from William Bradford's Puritans.

New attitudes about physical activity were part and parcel of a redefinition of family and sexual roles that accompanied the changing nature of the northern economy. Especially for a white middle class, the family became a unit distinct from the workplace, managed by women, with responsibility to serve as a haven in a heartless world and as a nurturer of character and values. Within it, sport and physical recreation emerged as new avenues for developing the proper values and character traits deemed necessary for the success and survival of a modernizing American society. For certain groups, defined both by ethnicity and class, associations in sporting organizations like the New York Knickerbocker Baseball Club, a German Turner society, or a college athletic club provided opportunities for status and community that inadvertently marked the onset of organized modern sport in America. These organizations also contributed to the development of particular sports in terms of the regularization of rules and the growth of regular competition. Although manifestations of colonial involvement in sport lingered in the South and on the western frontier, the ante-bellum years witnessed the beginnings of sport as an integral part of American culture.

Horse Racing, Ante-Bellum Style

Although horse racing enjoyed popularity in colonial America, it hardly compared to the attention the sport received throughout the United States between 1820 and 1860. Responding to new demands for leisure-time activities and the opportunity to make a profit, entrepreneurs throughout the country, especially in developing urban areas, had built some seventy formal race courses complete with tracks, stables and grandstands by 1842. In 1821, for instance, the Union Race Course was built on Long Island, New York, to accommodate crowds as large as 50,000 who might attend a day at the races. Organizers of these tracks charged admissions, publicized racing schedules in advance, and had the results of their contests reported in an increasingly expanding daily press. Specialized sporting newspapers such as William Porter's *Spirit of the Times* and the *American Turf Register* were created to cater to the interest of the nation's racing fans. Although people of all classes spent their time and money at the track, seating was often decided by class and sex.

The following description, taken from the May 5, 1845, edition of the *New York Herald*, details one of a number of intersectional races between northern and southern mounts that attracted particular attention in pre-Civil War America. Compare its account of the race to horse races described in earlier documents. What differences or similarities do you notice? Does the *Herald* account tell us anything about the kind of changes taking place in American society in the first half of the nineteenth century? How many people attended the race? From what classes? How did they get to the racecourse? What picture of urban society can you discern from this newspaper story? What does the *Herald's* distinction between work and play suggest about attitudes towards time, work, and life? Do they appear different from colonial times?

THE GREAT CONTEST: FASHION V. PEYTONA (1845)

THE GREAT CONTEST
Between the North and the South

PEYTONA, THE SOUTHERN MARE
VICTORIOUS

Tremendous Excitement on the Race Course
Immense Concourse of People

At a very early hour yesterday morning, New York showed by evident and significant signs, that it was no common day. It is well known that her industrious citizens are no long sleepers when business calls to resume the daily task. But say what we will, there is a difference between work and play, toil and enjoyment, care and sport. Yesterday was a day dedicated to the latter, and we again repeat that the thousands and tens of thousands who turned out for the Long Island races, showed clearly the meaning of the phrase, "life let us cherish."

It was an exciting, but very beautiful morning; exciting because the contest between the North and the South for the dominion of the turf was to be settled, before the shades of evening closed on the well-trodden race ground. It is well understood that the ambiguity of the relative pretensions of the two great sections of the country to this honor, is the natural result of former well balanced successes. The North beat the South twice, and twice the South returned the compliment; their yearnings then for victory were as keen as Damascus sword blades. In addition to the sectional feeling and the strong rivalry of sportsmen, and in one sense partizans—the vast sums of money pending on the race, attached a degree of absorbing interest to the result, quite proportionate to the great demonstration that took place.

More than three thousand persons crossed the South Ferry yesterday morning before 8 o'clock, for the races. As the morning progressed, the crowd increased rapidly, and a scene of tumult, disorder, and confusion ensued. Apple women's stands were overturned, an omnibus upset, fighting, swearing, pushing, screaming and shouting in abundance.—All seemed eager to reach the ground. Long trains of carriages, filled with all sorts of people, reaching to Broadway, lined Whitehall Street. Here was the magnificent barouche of the millionaire, full of gay, laughing, dark-eyed demoiselles, jammed in between a Bowery stage and a Broadway hack— here were loafers and dandies, on horseback and on foot—sporting gentlemen in green coats and metal buttons—Southerners from Louisiana, Mississippi and Alabama, with anxious faces, but hearts full of hope, "a pocketfull of rocks," and a calm determination to await the result. The whole Union had in fact sent delegates to represent it in the grand contest which this day ushered in—all business seemed laid aside—one spirit animated the vast multitude. Omnibusses of all dimensions, cabriolets, chariots, drays, wagons, and every description of vehicle were put in requisition. . . .

In short, the whole scene was of a very exciting and disorderly character. At the Fulton ferry somewhat similar occurrences took place, though no blame is to be attached to the proprietors of the ferries, or the gate-keepers. By 12'clock about 30,000 persons had passed over the South and 20,000 over Fulton ferries.

We saw many distinguished sporting characters, politicians, editors, reporters, managers, actors, printers' devils, &c., among the group. Tryon, of the New Bowery Theatre came down in a splendid vehicle—and "Mi Boy and the Brigadier" followed on the look out for news.

The first train started from the terminus of the railway, Brooklyn, at 7 o'clock, followed by others at 8, 9, 9¼, 9¾, and 10½ o'clock. With each of these trains one of our corps started, to not only note whatever might occur, but to afford the voyageurs the benefit of their presence, and also because it is fitting that the Herald should be represented, if not identified with all marvellous progressive movements of our race. A terrific rush from the ferry boats to the cars was the work of a moment, and another sufficed to pile them in, and about the cars, in all sorts of postures and attitudes. A large number of cars had been fitted up with temporary seats made of deal scantlings; some were placed transversely, others parallel with the length; whatever were their directions, however, happy was the wight, who got a seat, here or there, for forty minutes or so, for the lawful consideration of twenty-five cents. Our reporters on comparing notes found that there was no casualty of sufficient importance to publish to the world, and they were immensely gratified to learn that the vast migration of citizens took place under their judicious supervision, without any accident or misfortune to damp the ardor of the day's sport. It was observed that the moment the trains halted, the passengers bolted as though they were in danger of being blown up by retaining their seats one second after the wheels of the cars had ceased to revolve. It was moreover ascertained from accurate observations, that for the most part each passenger the instant his feet touched the ground, turned round and gave a parting glance of rather a contemptuous cast at the vehicles, and without an exception, save one each and every individual who had passed the time going out in smoking, threw away the stumps of their cigars; but he who persisted in tugging away at his, had his whiskers much singed by reason of the united heat of the weather, at the Course, and the blaze of the cigar. . . .

On the arrival of the two earlier trains, there was not a very remarkable degree of bustle. The passengers were set down immediately beside the course, to which admittance was procured through narrow entrances, about three or four hundred yards from the railway, on the edge of which are half a dozen of dwelling houses. These were all converted into dram shops and places of refreshment, and if they did not do more than their share of the business, they had the honor of an early call from a large portion of the race-going blades, who, after their dusty and perilous journey, per railway, were ready for a grateful draught of something or other to wash down the dust. From this point to the entrance of the course, and, as far beyond it, equal, perhaps to a fifth of the circumference of the course, was a continuous line of tents on one side of the thoroughfare—the other being bounded by the fence of the Course. This passage was about twenty yards wide, so that, there being a good deal of room to spare, it was occupied by all sorts of irregular forces, and indescribable camp followers, sutlers, loungers, rowdies, gamblers, and twenty other species of the genus loose fish. Here you saw a bucket of water, with two or three little negro boys for an escort; there baskets of oranges as thick as yellow gowans; piles of oysters reared their rough exteriors in huge profusion, and the confectionery peered up in tempting masses albeit in rather a melting mood on account of the sun's vertical rays, which spared nothing, sweet or sour, that memorable day. Business in the tents—the wigwams—the culinary camps and conventicles commenced at an early hour, and was carried on with a briskness that betimes looked like voracity, and fears were occasionally excited that the impetuosity of the hungry crowd might find a melancholy end in the prodigious tubs of lemonade and brandy punch that lay in elegant negligence around the tables, whose extended surfaces supported masses of ham, sandwiches, lobsters, loaves, decanters, glasses, and all the paraphernalia of drinking that could be condensed into the space. The rap of the hammer in erecting these tents mingled incessantly with the popping of corks, for a couple of hours, when the music of mastication reigned triumphant. During all this time, from the very beginning of the arrivals, gamblers of all descriptions swarmed about in every direction. In the space of a hundred yards we counted no less than seventeen ill-looking wretches, using their utmost cunning to cajole the natives with three cups and one ball. . . .

The enclosed area, whose circumference of a mile formed the Course, was the resort of the carriates and horsemen; and those pedestrians who declined to pay for a place on the stand, or who were able to screw up their self denial to leave the enticing precincts of the booths and tents we have spoken of to witness the potent contest between the horses. . . .

Immediately on the right of the Judge's stand, and the opposite to the great stand for spectators, on the other side of the course, a dense mass of vehicles of all descriptions congregated. Among these, the most striking were a number of the city omnibusses, which had been engaged for the day by a full complement of passengers, who, from the roofs of them were enabled to have a capital view of the race. As may be expected, the occupants of them were of a more mixed class than those who lolled in private carriages, or those engaged special for the occasion; accordingly, our friends of the omnibuses managed to while away time in a right free and easy manner. Here and there out of the windows might be seen protruding a rubicund visage, smiling complacently down on a jar of Old Jamaica, whose contents were being dispensed to a knot of thirsty looking souls beneath the shadow of the high carriage; in another quarter, the bowl of a huge Dutch pipe kept steaming away with less noise but more uniformity than the chimney of the locomotives on the road contiguous; whilst now and again a willing hand was stretched out to lay hold on that sparkling glass of grog, that the bountiful dispenser of the beverage below had raised to his friend inside. All over the face of the field the crowd was continually in motion; hundreds seated themselves on the grass, but by far the larger number went roaming up and down, seeking rest but finding none, until finding spirits more wicked than themselves, they entered into the swept and garnished groggery, and "verily, the last state of these men was worse than the first." . . .

On the stand there could not be fewer than thirty thousand persons; every train added countless hosts, for the first race of everybody who obtained admission, was to the grand stand, and the solicitude to secure places increased in the direct ratio of the difficulty of finding them, so that the onset of the last was impetuous in the extreme. . . .

About half past two o'clock, the bugle sounded to bring forth the horses. They shortly after showed themselves, and each were received with shouts that might have almost been heard from one end of the isle to the other. We have so often described them that it is almost needless to repeat it; suffice it to say that both looked as fine as silk, in first rate condition. Mr. J. Laird topped the pit-skin across Fashion, dressed in a purple jacket and red and gold cap. The "indomitable Barney" mounted Peytona. Two finer animals and abler jockies it is supposed there is not in the States. Having gone to the scales Laird made up his weight to 125 lbs.; and Barney his to to

118. Many thought that Fashion had "a leetle" too much upon her, but she appeared the same as ever.

After some endeavors on the part of those in authority, the track was well cleared as could be expected under the circumstances, thanks to the indefatigable Capt. Runders, Bill Harrington, Country McClusky, Yankee Sullivan, Don Casseau, or some such name, on his blind black mare. At 33 minutes past two o'clock the horses were saddled and mounted, and at the first tap they went forth in gallant style, Peytona having the poll, but a most beautiful start—nose and nose. They kept thus together round the bottom, Peytona gently falling off, but yet keeping her nose close to the tail of her rival, evidently waiting attendance. They kept thus to the first quarter, the same to the half. At the third quarter they were close together, Peytona making up, evidently waiting attendance; at the drawgate she came in front, and led to the judges stand a length and a half in front. For the second mile they appeared to keep in this position round the bottom, but owing to the clouds of dust prevailing just then, only an occasional glimpse could be caught of them; but they seemed to maintain a similar position round the top to the drawgate, where Fashion appeared to come in front, but on reaching the judge's chair, Fashion's nose was close up with that of Peytona, on the inside. For the third mile they kept well thus together round, to the nearing of the half mile post, where the heavy patch before alluded to occurs, Fashion appeared to gain somewhat, but shortly after Peytona reached her flank, nipping her hard, but Fashion appeared immediately afterwards to make the gap wider. At the drawgate, Fashion appeared two lengths in front, but on nearing the judge's stand, Peytona had her nose close on the flank of her opponent. It was now pretty evident that Barney had it all his own way, and could do just as he pleased with the affair, and faces became elongated, while others could scarce keep their feet. . . . Round the bottom they kept well together, but owing to dust, &c, there was no seeing further, until they reached the drawgate towards home, where Fashion appeared to have the lead, but it was immediately taken from her and Peytona came home two lengths in front, making the first heat in 7 m. 39 s., amid the most unbounded cheers.

The betting now took a very different turn—50 to 30 was offered on Peytona, but there was great shyness; 50 to 25 was taken to some extent. The course was kept in the best order possible, previous to the second heat, under all the circumstances—This was owing to the indefatigable exertions of Bill Harrington and others. A few light skirmishes took place previous to the commencement of the next heat, but after a sufficient dose of punishment having been administered, pro, and con, matters were adjusted, and every preparation was made for the succeeding heat.

At the first attempt they did not go forth, and were pulled short up, owing to what appeared a rather premature tap. They returned and commenced again, de novo. At the second attempt they went forth Peytona leading a neck, Laird well up round the bottom to the quarter; on approaching the half Fashion went in front, and led to the three-quarter. Here the crowd broke in at the lower drawgate, which caused some confusion for a few moments, but owing to the vigilance of those now engaged, was soon got under. Fashion led to the drawgate, where they came together to the Judge's chair, head and head, no telling who had the lead. For the second mile Fashion appeared to have the lead to the quarter, the other well up; they kept so up the back stretch; at the three-quarter it was just so. Fashion still kept the lead, closely waited upon by Peytona; it was thus round the top, but at the drawgate they were again well together, Fashion having the track, but at the end of the second mile, notwithstanding Fashion's advantage Peytona led to the Judge's stand a head in front. For the third mile they kept so so to the quarter; a table cloth might have covered the pair to the half-mile post. They kept just so to the three-quarters; at the drawgate Fashion led on the inside, but Peytona had got her and led her home a length in advance. "Now comes the tug of war." Peytona maintained her position, both well together; she gained a little on her round the bottom, but apparently with little effect; at the half they were well together, which was maintained to the three-quarters, but here the mob closed in so as to obscure sight from the club stand.—Fashion appeared to have the lead, but on approaching the drawgate, notwithstanding the mob closing on the track, Peytona led the way a clear length in advance in 7:45¼. We have only time to say that it was quite a waiting race; "Barney" knew what he had to do, and did nobly, and doubtless more he would have done if it had been required.

The following is the summary of the whole affair:

Miles	First Heat	Second Heat
First	1:54	1:58
Second	1:53	1:54
Third	1:57	1:55¼
Fourth	1:55¾	1:58
Total	7:39¾	7:45¼

SPEED OF PEYTONA, THE WINNER OF THE GREAT RACE:

	Distance miles	Distance feet	Time seconds	Distance pr sec'd	Strides pr sec'd
First Heat	4	21,120	459¼	46	2
Second Heat	4	21,120	465¼	45⅖	2

The horses at length appeared, and after the close of the first heat (an account of which we have given), when the word passed round that

Peytona, the southern favorite, was the conqueror, a most exciting scene was presented on the ground. The southern gentry having their most anxious expectations thus so nearly consummated, were loud in their rejoicing and hearty congratulations and warm hand shakings were seen on all sides among them, whilst the more cool and deliberate Northerners remained perfectly cool and easy, though certainly their spirits were not quite so buoyant as before this damper to their sanguine expectation however, the general excitement of the crowd on the Course was by no means allayed; in fact, if possible, it was more intense than ever, and the various groups walking up and down might be heard discussing with the greatest earnestness the chances and probabilities for and against their respective favorites and in some instances waxing so high in dispute as to cause apprehensions of a breach of the peace—but a few instances of fighting however came under our immediate notice, and as far as we could ascertain, but very few took place altogether. In the interim between the heats, quite an alarm was created in the gambling establishments underneath the stand by an ominous crack of the rafters overhead, and a most terrific rush from the tables took place money and game being alike forgotten in the horror of being crushed by the superincumbent mass of people on the stand. Luckily the alarm was a false one, and except the descent of a couple of sightseers from the stand above to the room below and the astonishment of a roulette table keeper at their landing on the top of his apparatus and disturbing his game, no damage was done. In the early part of the day, one of the stair cases leading to the stand broke down, but also in this instance the damage was slight, as all we could gather was the loss one unfortunate gentleman sustained in his wig, which, considering the warmth of the day, must have been no slight loss to the owner.

After the interval of twenty minutes the horses were again ready, and the crowd resumed their positions round the course; this time wound up to the pitch of frenzy, and, on the announcement of Peytona being again the conqueror, we can compare the universal cheer that broke forth to nothing that we have ever heard. The southerners appeared perfectly beside themselves with joy, and afforded quite a striking contrast to the northerners, whose lengthened faces were indicative of the shortening their purses and fame had undergone within the last few minutes. The result was soon announced from the judge's stand, and the time of the different heats marked in front of that building, and thus the south was declared the victor of the turf.

Both heats having been won by Peytona, and the necessity of a third heat being precluded, every one was busily engaging in making preparations for their return to town, and it was marvellous to see the astonishing celerity with which the ground was cleared of its thousands and thousands of spectators. One after another the various vehicles disappeared, and in a quarter of an hour the ground was almost deserted; though the booths and gambling establishments outside still had a number of customers, who remained till the train started for Brooklyn, at six o'clock, and though we thought the crowded state of the cars in the morning could not be exceeded, yet they were far more crammed and it not only required much agility to obtain a seat, but a good share of strength to keep it. However good, bad and indifferent, we all rolled off together, and a more dust-begrimed, dirty looking set of passengers we doubt have ever travelled on one train before. In consequence of the length of the train, it was seven o'clock before it arrived at the tunnel at Brooklyn, and the horrid screeches, yells and noises which they kept up during their passage through it, were well calculated to give an idea of Pandemonium. As might be supposed, the boats were crowded down with vehicles and passengers of every kind, and the day must have proved very profitable to the railroads and ferry boats on the route. Not the least gratifying fact is, the absence of any material accident among such an immense concourse of people.

The Camptown Races

Stephen Foster was one of America's most popular songwriters in the nineteenth century, best known for songs like "Dixie" and "Old Black Joe," which romanticized plantation life in the slave South. His "Camptown Races" (1850) suggests that familiarity with horse racing was common enough to integrate it into other forms of popular entertainment. What details about the sport can be learned from this song?

THE CAMPTOWN RACES

De Camptown ladies sing dis song,
Doo-dah! doo-dah!
De Camptown racetrack five miles long
Oh! doo-dah-day!
I come down dah wid my hat caved in
Doo-dah! doo-dah!
I go back home wid a pocket full of tin
Oh! doo-dah-day!

De long tail filly and de big black hoss,
Doo-dah! doo-dah!
Dey fly de track and dey both cut across,

Oh! doo-dah-day!
De blind hoss sticken in a big mud hole,
Doo-dah! doo-dah!
Can't touch bottom wid a ten foot pole,
Oh! doo-dah-day!

Old Mulley cow come onto de track,
Doo-dah! doo-dah!
De bobtail fling her ober his back,
Oh! doo-dah-day!
Den fly along like a railroad car,
Doo-dah! doo-dah!
Runnin' a race wid a shootin' star,
Oh! doo-dah-day!

See dem flying on a ten mile heat,
Doo-dah! doo-dah!
Round de race-track den repeat,
Oh! doo-dah-day!
I win my money on de bobtail nag,
Doo-dah! doo-dah!
I keep my money in an old towbag,
Oh! doo-dah-day!

CHORUS

Gwine to run all night!
Gwine to run all day!
I'll bet my money on de bobtail nag,
Somebody bet on de bay.

The Louisville Regatta

Anyone familar with the sleek eight-oared, graphite racing shells of today replete
with Adidas shoes, sliding seats and sound systems, may have a hard time
recognizing this description of a rowing race held in Louisville, Kentucky, and
reported in the July 20, 1839, issue of the Spirit of the Times. Yet in the 1830s,
1840s, and 1850s rowing was a popular spectator sport. Often involving sailors
from merchant ships, crews competed for cash prizes and occasionally for
national pride. By 1852, the first Harvard–Yale boat race signalled the emergence
of rowing as a major team sport for élite colleges and increased its popularity as
a spectator sport in the East.

As with other descriptions of ante-bellum sporting events, note the gambling
associated with the Louisville race. Does the attention to detailed reporting in this
account suggest anything about the interest and expertise of those who followed

the sport? Who attended the race? Does the fact that this story appeared in a newspaper devoted to coverage of sport and theatre for a middle class audience reveal anything about the popular appeal of sport in these years?

THE LOUISVILLE REGATTA, 1839

At half past 9 o'clock on the morning on the 4th, anxious hundreds swept in crowds towards the scene of action. The beauty and fashion of the city were there. Ladies and gentlemen, loafers and laborers, white folks and "niggers," steamboat cooks, scullions, cabin boys, clerks, mates, passengers and Captains, and all the paraphernalia of city life on an Independence Day, formed the contiguous parts of the heterogeneous mass that stood jammed and crowded upon the levee. Steamers were loaded down to their guards—boiler and hurricane decks, cabin lobbies, bow sprits, and chimneys were completely obscured, and the majestic boats towered from the water like solid masses of humanity. It was a great concentration of "mind and matter," though from the almost vertical rays of the summer sun, that shone steadily and fervidly down upon the scene, I should judge that the "matter" was the hottest portion of the focus. The eye, glancing upon the assembled crowds, was agreeably relieved from the monotonous and coommon-place display which may be observed in all such assemblages of ladies with their bonnets, ribbons, and bright eyes—gentlemen with their hats, canes, and cigars—Jehus with their hacks and horses—loafers with their white faces, and negroes with their black ones—by the beautiful regimentals, the drooping feathers, and bristling bayonets of the City Legion, composed of the male elite of Louisville.

As I stood gazing upon the oddly assorted multitudes from a small boat at the quay, a shout rolled up the air with a suddenness that was only equalled by the suddenness with which it ceased. I looked around—the fairy-formed barges were drawn to "the line." In point of men the "Ariel" had the advantage, and her strong and sinewy oarsmen bore a remarkable contrast to the comparatively weak and diminutive proportions of the "Stewarts." This disparity caused the bets to run greatly in favor of the eight-oared barge. Expectation was now on tip-toe—it was so intense that a silence, deep and impressive, fell pall-like over the multitude. There was a buzz—a hum throughout that mass, but no more. I never witnessed an apter emblem of the calm that precedes the outburst of the tempest. The feelings of the crowd seemed to sleep, to use the beautiful words of a poet.

" . . . like the passions in infancy's breast,
Till the storm should unchain them from out their dark cave,
And break the repose of the soul and the wave."

"Bang!" went the signal stroke upon the "gong," and in a second a long loud cheer—a rushing, crushing crowd—the trampling of feet—the curses of outraged pedestrians—the cries of excited hundreds, and the dash of oars overwhelmed me. I was unnerved—speechless, and absolutely blind. . . .

Bets were high, but equal. All had their eyes fixed upon the contending barges, which now dimly seen, seemed to dance upon the glittering waters, while their rapidly dipping oars flashed brightly in the sun-light. "The Ariel! the Ariel! shouted even the old river men, in anticipation of victory, and this shout was echoed to a deafening extent, when suddenly the "poor George Stewart" seemed to lose her distance, and her competitor shot still further ahead! Alas! the Stewart had broken a row-lock, but still pulled up with five oars. The tears started into the eyes of the debutants, but though all seemed lost, hope still nerved their arms. "The Infant," poor little fellow! was again the unfortunate person; his oar was now rendered useless, and his ambitious little soul swelled to such a pitch of agony, that for a few moments he was actually demented.

The Ariel reached the buoy, and rounded it. Up shot the Stewart, shouting for a row-lock. One was thrown from the buoy—it was caught—our little hero fixed it in its place again! Both boats were now on the descent. The excitement from this period of the race became more and more intense. Louder and longer swelled the shouts; men stood in the water to their knees; ladies from balconies and carriages waved their hand-kerchiefs; men threw up their hats and unfurled their silks, while other poor devils, who possessed neither of those articles, jerking off their coats, waved them encouragingly in the air. . . . the George Stewart is half a length—a length—a length ahead! Pull on! mind not the shouts! stretch to your oars! Another pull! "the line" is there! Another! it is crossed—the race is won! and the Ariel shoots in two lengths astern!

The five miles were run in 26m. 44s.

As the victorious Stewart crossed the line, the rapid discharges of musketry from the platoons of the military, mingled with the loud cheering of the excited multitude, rendered the scene at one moment the most stirring I ever beheld.

Prize Fighting

Although often attacked by middle-class moralists as a sign of civilization's decay and an activity beneath the dignity of respectable people, prize fighting enjoyed popularity in a variety of forms throughout the United States. Southern planters were known to pit their best fighting slaves against each other, much as they matched each other on horseback in earlier times. In the North, especially among working-class people, the sport, although prohibited by law in most communities, also was a diversion that provided opportunity to gamble and drink while affording a break from the arduous routine of work. Although matches were often held outside city limits, occasionally even on floating barges to avoid legal prohibitions and although critics often referred derogatorily to the sport's aficianadoes as "the fancy," there is ample evidence that the sport had a large following. In 1860, when an American Irishman named "Benica Boy" Heenan fought the British champion Tom Sayers to a 43 round draw, the *Spirit of the Times* published 100,000 extra copies to carry the news to its readers while *Frank Leslie's Illustrated* came out with an edition of 347,000 replete with five pages of drawings.

The following selection, from the October 15, 1859, edition of *Harper's Weekly;* offers a taste of both the action of a match and the criticism the sport engendered.

A TASTE OF THE ACTION

On Thursday, the 6th of October, the progress of our civilization was bravely illustrated by one of those exhibitions ever dear to degraded hearts, a Prize Fight. An event so hideous and revolting in all its relations is not to be approached without hesitation, yet there is that to be gained by a glance at its actual characteristics which the ordinary narrative reports to not afford. These, mostly aiming to satisfy the coarse tastes of the class who look upon the prize fighter as the loftiest embodiment of noble and digni- fied heroism, observe altogether from a technical pugilistic point of view, or deal generally with the agreeable aesthetics of brutality. They fail to set forward the truly horrible features of such displays, a tolerably faithful picture of which might perhaps awaken a deeper and more effective indig- nation against participators therein than now exists. In this belief we undertake to describe, as accurately as may be briefly done, the most recent of these offenses against law and humanity.

. . . The fight was between Edwin Euoch Price, of Boston, and James Kelly, of New York, two young men of splendid physical powers and good personal appearance. It occurred at Point Abino, a secluded spot on the Canadian shore of Lake Erie, fifteen miles from the city of Buffalo. The preparations were all conducted with great caution, in consequence of a reasonable apprehension that the authorities, in obedience to a law recently enacted to cover such cases, would take the first opportunity to seize upon all concerned, and to overthrow if possible, the entire arrangement. But by the care of artful managers every thing proceeded undisturbed, and on the morning of Thursday the appointed ground was covered with the rough and vicious crowd which gathers in regular force on such occasions. Most of the larger Northern cities contributed their share. For a day New York was relieved of much of its overflow of "fancy" feculence.

The Ring was planted in the centre of a sheltered grove, the surrounding trees of which were rapidly made to blossom thickly with anxious gazers. About the ring itself swarmed hundreds of congenial spirits, all eager, some almost frenzied with excitement. It was not a tranquilizing scene. Not a face but was seared with sin, or scarred with the record of some violent crime. Not an eye but glistened with evil impulses, betraying the desperate passions it reflected. Of first-class murderers there were two, each hemmed in by his band of fond admirers proffering adulations. By one of them stood stalwart Morrissey, showing in every attitude and gesture the burly ferocity of his nature. Not far away sat old Lazarus, long ago a fugitive from England, whence he fled after battering his opponent to death in just such a fight as this. His son beside him, trained to his father's vocation, and already in his youth a "champion," watched all that passed with critical frown. Of less glaring lights a multitude flickered around. Sympathetic lamentations were heard for "poor Joe Coburn," who, but for unkind detention at Sing Sing, would have been welcomed here in the name of his associates, as if, indeed, a stronger infusion of turpitude were needed in that crowd. . . . Price appears anxious and not quite at ease. Kelly, on the contrary, is given to manifestations of confidence, and takes arrogant strides, crying, "I will bet five hundred dollars that I win this fight!" "I will take seven hundred to one that he never knocks me down!" At this the crowd shouts lustily, and Kelly is moved to acknowledge its homage gracefull . . . meanwhile the betting progresses furiously. Morrissey, who rests his hopes on Kelly offers large odds in his favor. The youngest of the two murderers upon the ground displays heaps of bank notes, and declares that he, too, burns to prove his trust in Kelly, on whom, indeed, at this time, the great majority of all present appears to place reliance, while few voices are lifted up in Price's cause. . . . His [victim is] carried as tenderly as the case admits to his cottage. He groans piteously. Blood and cries of anguish issue together from his mouth. Physicians are summoned. They discover the fractured rib, and apply such remedies as are within their reach. The wounded man gives ceaseless utterance to his agony. His friends, sensitive souls when ridicule threatens, are shocked at his want of firmness. "Stop, Kelly, stop!" says one, "They'll be laughing at you, man." "My god. what can I do," cries the sufferer. "Die, man die, if you must," says another, "but give over this hellish howling." And thus the crushed and broken-hearted man is comforted.

Of the scenes of riotous revelry that follow, of the transfer of the thousands of dollars that takes place, of the weak and futile attempts of the Buffalo police to apprehend the participators, of the stampede in midnight trains, there is no need to speak in detail. Tis not too difficult to imagine all.

This was a prize fight. Do you find it brutal, barbarous, cruel, a disgrace to human nature, and a scandal to our nation's name? It is well to know, then, that, compared with the average of prize fights, this was a simple, weak, and trifling jest. The fraternity of "sportsmen" speak of it only with contempt. They do not care to conceal their disgust at its tameness. Why, here was one man who came out of the contest unharmed. For shame, Price, to disappoint the lively expectations of your audience. The affair of Heenan and Morrissey, though lasting only twenty-one minutes, while this was nearly twice as long, was richer a hundred times in all that stirs the soul with horror. One compensation is, that there was no rib broken then, as here, and over that consideration the "fancy" gloat with grim delight.

Frontier Sport: The Delicate Art of Gouging

While southern planters, northern working-men, and a growing urban middle-class might find the time to engage and watch a variety of sporting activities increasingly taking on the characteristics of modern sport, those Americans who pushed the physical boundaries of white settlement westward engaged in sporting activities reflective of the pace and conditions of the hard life they experienced on the frontier. Emphasizing the work skills and character traits necessary for survival in an isolated wilderness or a frontier town, frontier sport, although less organized and formal than what was developing elsewhere, provided opportunities to test individual hunting and strength skills while offering the chance for people to socialize with each other.

The following description of "rough and tumble" provides one example of sport on the frontier. It comes from Englishman Thomas Ashe's *Travels in America*, published in 1809. Although even less organized than boxing matches, this version of fighting gave Abraham Lincoln an early reputation as a formidable man.

ROUGH AND TUMBLE

. . . The quarrel took a smaller circle, confined to two individuals, a Virginian by birth, and a Kentuckeyman by adoption. A ring was formed, and the mob demanded whether they proposed to *fight fair*, or to *rough and tumble*. The latter mode was preferred. Perhaps you do not exactly understand the distinction of these terms. Fight fair, however, is much in the English manner; and here, as there, any thing foul requires interference; but when parties choose to *rough and tumble,* neither the populace nor individuals are to intermeddle or hinder either combatant from tearing or rending the other on the ground, or in any other situation. You startle at the words, *tear* and *rend,* and again do not understand me. You have heard these terms, I allow, applied to beasts of prey and to carnivorous animals; and your humanity cannot conceive them applicable to man: it nevertheless is so, and the fact will not permit me the use of any less expressive term. Let me proceed. Bulk and bone were in favour of the Kentuckeyan; *science* and craft in that of the Virginian. The former promised himself victory from his power, the latter from his science. Very few rounds had taken place, or fatal blows given, before the Virginian contracted his whole form, drew up his arms to his face, with his hands nearly closed in a concave, by the fingers being bent to the full extension of the flexors, and summoning up all his energy for one act of desperation, pitched himself into the bosom of his opponent. Before the effects of this could be ascertained, the sky was rent by the shouts of the multitude; and I could learn that the Virginian had expressed as much *beauty* and *skill* in his retraction and bound, as if he had been bred in a menagerie, and practised action and attitude among pan- thers and wolves. The shock received by the Kentuckeyan, and the want of breath, brought him instantly to the ground. The Virginian never lost his hold; like those bats of the south who never quit the subject on which they fasten till they taste blood, he kept his knees in his enemy's body; fixing his claws in his hair, and his thumbs, on his eyes, gave them an instantaneous start from their sockets. The sufferer roared aloud, but uttered no com- plaint. The citizens again shouted with joy. Doubts were no longer enter- tained and bets of three to one were offered on the Virginian. The Kentuckeyan not being able to disentangle his adversary from his face, adopted a new mode of warfare; and, in imitation of the serpent which crushes such creatures to death as it proposes for its food, he extended his arms round the Virginian, and hugged him into closer contact with his huge body. The latter disliking this, cast loose the hair and convex eyes of his adversary, when both, folded together like bears in an embrace, rolled several turns over each other. The acclamations increased, and bets run that the Kentuckeyan "would give out," that is, after being mutilated and deprived of his eyes, ears, and nose, he would cry out for mercy and aid. The public were not precisely right. Some daemon interposed for the biggest monster; he got his enemy under him, and in an instant snapt off his nose so close to his face, that no manner of projection remained. The little Virginian made one farther effort, and fastening on the under lip of his mutilator, tore it over the chin. The Kentuckeyan at length *gave out,* on which the people carried off the victor, and he preferring a triumph to a doctor, who came to cicatrize his face, suffered himself to be chaired round the ground as the champion of the times, and the first, rougher and tumbler. The poor wretch, whose eyes were started from their spheres, and whose lip refused its office, returned to the town, to hide his impotence, and get his countenance repaired.

America's National Game and the Beginnings of Organized Sport

Significant evidence that the ante-bellum years were critical to the development of modern American sport comes from the emergence of private clubs and college associations devoted to specific sporting activities. Invariably, the organization and membership of these groups reflected the particular social and physical needs of its members. In one way or another, their participation in particular sporting activities contributed to the sport's development and popularity.

The New York Yacht Club, for example, founded in 1844 by John Cox Stevens, limited its membership to New York's social and financial elite, charging its members initial dues of $40 for use of its sumptuous clubhouse and grounds where meetings and balls were held and where members were required to wear expensive uniforms. This organization, which began the America's Cup competition in 1851, not only aimed to satisfy the nautical interests of New York's elite but also to provide a sense of status and exclusion for them.

The operation of student-run rowing and baseball clubs on Eastern college campuses served similar purposes for its members just as the organization of German Turner societies and Scottish Caledonian clubs used athletic competition to satisfy the social and communal needs of particular ethnic groups. The sons of elite New Englanders at Harvard and Yale inaugurated intercollegiate rowing in 1852 when student clubs, operating without coaches or serious training, raced against each other on Lake Winnepesaukee. A high concentration of Scots in New York and Boston led to the birth of the Caledonians, clubs organized on a local basis that as early as 1836 held local and regional Highland Games competition emphasizing track and field events as well as traditional Scottish contests such as tossing the caber and putting the light stone. Always accompanied by music, dancing, and food, these games not only encouraged retention of Scottish identity and custom but inadvertently encouraged the development of formal track and field in the United States.

Even baseball, the first organized team sport in this country to gain popularity among both participants and spectators, owes its growth to this "associational" impulse. Contrary to the legend spawned by A. G. Spalding that baseball was "invented" by Abner Doubleday in Cooperstown, New York, in 1839, the game of baseball evolved in the United States from the English game of rounders. Its development as an organized team sport, however, owes much to the New York Knickerbockers, a social club of New York City middle-class professional men organized in 1842, and especially to Alexander Cartwright, the owner of a stationery and book store who founded the club, restricted its dues-paying membership to forty, and focused its activities on weekly games of baseball. Clubs like the Knickerbockers had rules that stipulated membership on the basis of class, insisted that players receive no pay for play or travel, and required that all expenses be covered out of membership dues rather than paid admissions. Matches scheduled on mid-week afternoons and followed by gala banquets and balls emphasized social occasion rather than intense competition.

By 1858, these amateur clubs had organized into the National Association of Baseball Players, formalized rules, and set the stage for the emergence of the professional game. As this selection from Charles Peverelly's *The Book of American Pastimes* (1866) indicates, the Knickerbockers and Cartwright were the first to codify rules of a game of "excitement and vim" described as well-suited to the quick pace of American life. A brief history of the Knickerbockers and their rules are included. Note the appeals to middle-class respectability as well as the suggestion of its appeal to the working class. Why does Peverelly see baseball as especially suited to Americans? Who watched teams like the Knickerbockers? What was the purpose of competition? How do the rules of the game compare to the present day version?

AMERICA'S NATIONAL PASTIME

The game of Base Ball has now become beyond question the leading feature of the out-door sports of the United States, and to account for its present truly proud position, there are many and sufficient reasons. It is a game which is peculiarly suited to the American temperament and disposition; the nine innings are played in the brief space of two and one half hours, or less. From the moment the first striker takes his position, and poises his bat, it has an excitement and vim about it, until the last hand is put out in the ninth innings. There is no delay or suspense about it, from the beginning to end; and even if one feels disposed to leave the ground, temporarily, he will generally waive his desire, especially if it is a close contest, from fear of missing some good point or clever effort of the trial.

An American assemblage cannot be kept in one locality for the period of two or three hours, without being offered something above the ordinary run of excitement and attraction. They are too mercurial and impulsive a race not to get drowsy and dissatisfied with anything which permits their natural ardor to droop even for a brief space of time. Hence their congeniality with, and partiality for Base Ball, which game caters to their inclinations and desires to a nicety; in short, the pastime suits the people, and the people suit the pastime.

It is also, comparatively, an economical recreation; the uniform is not costly, the playing implements, colors, and furnishing of a neat club-room, need not occasion an extravagant outlay when divided, pro rata, by the members of a full club. In aquatic organizations, either of Yachting or Rowing (both glorious sports), the expenses are necessarily heavy. The uniforms, boathouses, and boats, all necessitate liberal disbursement, and not unfrequent renewal. Base Ball does not demand from its votaries too much time, or rather, too great a proportion of the day. In the long sun-shiny days of summer, games are frequently commenced at four and even five o'clock in the afternoon, and completed some time before sunset. Consequently the great mass, who are in a subordinate capacity, can par-ticipate in this healthgiving and noble pastime.

The game stands today in a proud and fairly-won position—scarcely requiring eulogy from any source. Dating from the years when the old Knickerbocker Club, closely followed by the Gotham, Eagle, and Empire, gave their colors to the breeze as rallying points for the lovers of the game to muster at, it has grown with giant strides until its organizations are the pride of numberless villages, towns, and cities, all over the land. Wherever established, it has quickly had the sentiment and good feeling of the com-munity with it, and with scarcely an effort, achieved solid popularity. Hav-ing no debasing attributes, and being worthy of the presence of the good and the refined, it has everywhere been countenanced and encouraged by our best citizens; and of the thousands who gather at important matches, we have always noted with sincere gratification that the ladies constituted an honored proportion.

The game originated in Great Britain, and is familiarly known there as the the game of Rounders. We quote a description of the game. The reader will observe that it is the merest outline of what is now termed by the American press and public The National Game.

"Rounders.—This game is played with a ball and bats, or sticks some-thing of the form of a policeman's truncheon. A hole is first made, about a foot across and half a foot deep. Four other stations are marked with pegs stuck into the ground, topped with a piece of paper, so as to be readily seen. Sides are then chosen, one of which goes in. There may be five or more players on each side. Suppose that there are five. One player, on the side that is out, stands in the middle of the five-sided space, and pitches the ball towards the hole. he is called the feeder. The batsman hits it off, if he can; in which case he drops the stick, and runs to the nearest station, thence to the third, and all round if the hit has been a far one. The other side are scouting, and trying to put him out, either by hitting the batsman as he is running, or by sending the ball into the hole, which is called 'grounding.' The player at the hole may decline to strike the ball, but if he hits at it, and misses twice running, he is out. When a player makes the round of the stations back to the hole, his side counts one towards the game. When all the players are out, either by being hit or the ball being grounded, the other side get their innings. When there are only two players left, a chance is given of prolonging the innings, by one of them getting three balls from the feeder; and if he can give a hit such as to enable him to run the whole round, all his side come in again, and the counting is resumed. The feeder is generally the best player on his side, much depending on his skill and art. The scouts should seldom aim at the runners from a distance, but throw the ball up to the feeder or to some one near, who will try to hit or to ground, as seems the most advisable. A caught ball also puts the striker out."

We commence our sketches of the clubs of the National Association with a carefully prepared and interesting history of the pioneer Knickerbocker Club, of New York.

Knickerbocker Base Ball Club.

During the years of 1842 and '43, a number of gentlemen, fond of the game, casually assembled on a plot of ground in Twenty-seventh street—the one now ooccupied by the Harlem Railroad Depot, bringing with them their bats, balls, etc. It was customary for two or three players, occasionally during the season, to go around in the forenoon of a pleasant day and muster up players enough to make a match. The march of improvement made a "change of base" necessary, and the following year they met at the next most convenient place, the north slope of Murray Hill, between the railroad cut and Third avenue. Among the prominent players were Col. James Lee, Dr. Ransom, Abraham Tucker, James Fisher, and W. Vail, the latter better known in later years of the Gotham Club, as "Stay-where-you-am-Wail." In the spring of 1845 Mr. Alex. J. Cartwright, who had become an enthusiast in the game, one day upon the field proposed a regular organization, promising to obtain several recruits. His proposal was acceded to, and Messrs. W. R. Wheaton, Cartwright, D. F. Curry, E. R. Dupignac, Jr., and W. H. Tucker, formed themselves into a board of recruiting officers, and soon obtained names enough to make a respectable show. At a preliminary meeting, it was suggested that as it was apparent they would soon be driven from Murray Hill, some suitable place should be obtained in New Jersey, where their stay could be permanent; accordingly, a day or two afterwards, enough to make a game assembled at Barclay street ferry, crossed over, marched up the road, prospecting for ground on each side, until they reached the Elysian Fields, where they "settled." Thus it occurred that a party of gentlemen formed an organization, combining together health, recreation, and social enjoyment, which was the nucleus of the now great American game of Base Ball, so popular in all parts of the United States, than which there is none more manly or more health-giving.

The parent Knickerbockers claim for themselves the original organization, from which the succeeding clubs derived their rules of playing, and which was always ready to foster, encourage, and promote the pleasure of all who were desirous of enjoying the game. Its members have from its inception been composed mostly of those whose sedentary habits required recreation, and its respectability has ever been undoubted. The same standard still exists, and no person can obtain admission in the club merely for his capacity as a player; he must also have the reputation of a gentleman; and hence arises one of the causes of its not being what is called a match-playing club.

The organization bears date the 23d of September, 1845. Its first officers were: President, Duncan F. Curry; Vice-President, Wm. R. Wheaton; Secretary and Treasurer, Wm. H. Tucker.

Rules of the Knickerbocker Base Ball Club, Adopted September 23, 1845.

1st. Members must strictly observe the time agreed upon for exercise and be punctual in their attendance.

2d. When assembled for exercise, the President, or in his absence the Vice-President, shall appoint an Umpire, who shall keep the game in a book provided for that purpose, and note all violations of the By-Laws and Rules during the time of exercise.

3d. The presiding officer shall designate two members as Captains, who shall retire and make the match to be played, observing at the same time that the players put opposite to each other should be as nearly equal as possible; the choice of sides to be then tossed for, and the first in hand to be decided in like manner.

4th. The bases shall be from "home" to second base, forty-two paces; from first to third base, forty-two paces, equidistant.

5th. No stump match shall be played on a regular day of exercise.

6th. If there should not be a sufficient number of members of the Club present at the time agreed upon to commence exercise, gentlemen not members may be chosen in to make up the match, which shall not be broken up to take in members that may afterwards appear; but, in all cases, members shall have the preference, when present, at the making of a match.

7th. If members appear after the game is commenced they may be chosen in if mutually agreed upon.

8th. The game to consist of twenty-one counts, or aces; but at the conclusion an equal number of hands must be played.

9th. The ball must be pitched, and not thrown, for the bat.

DIAGRAM OF A BASE BALL FIELD.
Position of Players and the Measurements for Laying A Field Out

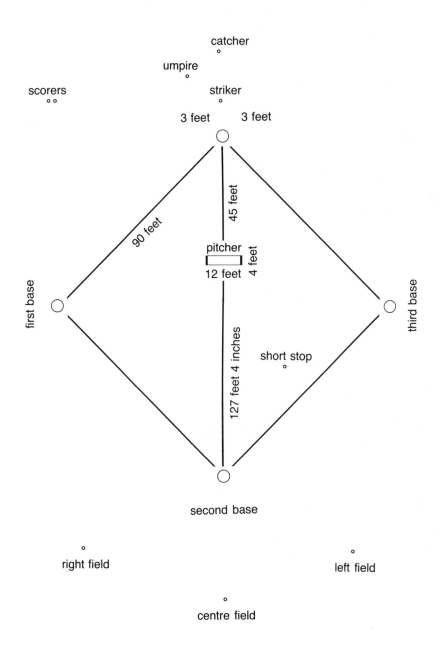

catcher

umpire

scorers   striker

3 feet   3 feet

90 feet   45 feet

pitcher   4 feet

12 feet

first base   third base

127 feet 4 inches   short stop

second base

right field   left field

centre field

Sport and Social Purpose

Acceptance of sport as legitimate activity in the ante-bellum years increasingly depended on the belief that participation served positive social purpose. Although full expression of the idea that there was a positive connection between physical and spirtual concerns or that sport could promote proper character awaited the decades after the Civil War, a number of articulate Americans began espousing these ideas earlier. Increased interest and participation in sport and physical recreation in the ante-bellum years, especially in the North, had clear connections to growing optimism about an expanding, modernizing society and the new leisure time some groups gained from a changing economy. Nevertheless, many middle-class Americans caught up and, enjoying the rewards of the transformation of American life, also expressed doubt about what was happening to them. For a whole range of health reformers, child guidance writers, and the authors of books about sport, sport and physical recreation were promoted as new ways to deal with the problems of a new society. Some argued that participation would encourage the development of character traits and values necessary for success. Others saw sport as providing relief from the rigors of the pursuit of wealth, allowing the individual to re-enter the battle with renewed energy. Others emphasized the importance of sport as an organized activity with rules and regulations that would reinforce ideas about order and stability in what appeared to some to be an increasingly unstable world. Whatever their argument, this growing literature on sport and social purpose underlined the growing importance and acceptance of sport as a distinct and significant part of everyday life.

The following selection from Robin Carver's *Book of Sports*, first published in Boston in 1834, offers an example of sports books written for middle-class urban adolescents that appeared in the 1830s and 1840s. Carver describes a wide range of athletic activities while gently suggesting the moral and spiritual benefits that could be gained from participation. Note the variety of activities listed in the table of contents and the detailed instructions offered for each activity. What message is presented about the benefits of participation in sport for both the individual and society? Do they have a modern ring? What difference or similarities are discernable between Carver's descriptions of nineteenth century ball games and contemporary versions? How do you explain the lack of attention given to girls? Already in these years, differences in male and female participation in sport reflected changing sexual roles and laid the foundations of discrimination against women's involvement in sport that marked the late nineteenth and the first half of the twentieth century.

SELECTIONS FROM *BOOK OF SPORTS*

Contents

Chapter I

Simple Sports and Pastimes

My young friends have often come to me, after they have been dismissed from school, and begged me to think of some new sport for their amusement. Now, though somewhat of an old man, I have not forgotten the games and pastimes of my boyhood. Many of the events of my youth are fresh in my memory, while those of later years have quite faded away. How careful should the young be to avoid every act, upon which they cannot always reflect with pleasure, when they know that the remembrance of it will last so long!

As I cannot have all my young friends about me at once, to tell them stories and assist them in their games, I have concluded to write a Book of Sports, purposely 'for American boys.' I would have you fond of exercise and of being in the open air; capable of bearing the winter's cold without injury, and of exerting yourselves with strength and agility.

There are many sports, which may help you to attain these desirable ends, and which are not only amusing but beneficial to young people.

In this little book, I intend to give you a description of such sports, as may be likely to afford you either healthful exercise or innocent amusement. I shall tell you some pleasant stories as I go along; and you will not be displeased if I occasionally mingle some useful piece of information with my descriptions. I shall begin with a very simple sport; but it is one, from which I dare say you have derived too much entertainment to think it unworthy of a place here.

Puss in the Corner

This lively game is played by five only. The place usually chosen for the sport is a square room or yard. Each of the four corners is occupied by a player: the fifth, who is called Puss, stands in the centre. The game now commences. The players exchange corners in all directions: it is the object of the one who stands out, to occupy any one of the corners, which may remain vacant for an instant during the exchanges. When he succeeds in so doing, that player, who is left without a corner becomes puss. This game may be played in any place, where there are four trees or posts, which may form the four corners of a square.

Chapter 3

Games with Balls

The use of the ball was well known to the children, who played many hundred years ago. It is a favorite game still, and offers a good opportunity for the exercise of the limbs and the muscles. The games with the bat and ball are numerous, but somewhat similar. I will mention some of those, which I believe to be the most popular with boys.

Base, or Goal Ball

This game is known under a variety of names. It is sometimes called 'round ball,' but I believe that 'base' or 'goal ball' are the names generally adopted in our country. The players divide into two equal parties, and chance decides which shall have first innings. Four stones or stakes are placed from twelve to twenty yards asunder, as a, b, c, d, in the margin; another is put at e. One of the party, who is out, places himself at e. He tosses the ball gently toward a, on the right of which one of the in-party places himself, and strikes the ball, if possible, with his bat. If he miss three times, or if the ball, when struck, be caught by any of the players of the opposite side, who are scattered about the field, he is out, and another takes his place. If none of those accidents take place, on striking the ball he drops the bat, and runs toward b, or, if he can, to c, d, or even to a again. If, however, the boy who stands at e, or any of the out-players who may happen to have the ball, strike him with it in his progress from a to b, b to c, c to d, or d to a, he is out. Supposing he can only get to b, one of his partners takes the bat, and strikes at the ball in turn. If the first player can only get to c, or d, the second runs to b, only, or c, as the case may be, and a third player begins; as they get home, that is, to a, they play at the ball by turns, until they all get out. Then, of course, the out-players take their places.

Fives

Fives may be played either single-handed or with partners. A good wall must be selected, with a round flat piece of ground in front of it. Three lines must be drawn so as to form, with the bottom of the wall, a square, to mark the bounds. A line must also be drawn on the wall, about three feet from the ground. The players toss up for innings. The winner begins by bounding his ball on the ground, and striking it against the wall, above the line, so that it may rebound vigorously. The other player then strikes it, in the same manner, either before it has touched the ground, or hopped from the ground more than once: the first player then prepares to receive and strike it at its rebound; and thus the game goes on, until one of the players fails to strike the ball in his turn, before it has hopped twice, or fails to strike it below the mark, or to drive it out of bounds. If the party who is in do neither of these, he loses his innings; if the other, then the in-player reckons one, on each occasion, towards the game, which is fifteen.

Nine-Holes, or Hat-Ball

Near a wall where the ground is level, dig nine, or a lesser number of holes, according to the number of players, large enough for a ball to be bowled in without difficulty. Number them, and let each player be allotted a number, by chance or choice, as it may be agreed. A line is drawn about five yards from the holes, at which one of the players places himself, and bowls the ball into one of the holes. The player to whom the hole, into which the ball is bowled, belongs, picks it up as quickly as he can, and endeavors to hit one handkerchief behind one of the players again. When he is fairly overtaken by the player behind whom he has last dropped the handkerchief, the latter takes his place, and he joins hands in the circle.

Chapter 5

Sports of Agility

A boy, who is quick and active out of doors, who is not seen lounging lazily in the sun, but who enters heartily into his sports, when the time and place are proper, may generally be looked upon as a good, or capable scholar. Habits of laziness and inactivity are to be carefully shunned by the young, lest in after life they reap their consequences in a feeble and sickly frame.

I once knew two brothers, of whom the eldest was named Arthur, and the youngest James. Arthur was a studious boy, but fond of the fireside, and averse to exercise in the open air. He was also very fond of lying in bed at morning, and would not leave the house till it was time to go to school. James, though quite a respectable scholar, was the foremost in all sports during play-hours, and lost no opportunity of improving himself in strength and agility. He was always up at an early hour, and forth in the fields, or performing some useful labor in the yard.

Years passed on, and the boys grew in size, and in mind. At last they both entered college, but Arthur had not been there a week before he was obliged to leave on account of his health, and he has remained an invalid ever since, regretting deeply his early habits of bodily sloth and inactivity.

James passed through his course of study at the university in a creditable manner, and unimpeded by illness or want of strength. He has since become eminent as a lawyer, and I have often heard him declare, that wealth and reputation are nothing compared to the blessing of 'a sound mind in a sound body.'

I would, therefore, my young readers, enjoin it upon you as a duty to avoid habits of inactivity and idleness. Rise with the lark, study while you study, and play while you play. Agility may be acquired by practice, but do not attempt fear which have in them anything dangerous, for they are unnecessary, and without benefit. It is best to advance by degrees; you will find it the sure means of success.—I will now go on with a list of sports.

Women's Amusements

Anxious about the consequences of a changing America but optimistic about the possibilities for success, northern middle-class Americans devoured an enormous literature offering advice on how to behave and succeed. A large portion of these advice books were aimed at instructing women in their new roles in an industrializing economy. Emphasizing the belief that women, by their different nature and for practical reasons, belonged in the home raising proper children and providing a haven from the rough world of work that men engaged in, writers like Catherine Beecher and William Alcott cultivated the ideas of separate spheres and the cult of domesticity. Sincerely and forthrightly, they argued that in a new American society, women's critical role in maintaining the republic lay not in the workplace, now set off as the exclusive domain of men, but at home.

Although such writers took seriously women's role, they reinforced notions that severely limited options and opportunities on the basis of gender that American women have been challenging down through the twentieth century. The following selection suggests that these distinctions also appeared in the area of physical recreation. This letter on "Amusements" comes from William Alcott's *Letters to a Sister, or Women's Mission* (1850). According to Alcott, why are amusements important for women? What activities does he suggest for them? How are they different from what Robin Carver offers young men? How do they correspond to the role and character of women, as Alcott understands them?

AMUSEMENTS

Closely connected with the subject of health is that of amusements; nor is it much less important. Few things demand more the serious attention of those who have the charge of the young of both sexes, at the present time—females no less than males—than the manner in which they are to amuse themselves. It is of course a subject of importance.

For amusement you must have of some sort or other. Your opening nature, bodily and mental, demands it. You need it as much as the kitten or the lamb. It has been a maxim, "all work and no play makes Jack a dull boy." So would all study, as well as all work. So would all *anything*. You cannot be deprived of your amusement, but at your peril.

I speak with the more freedom, in regard to amusements for the young, because there is the beginning of an awakening of the public conscience, which has so long slumbered, on this great subject. Good people, as well as others, are beginning to see that they have been guilty of a neglect, whose consequences have often pierced them through with many sorrows.

What, then, are some of the forms in which the young, especially those of more advanced years, like yourself, should amuse themselves?

Several things should be kept in view, in relation to this matter. Your amusements should be of such a nature as is compatible with health of body and mind. They should be such as afford exercise to those organs and faculties which are not otherwise called into sufficient activity. They should be such as are relished. They should have a good social and moral tendency.

It happens, by the way, that amusements which are peculiarly healthy to one person are often less so to another. This fact may be owing to temperament, mode of employment, inherited or acquired tendencies to disease, &c. While, therefore, all our directions we should keep in view the laws of health, we must by no means forget the varying circumstances of the individual.

Your temperament—nervous and sanguine, but not highly active—requires active exercise. You pursue household employments, in part, and these are highly favorable. Thus far considered, you would not seem to demand very active amusements. But then again, you do not highly relish your housework, while you are excessively fond of your garden, your walks, your pony and your carriage.

On the whole, you find yourself most benefited by amusements in the open air. You would not be profited so much by the dance, even if you could relish it, and could be made to believe it had a good moral tendency.

Your fondness for your garden, is very highly favorable. Continue that fondness. Your flowers, your vines, your fruit-trees, will all of them minister to your amusement. Whether watering, budding, pruning, hoeing, or collecting the products of your labor, you will still be amused, and both mind and body be greatly improved.

But this is not enough—it does not go far enough. You need something more active, as jumping, running, and the like. I will tell you what will be about the right amusement for you, beyond the garden and field. An occasional ramble with a friend or with a small party, in pursuit of rare flowers, plants, minerals, insects, or birds. And should you, in your zeal, so far compromise your dignity, as to forget the staid snail-like pace to which, ever since you entered your teens, society has endeavored to constrain you, as to walk a little more rapidly, or to even run, and clap your hands, and shout *Eureka*, do not think you have committed the sin unpardonable in Heaven's court; or that even the tribunal of your company will condemn you. You have your trial before a jury of the "sovereign *people*"—though it may not always be exactly twelve in number; be, therefore, of good courage.

Walking to do good—when your feelings are so much absorbed as to make you forget to measure your pace—is one of the best amusements of body and mind you can possibly have next, I mean, to those which have been just now mentioned. But mere walking, that is, walking for the *sake* of walking, is worth very little to you or any body else.

Exercise on horseback comes next. As you are fond of this, and as you require the open air, it is highly proper. Those, however, who incline either to pulmonary or bilious complaints, will, as a general rule, reap more immediate, solid advantages from it than you will.

I need not add to these hints. I need not interdict balls, assemblies, parties late at night, nor even a too frequent attendance on the lecture or the scientific experiments. Still less need is there that I should refer to the dance. Your own good sense and former habits are sure to decide right here . . . .

And thus it would be, through the whole circle of your acquaintance, were these real wants considered. One would require this exercise, another that. One would require this combination of exercise, another a different one. But then all, as a general rule, demand pure air, a cheerful mind, and a warm heart. All require their undivided energies for the time. You must not be half interested in them, but wholly so.

But I do not expect to give you a whole volume on amusements in the compass of a single letter. All I can reasonably hope to do is to establish in your mind a few correct principles, and then leave the application of these principles to your own good common sense. Happy will it be for you, and for all concerned with, or dependent on you, if you make the application wisely and judiciously.

One difficulty in relation to this matter, has been alluded to in connection with another subject. Young women are unwilling to think. Some are more averse to thinking than yourself. But all, or almost all, are faulty in this particular; and hence the importance of being frequently and earnestly admonished.

Is it necessary to remind you, that there is danger of amusing yourself too much? It would not be necessary to remind your bilious neighbor of it; she will never give up time enough to her amusements. her great, I might almost say morbid or diseased conscientiousness, would forbid it, if nothing else should. With regard to yourself, deep principle might be operative to restrain you; but not an over-active or high-wrought conscientiousness, except in case of diseased nerves and brain. And yet, though I am compelled to remind you that there is such a thing in the world as morbid conscientiousness, it is exceedingly rare. Most persons have too little rather than too much of this commodity. It is a fault of the age, so it seems to me, to ask, What will people say, rather than, What is right? or, What does God say?

Few among us come up to the requisition of the inspired penman. This is true, even in regard to the most sacred things; how much more so, in regard to the common every-day concerns of life! How few among us labor from day to day, from hour to hour, from moment to moment, to *do all to the glory of God!*

America's Muscular Christians

Thomas Wentworth Higginson was a minister, an abolitionist, and a vociferous supporter of John Brown. A firm believer in the importance of physical exertion and a patron of the poet Emily Dickinson, he once suggested to her that her poetry might improve if she lifted weights.

In 1858, Higginson published a short essay titled *Saints and Their Bodies*, which summarized his views about the importance of sport and anticipated Americans' acceptance of what was to be called "muscular christianity." What were the positive moral and social benefits Higginson saw from participation in sport? Does he offer different benefits for males and females? What do you think of his notion that the United States might become a "nation of athletes?" How would you compare his views about physical activity to those of the Puritans? Note his reference to Thomas Hughes' *Tom Brown's School Days*, a novel written by an Englishman that had a dramatic influence in popularizing the idea of muscular christianity in the United States.

SAINTS AND THEIR BODIES

Ever since the time of that dyspeptic heathen, Plotinus, the saints have been "ashamed of their bodies." What is worse, they have usually had reason for the shame. Of the four famous Latin fathers, Jerome describes his own limbs as misshapen, his skin as squalid, his bones as scarcely holding together; while Gregory the Great speaks in his Epistles of his own large size, as contrasted with his weakness and infirmities. Three of the four Greek fathers—Chrysostom, Basil, and Gregory of Nazianzen—ruined their health early, and were wretched invalids for the remainder of their days. Three only of the whole eight were able-bodied men,—Ambrose, Augustine, and Athanasius; and the permanent influence of these three has been far greater, for good or for evil, than that of all the others put together.

. . . It would be tedious to analyze the causes of this modern deterioration of the saints. The fact is clear. There is in the community an impression that physical vigor and spiritual sanctity are incompatible. We knew a young Orthodox divine who lost his parish by swimming the Merrimac River, and another who was compelled to ask a dismissal in consequence of vanquishing his most influential parishioner in a game of tenpins; it seemed to the beaten party very unclerical. We further remember a match, in a certain sea-side bowling-alley, in which two brothers, young divines, took part. The sides being made up, with the exception of these two players, it was necessary to find places for them also. The head of one side accordingly picked his man, on the presumption (as he afterwards confessed) that the best preacher would naturally be the worst bowler. The athletic capacity, he thought, would be in inverse ratio to the sanctity. We are happy to add, that in this case his hopes were signally disappointed. But it shows which was the popular impression lies.

. . . But, happily, times change, and saints with them. Our moral conceptions are expanding to take in that "athletic virtue" of the Greeks.

. . . Our American saintship, also, is beginning to have a body to it, a "Body of Divinity," indeed. Look at our three great popular preachers. The vigor of the paternal blacksmith still swings' the sinewy arm of Beecher;—Parker performed the labors, mental and physical, of four able-bodied men, until even his great strength temporarily yielded;—and if ever dyspepsia attack the burly frame of Chapin, we fancy that dyspepsia will get the worst of it.

This is as it should be. One of the most potent causes of the ill-concealed alienation between the clergy and the people, in our community, is the supposed deficiency, on the part of the former, of a vigorous, manly life. It must be confessed that our saints suffer greatly from this moral and physical anhaemia, this bloodlessness, which separates them, more effectually than a cloister, from the strong life of the age. What satirists upon religion are those parents who say of their pallid, puny, sedentary, lifeless, joyless little offspring, "He is born for a minister," while the ruddy, the brave, and the strong are as promptly assigned to a secular career!

. . . Physical health is a necessary condition of all permanent success. To the American people it has a stupendous importance, because it is the only attribute of power in which they are losing ground. Guaranty us against physical degeneracy, and we can risk all other perils,—financial crises, Slavery, Romanism, Mormonism, Border Ruffians, and New York assassins; "domestic malice, foreign levy, nothing" can daunt us. Guaranty us health, and Mrs. Stowe cannot frighten us with all the prophecies of Dred; but when her sister Catherine informs us that in all the vast female acquaintance of the Beecher family there are not a dozen healthy women, we confess ourselves a little tempted to despair of the republic.

The one drawback to satisfaction in our Public-School System is the physical weakness which it reveals and helps to perpetuate. One seldom notices a ruddy face in the school-room, without tracing it back to a Transatlantic origin. The teacher of a large school in Canada went so far as to declare to us, that she could recognize the children born this side of the line by their invariable appearance of ill-health joined with intellectual precocity,—stamina wanting, and the place supplied by equations. Look at a class of boys or girls in our Grammar Schools; a glance along the line of their backs affords a study of geometrical curves. You almost long to reverse the position of their heads, as Dante has those of the false prophets, and thus improve their figures; the rounded shoulders affording a vigorous chest, and the hollow chest an excellent back.

. . . To a well-regulated frame, mere physical exertion, even for an uninteresting object, is a great enjoyment, which is, of course, enhanced by the excitement of games and sports. To almost every man there is joy in the memory of these things; they are the happiest associations of his boyhood. It does not occur to him, that he also might be as happy as a boy, if he lived more like one. What do most men know of the "wild joys of living," the daily zest and luxury of out-door existence, in which every healthy boy beside them revels?—skating, while the orange sky of sunset dies away over the delicate tracery of gray branches, and the throbbing feet pause in their tingling motion, and the frosty air is filled with the shrill sound of distant steel, the resounding of the ice, and the echoes up the hillsides?—sailing, beating up against a stiff breeze, with the waves thumping under the bow, as if a dozen sea-gods had laid their heads together to resist it?—climbing tall trees, where the higher foliage, closing around, cures the dizziness which began below, and one feels as if he had left a coward beneath and found a hero above?—the joyous hour of crowded life in football or cricket?—the gallant glories of riding, and the jubilee of swimming?

The charm which all have found in "Tom Brown's School Days at Rugby" lies simply in this healthy boy's-life which it exhibits, and in the recognition of physical culture, which is so novel to Americans.

. . . Should it prove, however, that the cultivation of active exercises diminishes the proportion of time given by children to study, we can only view it as an added advantage. Every year confirms us in the conviction, that our schools, public and private, systematically overtask the brains of the rising generation. We all complain that Young America grows to mental maturity too soon, and yet we all contribute our share to continue the evil. It is but a few weeks since we saw the warmest praises, in the New York newspapers, of a girl's school, in that city, where the appointed hours of study amounted to nine and a quarter daily, and the hours of exercise to a bare unit. Almost all the Students' Manuals assume that American students need stimulus instead of restraint, and urge them to multiply the hours of study and diminish those out-door amusements and of sleep, as if the great danger did not lie that way already. When will parents and teachers learn to regard mental precocity as a disaster to be shunned, instead of a glory to be coveted?

. . . But so far as there is a deficiency in these respects among us, this generation must not shrink from the responsibility. It is unfair to charge it on the Puritans. They are not even answerable for Massachusetts; for there is no doubt that athletic exercises, of some sort, were far more generally practiced in this community before the Revolution than at present. A state of almost constant Indian warfare then created an obvious demand for muscle and agility. At present there is no such immediate necessity. And it has been supposed that a race of shopkeepers, brokers, and lawyers could live without bodies. Now that the terrible records of dyspepsia and paralysis are disproving this, we may hope for a reaction in favor of bodily exercises. And when we once begin the competition, there seems no reason why any other nation should surpass us. The wide area of our country, and its variety of surface and shore, offer a corresponding range of physical training. Take our coasts and inland waters alone. It is one thing to steer a pleasure-boat with a rudder, and another to steer a dory with an oar; one thing to paddle a birch-canoe, and another to paddle a duckling-float; in a Charles River club-boat, the post of honor is in the stern—in a Penobscot bateau, in the bow; and each of these experiences educates a different set of muscles. Add to this the constitutional American receptiveness, which welcomes new pursuits without distinction of origin—unites German gymnastics with English sports and sparring, and takes the red Indians for instructors in paddling and running. With these various aptitudes, we certainly ought to become a nation of athletes.

We have shown, that, in one way or another, American schoolboys obtain active exercise. The same is true, in a very limited degree, even of girls. They are occasionally, in our larger cities, sent to gymnasiums,—the more the better. Dancing-schools are better than nothing, though all the attendant circumstances are usually unfavorable. A fashionable young lady is estimated to traverse her three hundred miles a season on foot; and this needs training. But out-door exercise for girls is terribly restricted, first by their costume, and secondly by the remarks of Mrs. Grundy. All young female animals unquestionably require as much motion as their brothers, and naturally make as much noise; but what mother would not be shocked, in the case of her girl of twelve, by one-tenth part the activity and uproar which are recognized as being the breath of life to her twin brother? Still, there is a change going on, which is tantamount to an admission that there is an evil to be remedied. Twenty years ago, if we mistake not, it was by no means considered "proper" for little girls to play with their hoops and balls on Boston Common; and swimming and skating have hardly been recognized as "ladylike" for half that period of time.

Still it is beyond question, that far more out-door exercise is habitually taken by the female population of almost all European countries than by our own. In the first place, the peasant women of all other countries (a class non-existent here) are trained to active labor from childhood; and what traveller has not seen, on foreign mountain-paths, long rows of maidens ascending and descending the difficult ways, bearing heavy burdens on their heads, and winning by the exercise such a superb symmetry and grace of figure as were a new wonder of the world to Cisatlantic eyes? Among the higher classes, physical exercises take the place of these things. Miss Beecher glowingly describes a Russian female seminary in which nine hundred girls of the noblest familes were being trained by Ling's system of calisthenics, and her informant declared that she never beheld such an array of girlish health and beauty. Englishwoman, again, have horsemanship and pedestrianism, in which their ordinary feats appear to our healthy women incredible. Thus, Mary Lamb writes to Miss Wordsworth, (both ladies being between fifty and sixty), "You say you can walk fifteen miles with ease; that is exactly my stint, and more fatigues me"; and then speaks pityingly of a delicate lady who could accomplish only "four or five miles every third or fourth day, keeping very quiet between." How few American ladies, in the fulness of their strength, (if female strength among us has any fulness,) can surpass this English invalid!

But even among American men, how few carry athletic habits into manhood! The great hindrance, no doubt, is absorption in business; and we observe that this winter's hard times and consequent leisure have given a great stimulus to outdoor sports. But in most places there is the further obstacle, that a certain stigma of boyishness goes with them. So early does this begin, that we remember, in our teens to have been slightly reproached with juvenility, because, though a Senior Sophister, we still clung to football. Juvenility! We only wish we had the opportunity now.

CHAPTER THREE
THE EMERGENCE OF MODERN SPORT
1865–1910

Whether measured by the bicycling craze of the 1890s, the growth of organized, professional baseball, the rise of college football, the birth of the country club, the organized play movement, or the astounding expansion of the sporting-goods industry, there is no question that the last quarter of the nineteenth century witnessed an explosion of popular interest in sport. Sport as a spectacle for spectators became more prominent at the same time that participation in athletics reached new heights. Activities became better organized and rationalized as sports became lucrative as commercial venture. Major tendencies that were to mark the contours of twentieth century American sport are all evident in this period.

Historians are just beginning to appreciate what late-nineteenth century observers of American life understood first hand. For them, the rise of modern sport was directly related to the transformation of the United States into a modern industrial state and the confluence of events and movements that accompanied it: the close of the frontier, the growth of large cities, European immigration and an expanding immigrant working-class, the end of slavery, industrial expansion, and the rise of a new affluence. The commitment towards sport as a means of shaping proper citizens, evidenced in the writings of Thomas Wentworth Higginson and Robin Carver, received additional support in these years by a social Darwinist perspective that was used to justify the increasing division of wealth between social classes. This desire to preserve the savage instinct through organized sport and to channel it into a socially productive activity that would hone society's leaders complemented a belief that sport might serve as an "artificial frontier" where the American character could be tested and American values reaffirmed now that the real frontier no longer existed. In slightly different versions, moralists and health reformers, operating through agencies such as the settlement house, the YMCA, and the Playground Association of America also encouraged organized sport as a means of assimilating vast numbers of East European immigrants. Creative entrepreneurs who realized the potential for profit in the promotion of sport also persuaded Americans to participate in sport as spectators and as activists, contributing as well to sport's acceptance as a significant social and economic institution of American life.

The Strenuous Life

Theodore Roosevelt—outdoorsman, politician, and president of the United States—epitomized late-nineteenth century Americans' interest in the "strenuous life" and the growing acceptance of sport in developing strong and proper citizens. An avid sportsman known for his african safaris, hunting expeditions, and military exploits, Roosevelt advocated what he called the "strenuous life" as a means of nurturing solid and tough leaders for American society. The following selections come from two essays by Roosevelt collected in his *The Strenuous Life: Essays and Addresses*, published in 1900 while he was governor of New York and the newly picked vice-presidential running mate of William McKinley. Consider Roosevelt's arguments in comparison to Higginson's. What kind of personality and character did Roosevelt hope to develop in America's young men? What of his concern that the material success enjoyed by the nation's middle- and upper-classes might lead them to laziness and sloth? What views about society and progress are implicit in his comments?

THE STRENUOUS LIFE

In speaking to you, men of the greatest city of the West, men of the State which gave to the country Lincoln and Grant, men who preeminently and distinctly embody all that is most American in the American character, I wish to preach, not the doctrine of ignoble ease, but the doctrine of the strenuous life, the life of toil and effort, of labor and strife; to preach that highest form of success which comes, not to the man who desires mere easy peace, but to the man who does not shrink from danger, from hardship, or from bitter toil, and who out of these wins the splendid ultimate triumph.

A life of slothful ease, a life of that peace which springs merely from lack either of desire or of power to strive after great things, is as little worthy of a nation as of an individual. I ask only that what every self-respecting American demands from himself and from his sons shall be demanded of the American nation as a whole. Who among you would teach your boys that ease, that peace, is to be the first consideration in their eyes—to be the ultimate goal after which they strive? You men of Chicago have made this city great, you men of Illinois have done your share, and more than your share, in making America great, because you neither preach nor practise such a doctrine. You work yourselves, and you bring up your sons to work. If you are rich and are worth your salt, you will teach your sons that though they may have leisure, it is not to be spent in idleness; for wisely used leisure merely means that those who possess it, being free from the necessity of working for their livelihood, are all the more bound to carry on some kind of non-remunerative work in science, in letters, in art, in exploration, in historical research—work of the type we most need in this country, the successful carrying out of which reflects most honor upon the nation. We do not admire the man of timid peace. We admire the man who embodies victorious effort; the man who never wrongs his neighbor, who is prompt to help a friend, but who has those virile qualities necessary to win in the stern strife of actual life. It is hard to fail, but it is worse never to have tried to succeed. In this life we get nothing save by effort. Freedom from effort in the present merely means that there has been stored up effort in the past. A man can be freed from the necessity of work only by the fact that he or his fathers before him have worked to good purpose. If the freedom thus purchased is used aright, and the man still does actual work, though of a different kind, whether as a writer or a general, whether in the field of politics or in the field of exploration and adventure, he shows he deserves his good fortune. But if he treats this period of freedom from the need of actual labor as a period, not of preparation, but of mere enjoyment, even though perhaps not of vicious enjoyment, he shows that he is simply a cumberer of the earth's surface, and he surely unfits himself to hold his own with his fellows if the need to do so should again arise. A mere life of ease is not in the end a very satisfactory life, and, above all, it is a life which ultimately unfits those who follow it for serious work in the world.

In the last analysis a healthy state can exist only when the men and women who make it up lead clean, vigorous, healthy lives; when the children are so trained that they shall endeavor, not to shirk difficulties, but to overcome them; not to seek ease, but to know how to wrest triumph from toil and risk. The man must be glad to do a man's work. . . .

THE AMERICAN BOY

Of course what we have a right to expect of the American boy is that he shall turn out to be a good American man. Now, the chances are strong that he won't be much of a man unless he is a good deal of a boy. He must not be a coward or a weakling, a bully, a shirk, or a prig. He must work hard and play hard. He must be cleanminded and clean-lived, and able to hold his own under all circumstances and against all comers. It is only on these conditions that he will grow into the kind of American man of whom America can be really proud.

There are always in life countless tendencies for good and for evil, and each succeeding generation sees some of these tendencies strengthened and some weakened; nor is it by any means always, alas! that the tendencies for evil are weakened and those for good strengthened. But during the last few decades there certainly have been some notable changes for good in boy life. The great growth in the love of athletic sports, for instance, while fraught with danger if it becomes one-sided and unhealthy, has beyond all question had an excellent effect in increased manliness. Forty or fifty years ago the writer on American morals was sure to deplore the effeminacy and luxury of young Americans who were born of rich parents. The boy who was well off then, especially in the big Eastern cities, lived too luxuriously, took to billiards as his chief innocent recreation, and felt small shame in his inability to take part in rough pastimes and field-sports. Nowadays, whatever other faults the son of rich parents may tend to develop, he is at least forced by the opinion of all his associates of his own age to bear himself well in manly exercises and to develop his body—and therefore, to a certain extent, his character—in the rough sports which call for pluck, endurance, and physical address.

Of course boys who live under such fortunate conditions that they have to do either a good deal of outdoor work or a good deal of what might be called natural outdoor play do not need this athletic development. In the Civil War the soldiers who came from the prairie and the backwoods and the rugged farms where stumps still dotted the clearings, and who had learned to ride in their infancy, to shoot as soon as they could handle a rifle, and to camp out whenever they got the chance, were better fitted for military work than any set of mere school or college athletes could possibly be. Moreover, to mis-estimate athletics is equally bad whether their importance is magnified or minimized. The Greeks were famous athletes, and as long as their athletic training had a normal place in their lives, it was a good thing. But it was a very bad thing when they kept up their athletic games while letting the stern qualities of soldiership and statesmanship sink into disuse. Some of the younger readers of this book will certainly sometime read the famous letters of the younger Pliny, a Roman who wrote, with what seems to us a curiously modern touch, in the first century of the present era. His correspondence with the Emperor Trujan is particularly interesting; and not the least noteworthy thing in it is the tone of contempt with which he speaks of the Greek athletic sports, treating them as the diversions of an unwarlike people which it was safe to encourage in order to keep the Greeks from turning into anything formidable. So at one time the Persian kings had to forbid polo, because soldiers neglected their proper duties for the fascinations of the game. We cannot expect the best work from soldiers who have carried to an unhealthy extreme the sports and pastimes which would be healthy if indulged in with moderation, and to have neglected to learn as they should the business of their profession. A soldier needs to know how to shoot and take cover and shift for himself—not to box or play foot-ball. There is, of course, always the risk of thus mistaking means for ends. Fox-hunting is a first-class sport; but one of the most absurd things in real life is to note the bated breath with which certain excellent fox-hunters, otherwise of quite healthy minds, speak of this admirable but not over-important pastime. They tend to make it almost as much of a fetish as in the last century, the French and German nobles made the chase of the stag, when they carried hunting and game-preserving to a point which was ruinous to the national life. Fox-hunting is very good as a pastime, but it is about as poor a business as can be followed by any man of intelligence. Certain writers about it are fond of quoting the anecdote of a fox-hunter who, in the days of the English civil war, was discovered pursuing his favorite sport just before a great battle between the Cavaliers and the Puritans, and right between their lines as they came together. These writers apparently consider it merit in this man that when his country was in a death-grapple, instead of taking arms and hurrying to the defense of the cause he believed right, he should placidly have gone about his usual sports. Of course, in reality the chief serious use of fox-hunting is to encourage manliness and vigor, and to keep men hardy, so that at need they can show themselves fit to take part in work or strife for their native land. When a man so far confuses ends and means as to think that fox-hunting, or polo, or foot-ball, or whatever else the sport may be, is to be itself taken as the end, instead of as the mere means of preparation to do work that counts when the time arises, when the occasion calls—why, that man had better abandon sport altogether.

No boy can afford to neglect his work, and with a boy work, as a rule, means study. Of course there are occasionally brilliant successes in life where the man has been worthless as a student when a boy. To take these exceptions as examples would be as unsafe as it would be to advocate blindness because some blind men have won undying honor by triumphing over their physical infirmity and accomplishing great results in the world. I am no advocate of senseless and excessive cramming in studies, but a boy should work, and should work hard, at his lessons—in the first place, for the sake of what he will learn, and in the next place, for the sake of the effect upon his own character of resolutely settling down to learn it. Shiftlessness, slackness, indifference in studying, are almost certain to mean inability to get on in other walks of life. Of course, as a boy grows older it is a good thing if he can shape his studies in the direction toward which he has a natural bent; but whether he can do this or not, he must put his whole heart into them. I do not believe in mischief-doing in school hours, or in the kind of animal spirits that results in making bad scholars; and I believe that those boys who take part in rough, hard play outside of school will not find any need for horse-play in school. While they study they should study just as hard as they play foot-ball in a match game. It is wise to obey the homely old adage, "Work while you work; play while you play."

A boy needs both physical and moral courage. Neither can take the place of the other. When boys become men they will find out that there are some soldiers very brave in the field who have proved timid and worthless as politicians, and some politicians who show an entire readiness to take chances and responsibilities in civil affairs, but who lack the fighting edge when opposed to physical danger. In each case with soldiers and politicians alike, there is but half a virtue. The possession of the courage of the soldier does not excuse the lack of courage in the statesman, and, even less does the possession of the courage of the statesman excuse shrinking on the field of battle. Now, this is all just as true of boys. A coward who will take a blow without returning it is a contemptible creature; but, after all, he is hardly as contemptible as the boy who dares not stand up for what he deems right against the sneers of his companions who are themselves wrong. Ridicule is one of the favorite weapons of wickedness, and it is sometimes incomprehensible how good and brave boys will be influenced for evil by the jeers of associates who have no one quality that calls for respect, but who affect to laugh at the very traits which ought to be peculiarly the cause for pride.

There is no need to be a prig. There is no need for a boy to preach about his own good conduct and virtue. If he does he will make himself offensive and ridiculous. But there is urgent need that he should practise decency; that he should be clean and straight, honest and truthful, gentle and tender, as well as brave. If he can once get to a proper understanding of things, he will have a far more hearty contempt for the boy who has begun a course of feeble dissipation, or who is untruthful, or mean, or dishonest, or cruel, than this boy and his fellows can possibly, in return, feel for him. The very fact that the boy should be manly and able to hold his own, that he should be ashamed to submit to bullying without instant retaliation, should, in return, make him abhor any form of bullying, cruelty, or brutality.

There are two delightful books, Thomas Hughes's "Tom Brown at Rugby," and Aldrich's "Story of a Bad Boy," which I hope every boy still reads; and I think American boys will always feel more in sympathy with Aldrich's story, because there is in it none of the fagging, and the bullying which goes with fagging, the account of which, and the acceptance of which, always puzzle an American admirer of Tom Brown.

There is the same contrast between two stories of Kipling's: One, called "Captains Courageous," describes in the liveliest way just what a boy should be and do. The hero is painted in the beginning as the spoiled, over-indulged child of wealthy parents, of a type which we do sometimes unfortunately see, and than which there exist few things more objectionable on the face of the broad earth. This boy is afterward thrown on his own resources, amid wholesome surroundings, and is forced to work hard among boys and men who are real boys and real men doing real work. The effect is invaluable. On the other hand, if one wishes to find types of boys to be avoided with utter dislike, one will find them in another story by Kipling, called "Stalky & Co.," a story which ought never to have been written, for there is hardly a single form of meanness which it does not seem to extol, or of school mismanagement which it does not seem to applaud. Bullies do not make brave men; and boys or men of foul life cannot become good citizens, good Americans, until they change; and even after the change scars will be left on their souls.

The boy can best become a good man by being a good boy—not a goody-goody boy, but just a plain good boy. I do not mean that he must also love only the negative virtues; I mean he must love the positive virtues also. "Good," in the largest sense, should include whatever is fine, straight-forward, clean, brave, and manly. The best boys I know—the best men I know—are good at their studies and their business, fearless and stalwart, hated and feared by all that is wicked and depraved, incapable of submitting to wrong-doing, and equally incapable of being aught but tender to the weak and helpless. A healthy-minded boy should feel hearty contempt for the coward, and even more hearty indignation for the boy who bullies girls or small boys, or tortures animals. One prime reason for abhorring cowards is because every good boy should have it in him to thrash the objectionable boy as the need arises.

Of course the effect that a thoroughly manly, thoroughly straight and upright boy can have upon the companions of his own age, and upon those who are younger, is incalculable. If he is not thoroughly manly, then they will not respect him, and his good qualities will count for but little; while, of course, if he is mean, cruel, or wicked, then his physical strength and force of mind merely make him so much the more objectionable a member of society. He cannot do good work if he is not strong and does not try with his whole heart and soul to count in any contest; and his strength will be a curse to himself and to every one else if he does not have thorough command over himself and over his own evil passions, and if he does not use his strength on the side of decency, justice, and fair dealing.

In short, in life, as in a foot-ball game, the principle to follow is:

Hit the line hard; don't foul and don't shirk, but hit the line hard!

The Lighter Side of the Strenuous Life

The rapid expansion of intercollegiate sport, especially football, manifested popular interest in sport's role in building a strong America as well as anticipating many of the tendencies of twentieth century organized team sport. Begun on the college level as a club sport run by students for their own amusement in 1869, it became, by the 1890s, a full-fledged commercial spectacle marked by mass participation, huge crowds, the rationalization of rules, specialization, paid professional coaches like Amos Alonzo Stagg and Walter Camp, and an emphasis on winning. In the hands of university presidents like William Harper of the University of Chicago, it became a vital tool in attracting financial support and favorable publicity to the building of new universities.

Although a violent game that too often resulted in serious injury and even death, or perhaps implicitly because of such features, football was immortalized in prose and verse as a game that developed true muscular christians and that embodied the notion that sport was an important vehicle for developing the next generation of America's leaders. Not everyone, however, was convinced that football would be the savior of the nation's future. With tongue through cheek Edward Sanford Martin questioned the value of college football in his poem, "The Strenuous Life," from a collection called *The Athlete's Garland, A Collection of Verse of Sport and Pastime,* compiled by Walter Rice and published in 1905.

The Strenuous Life

I went down East to a football match; great game; I 'll go again.
There played a chap they called McBride, who had the strength of ten,
And divers more, whose names I miss, but they seemed to be all good men.

Thirty men or thereabouts competed there that day.
Thirty thousand anxious souls observed their urgent play.
All Harvard went prepared to yell ; all Harvard stayed to pray.

Bless me, how those lusty youths toiled round that leather sphere,
Lined up, rushed, tackled, bucked, and strove with ardour most severe,
While earnest lads in moving tones besought the crowd to cheer!

Governors, senators, ministers, judges, presidents of banks,
College presidents, mothers of families, matrons and maids, on ranks
Of benches steeple-high, sat round and watched those football cranks.

I sat next to a mossy fossil, forty years old, named Jim.
Neither one of us knew the game, but we went with purpose grim—
Yet humble, too—to see the show and learn—if it took a limb.

"They say it 's dangerous!" said I ; but he said, "I don't care ;
We 'll get back seats. I understand there 'll be policemen there."
So there we sat and viewed the whole preposterous affair.

It turned out safe enough for us, and as for those young chaps
Who played, they all made nothing of astonishing mishaps,
Enduring superhuman-seeming strains without collapse.

They 'd kill a player frequently, and on his corpse would pile
A score of them, and then pile off, and he 'd get up and smile,
And kick the ball ; the blessed crowd all hollering meanwhile.

A player 'd get the ball and run; another, just as fleet,
Would grab him passing, ankle-high, and throw him forty feet.
He 'd land upon his head, but still continue to compete.

"Sure that one 's dead!" I 'd cry ; and Jim: "What odds! there 's plenty more.
What stubborn brutes those Yale men are! Why can't our chappies score?"
"*Hi! Daly 's got the ball! Now go!* Down? Bless me! What a bore!"

Our beings to their cores were stirred that day by those young men,
Egregious heroes doing stunts far too sublime for pen.
Down to Yale's one-yard line they fought ; Yale fought them back again.

"And all that work and no one's game!" sighed I as we turned away.
"They jolly well got their exercise, you bet," said Jim, "this day.
In the strenuous life 't is n't wins that count, so much as how hard you play.

"Don 't bother about what 's gained, or whether you wollop the proper man,
In the strenuous life, to do hard things in the hardest way is the plan,
And to keep the biggest possible crowd as crazy as ever you can."

"Poor liver-saddened old croak," said I, "whose thews have lost their power ;
Whose muscles are soft and his spunk collapsed, and his spirit subdued and
        sour,
Grand is strife of the strenuous life, and the world 's best hope in this hour!"

"Granny!" said he, "those were fine young lads, and vigorous through and
        through.
They put commendable snap, I own, in the singular things they do.
Still, granting a sport is a right good sort, need we make it religion too?

"Must we add to the cross we 've had so long another upright pole,
And shove the bar along a bit, till it 's what they call a goal,
And say you must drive between the posts as you hope to save your soul?

"There 's more to life than hustling, man, though hustling has its place,
There 's virtue in contentment still ; tranquillity 's a grace ;
According to his legs and lungs, must each man set his pace."

I 've thought about it often since, and doubtless shall again.
The strenuous life 's a tip-top thing, I guess, for strenuous men
Whose necks are short, and whose heads are hard, and who have the strength
        of ten.

They 're skittish creatures anyhow; unless they have due vent
We 'll have them putting up on us with, maybe, good intent,
Hair-raising jobs, and to which we could not possibly assent.

To get them in between the shafts and let their shoulders feel
The public load, 's a scheme that well to prudence may appeal.
While we, the timid, stand by to clamp on brakes and shoe the wheel.

Our strenuous friends who can 't be cured, let them be strenuous still.
If they 'll be strenuous to our taste, we 'll cheer them to their fill,
And plank our dollars duly down to pay their long, long bill.

But as for us, the meek and mild, our racket 's to adhere
To docile virtue 's modest path, nor let ambition queer
Our sense, nor ever lure us off a strenuous course to steer.

To pose as strenuous half a day, and spend a week in bed
Would never do ; we 'd lose our jobs ; our babes would wail unfed.
Better to save our puny strength to earn our daily bread.

About one strenuous man to every thousand folks is right :
Five hundred lean and vigilant to keep him aye in sight ;
Five hundred fat to sit on him hard when he happens to want to fight.

Sport for Elites

In 1882 Boston's white Anglo-Saxon Protestant elite celebrated the opening of the Country Club of Brookline, the first of many exclusive domains of the rich devoted to outdoor sports such as fishing, hunting, and horsebackriding, and more importantly to distinguishing its members as a wealthy elite set off from the rest of society. With elaborate clubhouses and beautiful grounds designed and landscaped by America's leading architects, country clubs blossomed throughout the United States and soon became leading centers for the promotion of such sports as golf and tennis.

Clubs served to divide the rich from the masses of Americans by displays of conspicuous consumption, self-indulgence, and participation in sport and social activities that by time and price were off-limits to any but the elite. Memberships were restricted by high dues and race and religious requirements that barred blacks, Jews, and other ethnic groups.

The following selection, "Evolution of the Country Club," written by Caspar W. Whitney, first appeared in *Harper's New Monthly Magazine* in December, 1894. According to Whitney, how was the development of the country club related to late nineteenth century economic development? What advantages did country clubs offer its members? Who were they? What activities did they engage in? What attitudes about gender, class, and Americanism emerged from this selection?

EVOLUTION OF THE COUNTRY CLUB

It used to be said Americans did not know how to live, but that was before we were "discovered" by the journalistic missionaries of Great Britain. It used also to be said we did not know how to enjoy ourselves; but again, that was before the dawn of the country club. If we knew neither how to live nor how to enjoy ourselves until comparatively recent years, it must be acknowledged we have made excellent use of both time and opportunity since our enlightenment. Even yet our efforts to acquire more intimate acquaintance with the leisurely side of life are parodied by those who cannot understand the demands of this great throbbing work-a-day country of ours.

It must be admitted unhesitatingly that we are only just learning how to play; we have not been, nor are we yet, a nation of pleasure-seekers. We are a practical people; we build our living-house before undertaking landscape-gardening. If we have been long in turning our attention to material enjoyments, we have atoned somewhat for early indifference by modernizing the paraphernalia and investing in the pursuit all that earnestness which characterizes the American in whatever field he launches. Indeed, we have entered upon our recreation with such vigor, I often question if even yet we have attained wisdom with the recreative incentive. I confess to a doubt whether full enjoyment for our joys is an American attribute. We steal away for our holidays (likely as not with a portmanteau filled with work to do at odd moments), determined to rest and take life at its easiest; we promise ourselves to foreswear all thoughts of business and the outer world; to loll about under the trees, and seek some of the lessons nature is said to have for us. We hold bravely to our resolutions for a day or so, but the third or fourth is certain to find us bargaining for city newspapers. Perhaps our grandchildren may see the day they can separate themselves from the office as effectually as though it existed in name only, but the present-day American, at least he who fills any active part in this great progressive movement, has not yet reached that development in the cultivation of holiday amusement.

In this particular we may indeed learn from the Englishman, who knows to the fullest how to take his recreation; nothing hurries him; little worries him when he goes on his holidays, only collapse of the Bank of England would recall him to the business world. He has gone from town to enjoy himself, and he does so to the utmost of his capability, which is considerable. Truly it is restful to observe the Britisher at play; there is no doubting he is bent on recreation. Every movement bespeaks leisure. But then his disposition is and his training has been totally different from those of the American, to whom the Englishman's comfortable way of conducting his business would of itself be recreation. Even the boys at play reveal the difference in temperament; the American school-boy engages in his games with as much light-hearted enthusiasm as the English lad, but the former shortly exhibits the national characteristic when, as university undergraduate, he gives so serious a turn to his sports, making preparation for contest a matter of considerable expense and elaboration, and giving results the greatest possible importance.

We Americans do nothing by halves—perhaps we should enjoy life more if we did—and the history of the country club, as much as anything else, bears witness to our tendency to superlative development. From having not a single country club in the entire United States of America twenty-five years ago, we have in a quarter of a century, in half that period, evolved the handsomest in the world. But here at least the reaction has been beneficial, for the country club has done appreciable missionary work in bringing us in contact with our fellows, where another than the hard business atmosphere envelops us, and in enticing us for the time being to put aside the daily task. . . .

The country club in America is simply one of the results of a final ebullition of animal spirits too long ignored in a work-a-day world; it is nature's appeal for recognition of the body in its co-operation with the mind.

Only a careful study of our country's history and its social traditions will give us a full appreciation of what the country club has done for us. It has, first of all, corrected to a large extent the American defect of not being able or at least not willing to stop work and enjoy ourselves; it has brought together groups of congenial, cultivated people, that often as not might be sweltering in the midsummer sun in town, or at isolated country houses, or in crowded, ill-kept "summer hotels." It has given them a club and country villa combined in one, where, having practically all the comforts and delights of housekeeping, they are called upon to assume none of its cares or responsibilities. For here the steward attends to the early morning market, worries with the servants, and may be held to account for the shortcomings of the *chef*, and at a cost below that on which a separate establishment of equal appointment could be maintained.

It is impossible to overestimate the blessings of the country club in adding comforts to country living that before were utterly unattainable, and in making it possible to enjoy a degree of that rural life which is one of England's greatest attractions. I say degree, for we have not yet attained the full delights of suburban residence as they are enjoyed in England, where a large and wealthy leisure class make wellnigh every great hall virtually a country club. In its present development the country club is really an American institution; there is little occasion for it in England, and nowhere is it so elaborated in the Old World as in the New.

To Boston must be given the credit of first revealing the possibilities and delights of the country club. I never journey to the "Hub" that I do not envy Bostonians the geographical situation of their city, which is superior, from a sportsman's point of view, to that of any other in the United States. What with rural New England within a very few hours' railway travel, and the "North Shore," that ideal summer resting spot, at their very gates, there is out-door entertainment for those of every disposition.

What nature has done for the Bostonian, a visit to the "North Shore," or perusal of Mr. Robert Grant's charmingly realistic pen-picture of its beauties, alone can show. Really it was not very neighborly of Mr. Grant to awaken so abruptly to our rural shortcomings those of us who had pitched our tents on less-favored ground.

A quarter of a century ago the residents of the north shore of Massachusetts Bay—to which no self-respecting Bostonian nowadays, ever dreams of alluding otherwise than as the "North Shore"—differed little from those on the remainder of the much broken New England coastline. If you seek the pioneer in the modern movement you must go to Mr. Grant for information. I shall tell you only how by degrees the busy American began to appreciate that "all work and no play makes Jack a dull boy," and gradually to stop for a breathing-spell. And thus, one at a time, slowly at first, the value of wholesome air and a bit of relaxation made converts. Slowly the underestimated farms passed from rustic to urban ownership, and became at once the most economical and best sanitariums in America, while the erstwhile proprietors withdrew farther into the New England fastnesses. Gradually, too, the entire scene changed from the up-at-sunrise-to-bed-at-sunset monotony of the simple-minded country folk to the brisk atmosphere of refined people; Nature herself seemed to welcome the more congenial surroundings, and the country assumed a brightened aspect. Where the leg-weary family hack, silhouetted against the autumn sky had toiled over the hills to the solitary cross-roads store, the village cart now dashed along, drawn by a good-blooded horse, and driven by a fashionably gowned woman. Man and womankind improved in health, horseflesh in quality, and we began to learn how to use to advantage our opportunities for recreation and health. . . .

Probably the country club has rendered its greatest service in tempting us out of doors, and cultivating a taste for riding and driving that has so largely benefited both sexes. With the evolution of the country club we have been developing into a nation of sportsmen and sportswomen. Indeed, sport of one kind or another and the origin of the country club are so closely connected, it is exceedingly difficult to decide which owes its existence to the other. It may be asserted that country clubs, generally speaking, have been created by the common desire of their incorporators to make a home for amateur sport of one kind or another. Some grew directly out of sport, as, for instance, the Country Club of Westchester County, which was originally planned for a tennis club, the Rockaway, Meadow Brook, and the Buffalo clubs, that were called into existence by the polo and hunting men. Others owe their existence to a desire to establish an objective point for drives and rides, and a rendezvous within easy access of town like the Brookline and Philadelphia Country clubs. Others have been called into being as the centralizing force of a residential colony, as Tuxedo. And yet others have been created by fashion for the coast season, as the Kebo Valley, at Bar Harbor.

If sport had not been the *raison d'etre* of every club's establishment, it is at all events, with extremely few exceptions, the chief means of their subsistence. Practically every country club is the centre of several kinds of sport, pursued more or less vigorously as the seasons come and go. A few of them maintain polo teams, and all supply implements and encouragement for as many kinds of games as its members will admit.

Really, country-club life has two sides—its domestic, if I may so call it, and its sporting, and not every club has both. Nor do I mean social for domestic. Every club has a social side, and that of the country club is particularly festive in season. But the domestic side is given only to those that have been the magnet in the founding of a colony of residents. Its domesticity may not be of the nursery order, but it goes so far as apportioning a part of its house for the exclusive use of its women members, and in some instances, at the mountain and sea-side resorts, the house is common to members of both sexes. One or two in the West carry the domestic feature so far as to give it somewhat of a family aspect, which, it must be confessed, is a hazardous experiment. One roof is not usually counted upon to cover more than one family harmoniously. The one distinguishing feature of the country club, however, is its recognition of the gentle sex, and I know of none where they are not admitted either on individual membership or on that of *paterfamilias*.

Clubs like the Meadow Brook and the Rockaway, which were organized for hunting and polo pure and simple, have no domestic side and make no especial provision for women, though both entertain, the latter in its pretty little club, the former more often at the home of one of its members.

It is the sporting side of the country club, however, that gives it life and provides entertainment for its members; the club and our sporting history are so closely interwoven as to be inseparable. Polo, hunting, and pony-racing owe to it their lives, and to the members we are largely indebted for the marked improvement in carriage horseflesh during the past five years. They founded the horse show, made coaching an accepted institution, and have so filled the year with games that it is hard to say whether the country-club sporting season begins with the hunting in the autumn or with tennis in the spring, for there is hardly any cessation from the opening to the closing of the calendar year.

Once upon a time the country was considered endurable only in summer, but the clubs have changed even that notion; all of them keep open house in winter, some retain a fairly large percentage of members in residence, and one or two make a feature of winter sports. Tuxedo holds a veritable carnival, with tobogganing, snow-shoeing, and skating on the pond, which in season provides the club table with trout. The Essex Country Club of New Jersey owns probably the best-equipped tobogganslide in America, and on its regular meeting nights electric illumination and picturesque costumes combine to make it a most attractive scene.

Spring opens with preparation for polo, lawn-tennis, and yachting. Not all country clubs have polo and yachting, but every one has courts, and several hold annual tournaments that are features of the tennis season, and where the leading players are brought together. Of the country clubs proper, only Westchester, Philadelphia, Essex, Brookline, St. Louis, Buffalo, really support polo teams, besides which there are the Meadow Brook and Rockaway, the two strongest in the country, and Myopia hunt clubs. Two only enjoy yachting facilities, the Country Club of Westchester County and the Larchmont Yacht Club. The latter, although strictly speaking devoted to yachting, is, nevertheless, virtually a country club, with one of the handsomest homes of them all, a fleet second in size only to that of the New York Yacht Club, and a harbor that is one of the safest and most picturesque on the coast. Westchester has no especial fleet aside from the steam and sailing yachts owned by a few individuals of the club; but its harbor is a good one, and its general location very attractive.

All the clubs dabble in live-pigeon trap-shooting, which is regrettable, for it is unsportsmanlike, to say nothing of the cash prizes, professionalizing the participants. It is a miserable form of amusement and unworthy the name of sport; but it is not so popular as formerly, and that, at all events, is something in its favor.

The polo season begins in the latter part of May, and continues more or less intermittently to the middle of September, and sometimes even as late as the first week of October. But usually October sees the end of it, for by that time the interest in hunting is quickening, and active preparations are making for the field. Hunting and polo in the early days constituted the sole sport of the country-club members, but the introduction of other games in the last five years has divided the interest that was once given to them entirely. Neither has retrograded; but they have not expanded as they should. However, that's another story. Whatever may be lacking in its progression, polo is the game that furnishes the country club with its most spirited scenes. The rivalry between the teams is always of the keenest, and the spectators, made up largely of the members of the contesting clubs, are quite as susceptible to its enthusiasm as the players.

Probably the most characteristic country-club scene, however, is created by the pony-race meetings given on the tracks with which several of the clubs are provided. Here there is ample opportunity for the hysterical enthusiasm so dear to the feminine soul, and plenty of time between events for them to chatter away to their hearts' content. Here, too, there is the certainty of seeing one's friends not only in the carts and on top of the coaches that line the course, and on the temporary little grand stand, erected for the near-by residents of the club colony, but frequently riding the ponies. Formerly more gentlemen rode than is the case now, but one day some one, who evidently cared more for the stakes than for the sport, put a professional jockey on his pony, and many others with equally strong pot-hunting tendencies have followed the example. So to-day we go to a meeting expecting, hoping to see our friends, or at least club men, in the saddle, and find instead at least eight out of every ten ponies ridden by second-rate professionals or stable boys. . . .

Who shall deny the country club to have been a veritable blessing, what with its sport and pleasure and health-giving properties that have brushed the cobwebs from weary brains, and given us blue sky, green grass, and restful shade in exchange for smoke-laden atmosphere, parboiled pavements, and the never-ceasing glare and racket of the city? And womankind too has partaken of country-club as she should of all blessings, in relaxation from the petty trials of housekeeping, and the parade and deceits of "society," while the hue of health has deepened in her cheeks. It has been a wholesome growth all round. Beginning life as somewhat of a novelty, the country club has become so familiar an institution that we wonder, as about the New York elevated railway, how we ever managed to get on without it.

The Athletic Girl

The wives and daughters of America's new elite comprised one group that experienced new opportunities for participation in sport during the last quarter of the nineteenth century. Able to afford and enjoy the safety bike, they joined the bicycling craze of the 1890s in large numbers. At country clubs throughout the United States, they participated in golf, tennis, and horseback riding in unprecedented numbers. At colleges and universities that catered to this new class of women, they did gymnastics, rowed, and even played basketball. For some, new interest in physical activity for women opened up careers in physical education.

Although this involvement of a special class of women in sport was unprecedented, sexist attitudes about female participation first evident before the Civil War continued apace. Unlike their male counterparts who were encouraged to participate in college sports such as baseball or football in a highly competitive fashion and on an intercollegiate level as a means of preparing them for the battles of the real world of politics and business, women engaged only in intramural affairs in ways that defined their supposed special and fragile character.

The following August 1901 article from *Munsey's Magazine* by Ann O'Hagan correctly identifies and details women's increased involvement in athletics. Compare her comments about the benefits and purposes of athletics for women to other views about what it offers men. What women are left out of O'Hagan's story? Do her remarks suggest anything about the roles and relations of males and females in white Victorian American society?

ATHLETIC GIRLS

Not long since, a very entertaining writer, named Gerald Stanley Lee, who seemed to be suffering from an attack of that scorn of majorities which is inevitable in a country ruled by them, ridiculed the pretensions of the crowd, and jeered at the intelligence which sought to accomplish all things by monster mass meetings. He made numerous witty remarks on the convention as a cure all, and to prove how very slight is its influence, when compared with that of the single enlightened mind, he instanced the dress reformer and the bicycle. He declared that what conferences unnumbered and "movements" beyond the possibility of counting had failed to do had been quietly accomplished by the unaided efforts of the man who placed the first "ladies' wheel" upon the market.

There may be of course, some who will object to Mr. Lee's contention, and who will claim that the Hartford manufacturer owes as much to women as women owe to him; who will assert that only minds prepared by the discourses of the delegates to many conventions would have given open welcome to a toy requiring a marked change in attire.

However that may be, one point is indisputable; to whomsoever the athletic woman owes her existence, to him or her the whole world of women owes a debt incomparably great. Absolutely no other social achievement in the behalf of women is so important and so far reaching in its results. The winning of the Sacred Latchkey, from which such magnificent results were argued, and the half winning of the ballot, are far less important, even in the minds of those who fought for them. With the single exception of the improvement in the legal status of women, their entrance into the realm of sports is the most cheering thing that has happened to them in the century just past.

The Benefit to Body and Mind

In the first place, there is the question of health. The general adoption of athletic sports by women meant the gradual disappearance of the swooning damsel of old romance, and of that very real creature, the lady who delighted, a decade or so ago, to describe herself as "highstrung," which, being properly interpreted, meant uncontrolled and difficult to live with. Women who didn't like athletics were forced to take them up in self defense; and exercise meant firmer muscles, better circulation, a more equable temper, and the dethronement of the "nervous headache" from its high place in feminine regard.

The revolution meant as much psychologically as it did physically. After all, philosophy and ethics have a certain weak kneed tendency to form themselves upon tastes and desires instead of forming these; so that any course which inoculates a taste for wholesome living and a desire for simplicity and sunshine is of incalculable benefit even in the realm of morals.

In dress, since the day when the Greek girdle became the Teutonic corset, no boon has been granted to woman so great as the privilege of wearing shirt waists and short skirts. When the tennis players of ten or fifteen years ago first popularized that boneless, free chested, loose armed bodice they struck a blow for feminine freedom compared with which the vigorous assults of Mrs. Jenness Miller and Mme. Sarah Grand were puny thimble taps. The woman who plays golf has made it possible for the woman who cannot distinguish between a cleek and a broom handle to go about her marketing in a short skirt; she has given the working girl, who never saw a golf course, freedom from the tyranny of braids and bindings; she has made wet ankles an unnecessary evil, and restored to the street sweeping department entire responsibility for the condition of the thoroughfares.

To have improved half the race in health, disposition, and dress would seem almost enough for one movement to have accomplished. But athletics have done more than this. They have robbed old age of some of its terrors for women, and they promise to rob it of more. The golfing grandmother is a subject upon which the humorist occasionally whets his wits; but those in whom the sense of humor is not so strong can only rejoice in everything that adds to the pleasure, the interests, and the health of the good lady who for generations has been forced to consider herself amply repaid for the trials of a long life by the privilege of taking care of her grandchildren whenever their parents needed a holiday. It is a magnificent institution which has exchanged her felt slippers for the calfskin boots of the athlete, and has delayed for fifteen or twenty years the purchase of the lace cap of her decrepitude. Any one who can see, in the spectacle of a gray haired couple wheeling along in the spring sunshine, only an object for mirthfulness, has developed his sense of humor at the expense of other and even more valuable senses.

When "Play" Was "Wisely Banished."

There was a time, which one does not have to be an Oldest Inhabitant to recall, when American women took no part in outdoor sports or in any form of exercise. It is not a quarter of a century since the round eyed children of Washington used to press their faces against the iron fence surrounding the British legation grounds and gaze in wonder and awe at the young Englishwomen playing tennis. They could see croquet without pausing in their own occupations to gape and to speculate concerning its nature, but any more violent sport was unfamiliar to them. Now it would require an open air trapeze performance to stir their wonder.

Twenty five years ago a woman so fortunate as to live in the country probably rode on horseback—primarily as a means of locomotion, however. She could also play croquet. The city woman might walk, and she too might play croquet, if she had a large enough lawn; but that was about the sum of the sports permitted.

The change began with the gradual introduction of physical training into the schools. Today there is not a girls' school of any standing that does not include in its curriculum a course in gymnastics, and encourage or insist upon some sort of outdoor exercise. In the public schools in the large cities supervisors and instructors of physical culture are chosen as carefully as the teachers of mathematics and history. Boards of education require that the newer school buildings shall be properly equipped with gymnasiums. It is a long journey to this condition from that which prevailed when one of the most public spirited of our early citizens said exultingly of a Maryland college: "The Methodists have wisely banished every species of play from their college."

That was Dr. Benjamin Rush's opinion about a hundred years ago, and it prevailed so widely that there was no physical training in any American institution, except West Point, until 1825. As for physical culture for girls—our good forebears would have expected a thunderbolt from heaven to answer the impious suggestion.

Dio Lewis and His Work.

Until the time of Dr. Dio Lewis no attempt worthy the name was made to apply the "sound mind in a sound body" saw to the education of girls. Probably it was deemed unnecessary for them to have sound minds. Miss Catherine Beecher, in 1837, had introduced into a Cincinnati school a set of calisthenic exercises whose sole aim was to give gracefulness "without dancing." They were mild exercises and rather futile ones, but Miss Beecher thought them all that a well regulated young person of the then gentler sex should have. Later, she expressed her disapproval of Dr. Lewis' exercises. "They were so vigorous and *ungraceful*," she wrote, "as to be more suitable for boys than for young ladies." It is disturbing to imagine what Miss Beecher's feelings would be if she could read the daily newspapers now, with their reports of fashionable women riding astride and of college girls temporarily disabled in basketball games.

When Dr. Lewis' Normal Institute for Physical Education was opened in Boston in 1861, with President Felton of Harvard as its presiding officer and its active supporter, people breathed a sigh of relief and sank back convinced that the relation of women to exercise was settled with dignity, finality, and gentility.

A full course of training at this establishment took just ten weeks, and consisted in the familiar dumb bell and club movements. Today a normal course in physical culture occupies two years of eight months each and includes instruction in such airy branches as anatomy, anthropometry, physiology, and physical diagnosis.

An Awakening in the Colleges.

In 1878 the Hemenway Gymnasium was established at Harvard, under Dr. D. A. Sargent, the most accomplished athlete of his time at Bowdoin, the stroke oar of the college crew, and afterwards a successful physician and teacher of gymnastics at Yale; and the cause of women's exercises looked up as well as men's. At that time women's colleges had not quite proved themselves. They were taking serious pains to make their course no less thorough than that of the masculine institutions. If Harvard had such a gymnasium and such an athletic instructor, then Vassar and Wellesley and the rest must bestir themselves on the physical culture side. Today the Hemenway Gymnasium is itself important to women, being open to them, with the rest of Harvard, for the summer school work.

The result was a gradual supplanting of the old two by two walking system of the seminaries. Today no college for women would think of sending out a catalogue without its alluring half tone cuts of the interior or exterior of its gymnasium, its duly set forth attractions in lake or river, tennis and hand ball courts, golf grounds, and the like.

That the gymnastic and athletic work at women's colleges is a real factor in promoting health, and not merely an unimportant though natural catering to a prevalent craze, is shown by statistics. At Wellesley, where rowing is the chief of the outdoor amusements, and where class and college crews practice during five winter months in the gymnasium, as well as on the lake, measurements were kept for many seasons. The average girth of chest in November, in the case of forty students, was 31.5 inches, and the average shoulder measurement 14.4 inches, while the average strength of the back was represented by a hundred and forty five pounds. In May, after five months of gymnasium training for the lake and one month of actual rowing on it, the chest measurement was 33.4 inches; shoulder measurement, 15.3: strength of back, a hundred and sixty two pounds.

Forty other students, who had not been in the crews, but who had taken a course of Swedish gymnastics, showed an increase of chest girth from 31.6 to 33.4 inches: of shoulder girth from 14.6 to 15.4 and of strength in the back from a hundred and forty five to hundred and sixty six.

Another forty girls, excused for various reasons from all gymnastic and athletic work, showed no increase whatever in the average chest measurement of 31.6 inches, or in the average shoulder measurement of 14.9 inches, while the average back strength decreased from a hundred and forty six to a hundred and eighteen pounds.

Measurements kept in another woman's gymnasium show that in six months of regular exercise of about three hours a week, there was an average gain of about two inches in chest girth, and as much in chest depth; an average gain in lung capacity of about seventeen cubic inches: an increase in shoulder measurements of about one and a quarter inches, while the increase in back strength was about forty pounds, and in leg strength about sixty pounds.

Even women long past the age for striking changes in physical measurements are affected by the regular exercise of the gymnasium. Dr. Mary Taylor Bissell, one of the most prominent physicians in New York, who has been connected with gymnastic work for women for many years, cites the case of a woman of thirty seven, who, after a seven months' course of two hours a week in a gymnasium, found that her chest increased four fifths of an inch, her waist lessened one and four tenths inches, and her hips two inches, while her lung capacity increased thirty cubic inches.

The Growth of College Sports.

From being the chief factor in the athletic life of the women's colleges, the gymnasiums have grown to be distinctly subsidiary. They supplement the outdoor exercises which the location of most of the institutions for higher education makes so natural and attractive. Each has its specialty in the line of sport, and the young woman who wins a championship in rowing, swimming, track events, basket ball, bicycling, or whatever it may be, is a lionized creature who tastes for once the sweets of the cup of utter adulation.

At Wellesley, where the distinctive sport is rowing, Float Day is the banner festival of the year. No girl is allowed to row upon the crews who is not able to swim, but, even with this wise precaution, the only contest permitted is in rowing form, not in speed. Bryn Mawr has by far the most complete and elaborate of the gymnasiums connected with the women's colleges, and its basket ball is famous wherever college women, past, present, or to be, are gathered together. Vassar's tennis vies with her basket ball in the hearts of her students. At Smith, in addition to all sorts of general outdoor sports, there is snowshoeing. At Mount Holyoke, a rink polo club is a feature of the winter life. Vassar's ice carnival is as famous as Wellesley's aquatic festival. . . .

Once upon a time the young woman who came out of college was somewhat at a loss how to expend her energy and to keep up her sports. Bicycles, golf, and the country clubs have altered that. Moreover, for those seasons when the rigors of the miscalled temperate zone make outdoor exercise almost an impossibility there are, in the large cities at any rate, excellent gymnasiums. In New York for instance, apart from the gymnasiums in all the schools, in the working girls' clubs, and in the various branches of the Young Women's Christian Association, there are at least six well known private gymnasiums where women may pursue physical culture to their hearts' content and the good of their bodies. Many systems have been developed since Dr. Lewis first tackled the problem. You may go to a Swedish gymnasium, where no small apparatus is used, but only body movements and exercises on the larger apparatus are practised. You may go to a place where the German system is in vogue. Athletics in this country, by the way, owe a great deal to the German citizens, whose "turn versins" were among the earliest athletic associations.

In gymnasiums managed on the German plan, all sorts of apparatus are used. In the Delsartean schools of grace there is no apparatus at all. The Delsartean's secret of a happy life is relaxation, and she does not believe that a wooden horse or a vaulting pole is an aid to relaxation. The American system, as the one developed by Dr. Sargent at the Hemenway Gymnasium is called, is, in a way, a combination of all. It is almost universal in this country, forty eight of the leading gymnasiums having adopted it.

Between three and four hundred women are enrolled as pupils of the Savage Gymnasium, which, both in attendance and equipment, is the largest in New York. There are classes and there is individual work. Fencing and boxing, both of which have many ardent disciples, are taught privately. Girls of five and women of fifty and sixty are among the patrons. It is an encouraging fact that the gray haired women look almost as well in their blue and crimson bloomers and blouses as the little girls.

The cost of being a gymnast in New York varies. There is one gymnasium with pillowed couches about the room, soft, lovely lights, and walls that rest weary eyes; where a crisp capped maid brings the exerciser a cup of milk during her rest upon the divan, where her boots are laced or buttoned by deft fingers other than her own. For these privileges and the ordinary ones of gymnastic training the charge is a hundred dollars a year.

Forty dollars covers the cost in less Sybaritic circles, and if one has the distinction of being a working woman, ten dollars will pay for gymnastic instruction and privileges. The gymnasiums connected with the Christian Associations, the working girls' clubs, the settlements, and the like are even less expensive.

What New York offers women in gymnastic opportunities, all the other large cities duplicate. Chicago, indeed, is in advance of the metropolis, for it has a woman's athletic club, the only large and successful one now in operation in this country. It was started more than a year ago through the efforts of Mrs. Pauline H. Lyon, who interested Mrs. Philip Armour, Mrs. Potter Palmer, Mrs. Emmons Blaine, and other wealthy women in the project. A business building was remodeled to fit the needs of the club, the cost being about sixty thousand dollars. In addition to the gymnasium proper, a swimming tank, sixty five feet long, eigthteen feet wide, and nine deep, has been constructed. It is constantly filled with filtered water, and mirrored sides and ceilings add to the glittering effect. A Swedish teacher of swimming was engaged, and the gymnasium instructor is also a graduate in Swedish methods. There are bowling alleys, rooms for fencing, a Turkish bath, parlors, library, a tea room, diningroom, and everything that such a club could possibly require. And—a crowning glory—there are absolutely no literary or social annexes to the athletics.

With the gradual athletic development of women, the tendency of men to regard their gymnasiums and country clubs as closed corporations from which women must be barred at any cost, is disappearing. Of all the twelve hundred golf clubs which dot the United States with red and white flags, only one was instituted upon the monastic principle of excluding women. A club near Chicago was guilty of this painful lack of gallantry, and there was, at the time of its formation, not much hope that it would be long able to resist public sentiment.

There are however, many courses where women are not allowed to play on Sundays and holidays. There is excellent and almost universal masculine testimony to the fact that on crowded days nothing so discourages a man as women playing before him on the golf links. In England, where women have had their own golf associations since 1867, this difficulty was settled to the entire satisfaction of the men by providing the women with small separate links of perhaps five holes, where they could very comfortably play a sort of ladylike golf, a close relative of croquet.

There is something to be said in favor of the separate course, though not of such as those early English ones, now happily abandoned. The best drive of the champion women players is equal in distance to the average drive of the average man. In other words, Miss Beatrix Hoyt, of the Shinnecock Hills Golf Club, three times the national woman's champion, has a drive of from a hundred and twenty to a hundred and sixty yards. The men who are champions drive off from two hundred to two hundred and fifty yards. A good average drive for a man is a hundred and fifty yards. Therefore it often happens that the woman playing on a course laid out by men and for men either drives into the bunker and wastes several strokes to get out, or, playing purposely short, loses a stroke at once in endeavoring to avoid the bunker.

In driving, skill counts most, but muscle undoubtedly counts for something also. In the rest of the game the well trained woman has an equal chance with a man. Still, most women would rather lose that extra stroke from the tee than be banished to a nursery course, as it were. At Shinnecock Hills there is a separate course for women known as the "red" course. It is of nine holes, but the distances are not short. Until a woman has played this course at least three times in a certain minimum number of strokes, she is not allowed to play upon the "white," or eighteen hole course. The red course has turned out some admirable players, Miss Hoyt and Mrs. Charles Turnure being graduates of it.

In some places women have been more enterprising than men in the matter of forming clubs. The Morris County Club, of Morristown, New Jersey, was started and managed by women alone. In the associations of golf clubs there are both women's and men's. There is a Women's Metropolitan Association, under whose direction the women's championship matches have been played. There is a women's association of the clubs around Boston, though there is not yet a men's.

Every country club nowadays has its golf course, and perhaps three fourths of the country clubs are merely golf clubs. All this has come about in a very short space of time. St. Andrew's, near Yonkers, was the first golf club in this country, and the links were laid out only fifteen years ago amid much derision. Up to that time a country club was generally either a riding and driving or a hunt club, and women were admitted by courtesy, or, in a few instances, through actual achievement.

The membership was of the rich leisured class, the healthy spirit of democracy that characterizes the golf club being utterly unknown.

Women Afield and Afloat.

On Long Island, women have ridden to hounds, after the satisfactory fashion of their English cousins, for a long time. Occasionally the newspapers have recorded an accident in the cross country runs of the women on Hempstead Plains, or at Lakewood or Aiken, but on the whole the casualties have been infrequent.

In water sports the American woman is not so proficient as her cousin across the Atlantic. Most Englishwomen can row; many race their own yachts, and not a few have reputations as swimmers. Lady Constance McKenzie is the swimming champion of the Bath Club, mentioned before, and there are cases on record where young Englishwomen, challenged to jump overboard from a yacht and swim to shore in the full regalia of serge and calfskin, have not hesitated to plunge in and cover themselves with glory and water. Only the "lady matators" of the dime museums would be likely to do that in this country.

Water tournaments in general are little known here, although the number of those who dare great feats in the waves is increasing. The Newport colony, too, has several women who can sail small craft, and a race with feminine skippers takes place every year.

Of course there is not any equality between the athletic accomplishments of women and those of men. The best Vassar "dasher" could not do a hundred yards in less than thirteen seconds, while the men's college record is nine seconds and four fifths. Vassar's running high jump is four feet and five inches, instead of six feet and two inches like the University of Pennsylvania, and so on. But this is no more to be deplored than it is to be wondered at or changed. In gymnastic work the record breakers, according to the medical authorities, generally find their reserve strength gone by the time they are forty five. The aims of athletics among women has been the establishment and maintenance of a high general standard of health and vigor, rather than some single brilliant achievement. So far, with a few notorious exceptions, like the triple century rulers, women have made freedom and fun their objects in athletics; and there are certain indications that this temperate view of the subject is gaining ground even in the ranks of the record breaking sex itself.

A. G. Spalding and the Rise of Baseball

A. G. Spalding was one of the most recognizable men in American sport at the turn of the century. As a pitcher for his home town team in Rockford, Illinois, and then with the Boston Red-Stockings, he helped popularize baseball and change it from an amatuer club game to America's first professional team sport. He was professional baseball's first 200-game winner, captain, manager, and principal owner of the Chicago White Stockings, the game's most successful team in the 1880s; and, in 1876, co-founder of the National League. His role in shaping league policy, enforcing the reserve rule, keeping blacks out of the National League, and putting down a player's revolt in 1890 known as the Brotherhood War, set important precedents for the development of professional sport in the twentieth century. He even was responsible for fabricating the myth that Abner Doubleday had invented the game of baseball at Cooperstown, New York, the location of today's Baseball Hall of Fame where Spalding was enshrined in 1939. More than any other person, he pushed professional baseball as a commercial venture and helped rationalize and organize the game into a mass spectator sport controlled by owners and promoted as a game that was both respectable entertainment and a shaper of American values. Without question he was the critical figure in establishing the white world of professional baseball as a viable commercial enterprise and acceptable pastime in late-nineteenth century America.

Spalding was also a shrewd businessman who cashed in on his baseball fame and helped shape a new industry in sporting goods dominated by the company he formed in 1876 that still bears his name and that made him a multimillionaire by 1890. The following excerpt from Spalding's autobiographical account of baseball, "America's National Game", published in 1911, contains an interview that Spalding gave to a New York Times reporter named Edward Marshall. What were Spalding's views on the benefits of professionalism, baseball's positive impact on the development of the American character, and even on the growth of capitalism? Does his emphasis on the role of the expert and the necessity of organization reflect tendencies apparent in other areas of American life during the so-called "Progressive era?"

OUR NATIONAL GAME

I have thought best to conclude this book with an article written by Edward Marshall on "The Psychology of Base Ball," and which appeared in the Sunday issue of the New York "Times", November 13, 1910.

My reasons for giving space to this article are:

First—Because it deals with a side of the subject (the psychological) which had been heretofore overlooked, and

Second—Because it contained many thoughts that had existed in my mind for years, but had never before been expressed in words.

Mr. Marshall has the happy faculty of interviewing one in such a searching manner that, without apparent effort, he enters the recesses of his subject's mind and brings to light the inmost thoughts of the one interviewed.

The circumstances leading up to the interview came about in this way: Mr. Homer Davenport, the celebrated cartoonist, and a great admirer of the American national game, said to me one day that Mr. Edward Marshall, the well-known author, had expressed a desire to "interview" me on the "Psychology of Base Ball," and asked if he might bring Mr. Marshall to call at my New York hotel for that purpose. I consented, and a meeting was arranged for the next evening.

Mr. Marshall explained the object of his visit and the general lines of the information he was seeking, incidentally remarking that he had never seen a game of Base Ball.

In answer to my surprised inquiry, "Where have you lived all these years?" he replied that he had been a war correspondent and had spent most of his time in Europe, and more recently in Cuba.

Here was I, facing a man who had never seen a game of Base Ball; yet this man wanted to write an article on the "Psychology of Base Ball," which, so far as I knew, although I had been connected with the sport almost from its inception, was a phase of the subject that had never before been brought out.

While he was arranging his shorthand notes, seated in an easy chair, with a pad carelessly resting on his knee, I confess that I had some misgivings as to his forthcoming article, and as a precautionary measure requested him to show me proof of the same before it appeared in print. To this he assented.

Shortly after this first and only interview with Mr. Marshall I was suddenly called to my home at Point Loma, California, and never saw the article until some days after it had appeared in the New York "Times" of November 13, 1910. Had I seen the proof I would certainly have blue-penciled some of the personal references. I do not claim to have the face of a "Greek Hero"; I do not assume to resemble a Bishop of any church, and I could not be the father of a game whose birth antedated mine by ten years. Following is the article in full:

The Psychology of Base Ball Discussed by A. G. Spalding.

THE GAME ELEVATES AND FITS THE AMERICAN CHARACTER—IT BRINGS INTO PLAY THE EMOTIONAL AND MORAL AS WELL AS THE PHYSICAL SIDE OF MAN'S NATURE.

By Edward Marshall

His face is that of a Greek hero, his manner that of a Church of England Bishop, when I talked with him he was a candidate for United States Senator from California, and he is the father of the greatest sport the world has ever known.

You don't know him? You are unfortunate. There are in the United States at least a million men who do and who will yell at sight of him. I am writing now of A. G. Spalding, and he talked to me, the other evening, of the game's psychology.

"The psychology of Base Ball?" he said, thoughtfully. "I confess that the 'psychology of Base Ball' is a new one on me.

The Mind and the Game.

"I take it that you are trying to find out what effect the game has on the mind, and what effect the mind has on the game. The general impression among those who do not know, and, although there are several million people in this country who do know, still there remain a few who don't, is that Base Ball is simply a form of physical exercise which is interesting to watch and to take part in. Those who have played the game know well that it is more—much more. They know that it is quite as much a mental as it is a physical exercise.

"As a matter of plain fact, it is much more a mental exercise than a mere physical sport. There is really no other form of outdoor sport which constantly demands such accurate co-ordination between the mind and body as this national game of ours. And that is rather fine, when you come to think about it.

"Base Ball elevates, and it fits the American character. The emotional and moral as well as the physical side of a man's nature are brought into play by Base Ball. I know of no other medium which, as completely as Base Ball, joins the physical, mental, emotional, and moral sides of a man's composite being into a complete and homogeneous whole. And there is nothing better calculated than Base Ball to give a growing boy self-poise and self-reliance, confidence, inoffensive and entirely proper aggresiveness, general manliness. Base Ball is a man maker.

"Of course the professional Base Ball player is the one known to the non-playing public; he attracts attention through his superior talent, just as a great actor or a great singer does; but a great actor or great singer may start late, while a Base Ball player cannot. I do not believe there is a single player in the major leagues who had not demonstrated a peculiar fitness for the game, and made a reputation as a skillful player among boy associates, before he was fourteen.

"Yes; certainly the game has its psychology—a part of the fine, healthy, undegenerate psychology of the whole Nation. The professional Base Ball player is no thug trained to brutality like the prizefighter, no half-developed little creature like the jockey, no cruel coward like the bull fighter. He is the natural development of the American boy's inborn love of manly, skillful, outdoor sport—sport busying brain and body and not harming any one or anything. The average boy who loves Base Ball is not the sort of boy who loves to go off with a gun intent on killing some poor bird. Base Ball has done a lot to keep the Yankee lad from being brutal.

"And he revels in Base Ball, does this American boy—good luck to him: No one ever has to urge the normal Yankee lad to participate in this clean game. He takes to it as a duck to water. He knows its rudiments before he learns to read and write. His father played Base Ball before him, and, of this generation, most of his forefathers. And it is a sport which parents may encourage, for it is neither dangerous nor demoralizing.

"The professional Base Ball player is doing more for his native country than any one engaged in any form of sport has ever done for any country in the past. They say horse racing has resulted in improvement in horse breeding; well, Base Ball has done something better, it has resulted in improvement in man breeding. Aside from giving outdoor recreation to the public, the professional Base Ball player is, by his example, encouraging the boy to healthy sport with which not one unpleasant feature is connected. Little gambling is associated with Base Ball. When the game first started as a professional sport there was an effort made to saddle it with all the gambling features which beset the race tracks—pool-selling and all—and from 1870 to, say 1873, the gamblers practically had control of our professional Base Ball. Every Base Ball park had its betting ring. This made decent people stay away, and interest in the game fell to a low ebb. Every error made was charged to crookedness upon the player's part, and not always, probably, unjustly. William A. Hulbert, of Chicago, had become interested in the game, and I explained this all to him. I was actually afraid the game would have to go. He wanted me to take my winning club on from Boston to Chicago, and I told him that I would if he'd clean out the gamblers, and not otherwise. He said he'd try, and he did try, to mighty good effect. That saved the game, undoubtedly, and in the winter of the following year the National League was organized, and has been getting more and more important to the life of all America with the passage of each day since then.

Gambling Driven Out.

"The elimination of the betting evil was the cornerstone of the success of Base Ball as an exhibition game. The fight against it was a fierce one, lasting four or five years. Then we triumphed, and the cleanest game on earth had been established. No betting, no Sunday playing, no liquor sold upon the grounds! It was a revolution in the world of professional sport. Base Ball is the only game which suits the mighty populace and yet is wholly free from ties to bind it to the gambling and the liquor-selling element, whose aim it is to victimize that populace.

"That's part of its psychology—it is clean-souled. Another and important part of it is that it is a leveler. That makes it, in the truest sense, American. It is almost, if not exactly, the same game in all parts of the United States, and nowhere is it cursed by caste. Caste may not wreck a sport in countries where caste dominates the social life, but it would surely wreck Base Ball in this country. That's the finest thing about Base Ball. Its spectators, once they settle in their seats and glue their eyes upon the diamond, are absolutely equalized by their delight in what they see. The hod carrier, if his seat so placed him as to make it possible, would be pretty apt, in case of a good play, to beat the President upon the back in his enthusiasm with a cushion or his hat, and the President would almost surely turn and grin at him. I don't know that that has ever actually happened, but I have known a workingman in jumpers to so lose his memory of social and financial and political rank as to biff thus a grave Senator. It was a fine and significant spectacle, because—note this—the Senator was not offended. He couldn't clear his mind of frantic joy in time to be offended, and, better yet, he would not have been offended if he could have cleared it."

Right here I ought to explain something. This interview was quite a family affair. Across the room from me sat Mr. Spalding's nephew—a young scientist—and at my right, upon a couch, was Mrs. Spalding. She is a fit mate for her classically featured husband. She is really very handsome, has a notably delightful voice—soft, cultured, vibrant—and she does what the "advice to wives" departments in the women's magazines always urge young wives to do; she takes an interest in her husband's soul-enthusiams. Interest? Well, some.

Two Cranks in a Family.

"Men at Base Ball games, all men at Base Ball games, are brethren, equal shares in whatever joy or woe or protest the great game may bring," said she. "And utterly irreverent. Ban Johnson, the president of the league, was sitting near us in the stand, and a man wanted to make a photograph of him. Did the crowd sit awed and reverent? Not notably. That crowd admired Ban Johnson and, in a way, revered him, but the camera man was an obstruction. What a cry went up? 'Too much Johnson! Too much Johnson' roared instantly unto the vaulted heavens."

Mr. Spalding smiled at her. "Two cranks in a family means domestic bliss, if they are both Base Ball cranks," he commented, thereby adding to his exposition of the game's psychology.

"Any one who blocked a crank's view of the game would meet with instant criticism," he said proudly. "and if Teddy himself were playing and made an error he'd be roasted by the best friends he possessed upon the bleachers.

"But, in spite of this, Base Ball is the most good-natured pastime in the world.—Partisans will rave and tear their hair, but how often do you hear that one of them has torn another's hair on Base Ball grounds? In the history of the world no such great crowds have gathered to watch anything the world has ever known—sport or anything else—with so few fights. Base Ball, you see, arouses no brutal instincts. It is a turmoil rather than a battle. It is more a war of skill than a war of strength. Foot ball often breeds fierce fights. That game calls for heavy muscles, don't you see? as well as skill, and I shall dare some critics when I say that foot ball science is less delicate than Base Ball science. Brute strength in one foot ball player can, and often does, overmaster the pure science of another: In Base Ball this could not possibly occur.

The One Game in the Open.

"The game is in the open, too. Twenty thousand people can cluster round a diamond and see every move the Base Ball players on it make. There is no chance for secret cheating, therefore there is no tendency in that direction. It is not alone the umpire who can see what happens on the field, but every newsboy, every millionaire, among the spectators. In foot ball there is often chance for hidden fouls.

"Professionalism has not wrecked Base Ball—it has merely brought about a higher degree of skill in players by offering them an income which permits them to keep up, after they have become men, the sport in which they have excelled as boys. The professional is merely a grown boy, and, in the minds of a large number of his fellows, a very lucky boy at that. His profession is his sport a little glorified. He is the natural outcome of the boy's love for the game—ah, how that same boy loves it!

"And it is the only professional sport I know of which it does not hurt a boy to revel in. He worships the professional who wins, and, doing this, he never worships a plug-ugly or a thug. Drunkards and all other moral undesirables are barred from real success upon the Base Ball field by the very nature of the sport. The men whom the boy 'roots' for are a very decent lot of fellows—such a decent lot of fellows as no other professional sport the world has ever known could show. The professional Base Ball player, by his example, does not encourage his young devotees to anything unworthy. That's a fine detail of our national sport. Parents need not be alarmed if their young sons announce at breakfast some fine morning that they plan to be professional ball players when they reach maturity. In the first place, out of 500 boys who may express that firm determination, only one, upon an average, will ever make good in a major league, or minor league for that matter, and, in the second place, that one of the 500 will not, by making good, prove himself to be anything at all unworthy. Success as a Base Ball player does not plunge a youth into a vicious or a dissipated life, but on the other hand, insures him from that sort of a career.

Professionals Lucky Chaps

"Indeed lucky is the boy who can develop sufficient skill to get a place on a league team. That means a mighty good salary and a pleasant, clean and healthful life. The professional Base Ball player is no mollycoddle—there are no mollycoddles in the game; but neither is there any room for thugs in it. No training could be more severe than that of the league player. Under the present system of organized Base Ball, he must conform to the strictest mental, moral and physical discipline, and must develop wonderfully in patience, self-reliance and fair-mindedness. He must keep at the top notch in all these details of fine character if he would keep position in the game. Ability to take criticism cheerfully is one of the great requisites of real success in any line. I know of no profession which requires of those who win in it the disposition and ability to do this which Base Ball requires.

Base Ball and the Mind

"Now, as to the effect of Base Ball on the mind of the boy player. If a boy is naturally selfish, peevish or crab-minded the members of the team he plays with will soon knock that out of him, or drive him from the team. He won't want to leave the team for Base Ball, you must remember, is ingrained in his blood. If he is inclined to be hot-tempered, the loss of a few games and the respect of his associates as the result will help mightily toward correcting it. If he is prone to be a cud, to put on airs, to assume a superiority over his fellow-players as a result of the social or financial standing of his family, a little joshing from his fellows on the errors he made upon the field will soon bring him down to earth again. If he is unduly timid and shows cowardice in a pinch, his mates will quickly cure him or eject him. If he is apprehensive, pessimistic—and no trait is more entirely un-American—he will soon lose his place upon the team. The lad who is continually predicting a defeat will not last long in Base Ball. And the beauty of the thing is, that rarely will he let his faults go far enough to bar him from his game—his love of it is too instinctive and too real. Rather will he let the game correct the faults. And there you are. It's a man as well as a soul builder."

"The psychology of Base Ball? It is the psychology of success. "I know of nothing which more fitly trains the body, mind and soul. The game plays havoc with a boy's or man's emotions. In a day the player may well rise to the fine heights of victory and sink to the dark depths of black despair in a defeat. And it must be the one or the other. There is no midway station. The score is 5 to 3. You win or lose, and quickly learn that nothing is accomplished by trying to lay the blame, if defeat comes, upon the umpire or upon your fellow-players. Pleading a sore finger or strained muscle or tendon wins nothing for the vanquished player in his own mind or the minds of his associates. That is a good thing. After many victories, and the defeats which are quite certain to go with them, a player must, of sheer necessity, achieve self-poise, learn to take winning calmly, and lose philosophically. He may well reach that super-point where he looks grave in victory and smiles with hope when he is vanquished.

Important in Education

"Base Ball has for a long time been important in the education of our youth—far more important than most people think—and it is destined to become still more important. The day will come, I think, when all American school authorities will supply the necessary grounds to play the game on as an essential adjunct to every public school. The game means countless benefits, and not a single danger to the boy who plays it. You may have gathered from what I have already said that I consider it the greatest game on earth. I do, and doing so, am proud of my good judgment. There should be Base Ball grounds adjacent to or very near each public school building in the United States.

"Base Ball is the only sport which is severe enough to benefit and not severe enough to overstrain. Base Ball players live to good old ages, almost always. I wish I had the list at hand. The longevity of ex-professionals would surprise you. I myself began to play on the advice of my physician, and I made a business of it in the end.

"Prizefighters, jockeys, football players, oarsmen, even college athletes, are not long-lived."

I had not asked so very many questions. They had not been needed. Mr. Spalding put his words across the plate as accurately and as logically as, in the old days, he pitched his balls. But now I asked one.

"Even if the game had not resulted in wealth and fame for you, would you still be glad you took it up?"

He laughed. The Greek countenance framed with white hair, broke into a particularly winning set of wrinkles; the Bishop's face became that of the jolly monk in the world famous picture.

"I'm a candidate for Senator," he said, "and ought not to use slang, but—I—sure—would. Glad? Why, I tell you it meant health to me—the biggest thing of all. It has taken me around the world again, and yet again;

it has thrown me into contact with the finest set of men this country ever has produced. It has taught me that humanity is, at the bottom, clean of mind and soul. It has made me a rank optimist—and it has kept me one. It is the only sport on earth. The prizefighter is brutalized and his heart bothers him; the rowing man is almost certain to be most unequally developed physically, and his heart, also generally goes wrong; foot ball maims and brutalizes; horse racing sends its devotees to pieces morally and gives them little of the compensation coming from good exercise and honest rivalry. It is and always has been founded upon gambling.

Old Players Now Important

"Find fifty men from all these sports who have outgrown them and reached real importance in the world! You can't. I could name a hundred Base Ball players—yes, two hundred and then more—who have become important, worthy, and respected men in later years. There's John M. Ward, for instance. Senator Gorman was a Base Ball player once. John K. Tener, who as we talk is a candidate for Governor of Pennsylvania, was a professional and went around the world with us in 1888. Senator Bulkeley, of Connecticut, was a player first and then first President of the National League. Base Ball for a few years is one of the best character builders I can think of. An able boy's blood always runs high and the first thing he must learn, if he is to win success, is to control it. Base Ball teaches that, first, last and all the time.

"The game was fortunate from the beginning. It was spread throughout the country by the soldiers returning to their homes after the Civil War. Now it is in its third generation. I hesitate to guess what it will be when it has reached its fourth. The crowds today are big; the crowds of future days will be much bigger. Every boy, you see, plays Base Ball, and the players of to-day are the spectators of to-morrow. The human being who has ever got the germ of Base Ball in his blood, whether the infection comes when he is young enough or after he has reached maturity, never get it out."

Base Ball and Business

"Has your Base Ball training helped you in your business?" I inquired.

"I never struck anything in business that did not seem a simple matter when compared to complications I have faced on the Base Ball field," said Mr. Spalding. "A young man playing Base Ball got into the habit of quick thinking in most adverse circumstances and under the most merciless criticism in the world—the criticism from the bleachers. If that doesn't train him, nothing can. Base Ball in youth has the effect, in later years, of making him think and act a little quicker than the other fellow.

"They have now, in colleges, a course in which they call experimental psychology. The relation between thought and action is recorded by delicate instruments. These instruments, in the psychological laboratories of the colleges, show that the mental reactions of the athletes are quicker than those of any other students. And that of the Base Ball player is quicker than that of any other of the athletes. The sprinter, don't you see, has but to go from place to place. His thought is intent on the one thing—on getting there. The thought of the Base Ball player must take many other things—a thousand things—into consideratrion. He must think while he is going.

"Folks marvel at the great throngs which attend important Base Ball matches. They really need not be wondered at. The public likes the game, and more than that, it knows that this one game, of all sports, is certain to be absolutely on the square. The spectators have been players, most of them, and understand not only the first principles but the fine points of the sport.

"Here, again, is the effect of the evolution of the game up through the boy into the man. The boys of the past generation are the spectators of this; the boys of this one will be the spectators of the next. So, like an endless chain, Base Ball will last and grow as long as these United States shall last and grow. Each generation will produce a little higher type of citizenship than that which went before it and Base Ball and the principles which underlie it will help to bring this about."

The old Base Ball player, the successful business man, the candidate for Senator, stopped talking. I looked at him inquiringly.

He said:

"PLAY BALL."

Papa Jack and the Great White Hope

So explosive was interest in and acceptance of sport in the last quarter of the nineteenth century that even prize fighting became more acceptable to segments of American society that had previously scorned it. Support by urban elite athletic clubs who sponsored fighters and hired boxing instructors as well as by fight promoters brought changes in local laws that legalized boxing "exhibitions" and that even altered the nature of the sport itself. By the 1890s most boxing matches in the United States were fought under the Marquis of Queensbury rules that required the use of gloves and three minutes rounds.

The ring exploits of boxing champions like Gentleman Jim Corbett and John L. Sullivan identified boxing in these years with the Irish. Indeed some even believed that the success of Irish fighters proved that America was truly a land of opportunity for new immigrants and that sport could serve as one vehicle for social mobility and advancement.

Blacks also made their mark in the ring. Boxing stood as one of the few areas in American life or sport that did not totally deny them opportunity in an era replete with racial violence and bounded on one end by the emancipation of slaves (1863) and on the other by a Supreme Court decision, Plessy vs. Ferguson (1896) that formally sanctioned segregation and discrimination.

The success of Jack Johnson, however, revealed the real limits of tolerance at the turn of the century. Although black and white fighters often did battle against each other, white American heavyweight champions like Sullivan, Corbett, and Jim Jeffries refused to fight against blacks in championship matches. In 1908, however, the reigning heavyweight champion, an Australian named Tommy Burns, fighting in his native land, lost to Johnson for a guarantee of $30,000.

Johnson's easy victory and a lifestyle that included love affairs with white women and an unwillingness to accept the docility and second-class status that white Americans expected from blacks, was anathema to them. At a time when white Americans were reading books like Madison Grant's *The Passing of the Great Race* and expressing concern about immigrants diluting the strength and purity of the American character, Johnson's ascension to the heavyweight throne, the symbol of ultimate male supremacy, was unbearable. Exhortations to find a "Great White Hope" to dethrone the black champion persuaded Jim Jeffries to come out of retirement and do battle with Johnson in Reno, Nevada, on July 4, 1910. Johnson battered the former heavyweight champion for fifteen rounds until the fight was stopped.

Papa Jack's victory initiated a series of race riots and legal actions that demonstrated the hysterical nature of white fears and the degree of racial hatred and tension that existed in America. Eventually prosecuted and found guilty of violating the Mann Act, Johnson fled from authorities and spent the next five years of his life traveling through Europe and South America, a defrocked champion who survived on boxing exhibitions and vaudeville presentations of "Uncle Tom's Cabin." In 1915 he agreed to fight a new "White Hope," and lost by a knockout to Jess Willard in Havana, Cuba. Although Johnson claimed that he purposely threw the fight to better his chances of returning to the United States, most boxing experts believe he was fairly beaten. Johnson eventually returned to America in 1920, served his sentence at a federal penitentiary in Levenworth, Kansas, but found that no one had any more interest in him as a fighter.

The following account of the Jeffries-Johnson fight by Arthur Ruhl appeared in *Collier's Magazine* in July 23, 1910 (Vol. XLV, pp. 12, 13, 22). What insights does it offer about racial attitudes in the United States in 1910? Does Ruhl's account suggest anything about the commercial possibilities of professional boxing as it became more acceptable as a spectator sport?

JEFFRIES VS. JOHNSON

RENO, NEVADA, JULY 4, 1910.

The battle about which whole wood-pulp libraries have been written during the past few months is over, and the great Jeffries myth has vanished into the bright Nevada sunshine. As Mr. Jeffries himself and innumerable experts have stated repeatedly that one-time champion was never fitter in his life, one novice hesitates to dim the luster of his rival's achievement by concluding that he didn't "come back." Nevertheless, the fact remains whether or not the result was due to Mr. Johnson's admittably exquisite technique or to his possession of that divine fire of youth which once lost is never found again, that in the fifteenth round the "hope of the white race," with his crouch and his glare and all his hairy brown bulk, hung over the ropes by his knees in a position quite primordial enough to satisfy even the red-blood novelists who have written so eloquently of late in the sporting pages of neolithic men and the jungle-born. And above him, with superb muscles of that terrifying left arm and shoulder taut and trembling to continue the battle of need be, stood the black man, Johnson—"Lil' Artha," with the queer, flat-footed shuffle that only masked the quickness of a cat, "Lil' Artha" of the bass-viol and the crap-shooting and the half-puzzled, pleading, rather wistful smile—the undoubted champion.

As a mere fight, this battle for the greatest purse that two boxers ever fought for was, I suppose a pretty sad affair; but as an event, a drama of temperaments, an example of the phenomena possible in this year of grace 1910, it was as strange and as wildly romantic as any one child could desire.

I wonder what simple old gladiator of the pre-Sullivanite days—Randall or Tom Cribb, Sayers, Heenan, the Tipton Slasher, or Jim Belcher, the Pet of the Fancy—would have thought of a purse of $121,000 and moving-picture royalties, vaudeville engagements, and so on which meant to the winner, if the white man had won, something over a half-million dollars? Of wine agents and war correspondents, and all the curious, top-heavy accessories which surrounded this argument between two not particularly indispensable citizens?

Every night for a week before the fight between 100,000 and 150,000 words—two popular novels—to be doubled many times before they reached the newspapers to which they were telegraphed—went out to the world from Reno.

In addition to the regular war correspondents, most of the prize-fighters temporarily disengaged from the practise of their profession were also writing daily critiques for the papers. Some, to be sure, merely contributed the color of their signatures and photographs while weary but more articulate reporters did the actual work; but there was at least one shining exception and the sight of Mr. Battling Nelson, with his cauliflower ears growing redder and redder as he struggled nightly in the intricacies of the literary art with the public stenographer in the crowded lobby of the Hotel Golden, was one of the fight's most fascinating pictures.

And this had been going on more or less similarly not only for days but for months. Several newspapers had regular office headquarters, as at a political convention. One San Francisco paper had fourteen fabulously-paid special writers, including two red-blood novelists, one of whom was accompanied by a manager at least, if not by a trainer, and all trying to say each day the same thing in fourteen different ways. One of its rivals, not to be outdistanced, threw its papers off the train into an automobile on the west side of the Sierras and shot through the night over Nevada and to Reno two hours ahead of the train. These two newspaper automobiles raced over the same course, and after that another paper loaded its papers into an automobile as they fell from the presses in San Francisco at two o'clock in the morning, flew clear across California and over the mountains, and arrived in Reno the next afternoon considerably ahead of the train.

There were correspondents from London and Australia, and even M. Dupuy, of the Paris "Figaro," traveled across those American deserts, mysterious and immeasurable, "to observe M. Jeff and M. Jack Johnson make the box." One overland train, white with alkali dust, would pull in with Big Tim Sullivan of New York or Charlie Millet of Mullen Centre, Iowa, and his friend Bill. Another would come in from the West and out would step a little band of Australians, speaking a quaint, modified cockney of the colonies.

And fighters were so thick that as you pushed through the mob in front of the Golden, with the faro chips and roulette wheels clicking in Jim May's and the Fafner-like bellowing of the megaphone filling the street with betting odds, you always looked first at each man's left ear to see whether it was lopped over and grown together like an oyster or the ear of the ordinary non-fighting man.

No one who was not there can easily understand what a curiously enthralling drama a simple fight can be made into when thus isolated in a quiet little desert city and analyzed, colored, and vitalized by the nervous cumulative intelligence of two or three hundred keen and imaginative men with nothing else to do. All the raw material was there. They only needed to be made interesting.

On the one hand was this brown Colossus of a white man, not a fighter in the "scrappy" sense of the word, rather a sort of grizzly bear, bored by people and photographers and noise, and much preferring to bury himself in the mountains and fish. He didn't want to fight again. Public clamor made him.

And yet you had but to look at that vast hairy body, those legs like trees, the long projecting jaw, deep-set scowling eyes, and wide, thin, cruel mouth, to know that here was an animal who would stand up and give battle as long as it could see, whom cleverness could not ruffle, nor blows dismay.

A Caged Bear

There was nothing winsome about Jeffries. He was as surly and ugly as a caged bear. He would ride past you on a country road, returning alone from a fishing trip crouched in the rear seat of his automobile, swarthly, glowering, chewing gum, and never so much as notice your greeting by the flicker of an eyelid. After the machine had stopped at the gate of his training quarters and a crowd of harmlessly demented admirers had gathered about it, he would sometimes sit there without moving for five or ten minutes, still glowering straight ahead, chewing gum and seeing only, as it seemed, the vision of his black rival coming to meet him across the ring. There was something peculiarly sinister in this static ferocity, and he did not lessen the impression when he climbed down at last and walked slowly away, seeing no one, with his huge right arm partly contracted and slowly sawing the air as if aimed for a blow.

"He's John Ridd," said Mike Murphy to me one day. "You've read 'Lorna Doone.' He's another John Ridd."

"Lil' Artha" Johnson, the negro, was as different as could be. About twenty pounds lighter than Jeffries, with a rather lathy underbody and superb shoulders and arms, he was as smooth and sleek and supple as a seal just coming out of the water. Light-hearted, humorous, witty even as he showed—even during the thick of the battle—when any one ventured to engage him in repartee, he yet had the good sense or cleverness to keep the respectful ingratiating ways of the Southern darkey. He was quiet, well-mannered, generous in what he said of his opponent, and, indeed, not without an almost winsome charm.

In the ring he at once became fascinating. There was mystery in that slow, flat-footed shuffle, in the way his gloves, moving slowly about his opponent's biceps, turned like lightning either to block a lead or shoot in a blow. With seemingly indolent grace and his drowsy smile, he would stand up before George Cotton, his big black sparring partner, and catch and turn aside a rain of blows as easily as a big brother might play pease-porridge-hot with his little sister. Once during the fight, when Jeffries started a left swing for the wind that looked enough to fell an ox, the negro caught it in just the same way, and Jeffries's arm stopped as his biceps met the black man's right as neatly as if it were a ball settling into a catcher's glove.

The Impulse of Traditions

But what it was thought he didn't have—and this is what made the fight between the mature thinking white man and the light-hearted, seemingly careless, negro most interesting—was that dogged courage and intellectual initiative which is the white man's inheritance. For in any supreme effort there comes a moment when cleverness and technique count for nothing and the issue is decided by that something which goes down through panting lungs and beating heart and straining muscles and calls for the very core and soul of the man. And it is here, other things being equal, that a negro is always at a disadvantage. He has no traditions behind him. He stands alone. The white man has thirty centuries of traditions behind him—all the supreme efforts, the inventions and the conquests, and whether he knows it or not, Bunker Hill and Thermopylae and Hastings and Agincourt.

You should have seen Mr. Mike Murphy throw back his head, close one eye tight shut, and with just a crack showing in the other like the eye of some curious withered, wise old bird, and with insight gained from training generations of runners and football men, go straight to the heart of things in his crackling, half-quizzical drawl. He didn't believe even when the talk was wildest, that Jeffries could come back. "No man ever did," he would say, "and no man ever will. There are three things you can't beat—nature, instinct and death."

Fighting with the Mind

He thought the negro ought to win. He had the strength and skill, yet he couldn't quite make himself sure of that seemingly vague good-humored will.

"*Mind!*" he said to me one day, squinting through the half-opened eye and tapping his temple with one finger, "it's all mind. If you go into a contest with your mind right, you've got the other man beaten already. And that negro," he waved his hands vaguely, "loose! No concentration. If he don't wake up, he might get knocked out in the first round. Look at Jeffries. He's going into a fight. Temperament, that's the whole thing. Give me eleven men and time enough and I'll put into their hearts the idea that they are going to win and you can't beat 'em. That's what training is. Roosevelt would make a good trainer."

"Ha!" he crackled, "that's the way we used to beat Harvard—we had 'em beaten when we came onto the field." He tapped his chest mysteriously. "Here."

Here was a man of imagination and parts. In the contagious bite and snap of his words was the very mysticism and poetry of fighting.

On the Saturday before the fight, Mr. Tom Shevlin, who used to do terrific things to the Harvard line, now a glittering lumber king or something of the sort, came to cast his practical eye over the warriors. As the three of us rode back to town together, the old trainer tapped his head and murmured the one word "*Bad!*" Mr. Shevlin put his mouth close to Murphy's ear—for the latter is hard of hearing now—"*Rotten!*" he shouted. "No concentration. He going up against a locomotive for two hours, and he don't know it. I want to see a man worried. Go out by himself and not want to talk to people. When I played football"—he tapped his dove-colored waistcoat—"All gone here. Couldn't eat, couldn't sleep. Took two months to get my digestion back after the season was over. But when I went out into the field"—Mr. Shevlin lifted his excellent shoulders inquiringly, and as I had enjoyed the sad pleasure of seeing him hit the Harvard line, he needed to say no more. "Good heavens, that man's going into a batttle, and he don't know it yet!"

"Reno or Bust"

Well, no ride with Tom Turtle on top a stage-coach through the finest English country in the snappiest fall weather could have been more splendid and exciting than the morning of the fight. The day dawned spotlessly clear, one of those still crystalline mornings which come in the thin dry air of the mountain desert country. The town was jammed. Miles, it seemed, of dusty Pullmans stretched down the tracks, above their dining-car roofs the blue smoke of the breakfast fires. From east and west other trains kept pouring in and dustier still and honking gaily as they came, touring cars with ragged signs of "Reno or Bust."

There were Indians, Chinamen, Hindus, New York wine-agents, and other queer fish, but above all it was a man's crowd—of husky men, boyish, in high spirits, talking at a great rate, and in the liveliest good humor, about the difficulties of getting breakfast, getting a shave, and about the prospects of the fight. You must imagine a bright green little oasis, ten or fifteen miles across, set in a sort of dish of bare enclosing mountains—brown mountains with patches of yellow and olive-green and exquisite veils of mauve and amethyst, and at their tops, blazing white through the clear air, patches of austere snow. In the center of all this a great pine bear-pit had been raised, glaring white and hot in the blazing desert sun, and into this at 1.30 o'clock that afternoon 20,000 men were crowded with their eyes fixed on a little roped square in the center.

The betting was 10 to 6 or 7 on Jeffries and the talk about 1,000 to 1. You couldn't hurt him—Fitzsimmons had landed enough times to kill an ordinary man in the first few rounds, and Jeffries had only shaken his head like a bull and bored in. The negro might be a clever boxer, but he had never been up against a real fighter before. He had a yellow streak, there was nothing to it, and anyway, "let's hope he kills the coon."

A Scowling Brown Colossus

That was about the mental atmosphere as Lil' Artha', wrapped in a dressing-gown and smiling his half-puzzled, rather pleading smile, climbed into the ring. Old Billy Jordan, who has been announcing fights for fifty years or so, was just introducing the negro to the buzzing, hostile audience, when Jeffries, with a cloud of seconds and camp-followers behind him, climbed through the ropes.

I had a seat at the ringside, directly opposite him, and I can unhesitatingly state that I have never seen a human being more calculated to strike terror into an opponent's heart than this scowling brown Colossus as he came through the ropes, stamped like a bull pawing the ground before his charge, and chewing gum rapidly, glared at the black man across the ring.

If looks could have throttled, burned, and torn to pieces, Mr. Jack Arthur Johnson would have disappeared that instant into a few specks of inanimate dust. The negro had his back turned at the moment, as he was being presented to the crowd on the opposite side. He did not turn round, and as he took his corner and his trainer and seconds, crowding in front of him, concealed the white man a sort of hoot, wolfish and rather terrible, went up from the crowd. "He darsen't look at him! *O-o-o!* Dont let him see him! Don't let him see him!" And when Jeffries pulled off his clothes with a vicious jerk, and standing erect and throwing out his chest, jabbed his great arms above his head once or twice, I don't suppose that one man in a hundred in that crowd would have given two cents for the negro's chances.

Nor did many suspect until Johnson's left shot across to the white man's right eye in the sixth round and closed it—so strong and convincing was the Jeffries tradition, the contagion of the atmosphere, and that crouching, scowling gladiator—that the negro's finish was anything but a matter of time.

They had all seen or heard of that short, rather slow, piston-rod-like punch which the white man knew how to send with a tremendous, if not spectacular, force into his opponent's side just under the lower right ribs. They saw him send it in, time and again apparently, and each time the crowd gave a sort of subdued, exultant grunt. When Johnson supposed he must be shamming, and when those uppercuts of his shot up like lightning, they thought it was merely pretty, but didn't hurt.

When that blow got across in the sixth round,however, the cynicism of the white man's glare suddenly went dead and changed. His right eye blackened and closed, and the blood began to run down from his right nostril. He was fighting after that not to finish his opponent, but to save himself, to stave off what he probably knew, if the crowd did not yet suspect, nothing but chance could save him from. Mr. Jim Corbett, who as Jeffries second and following the quaint sportsmanship of the ring, had gone across to the corner nearest the negro between each of the earlier rounds to fix him with a sneering eye and wittily taunt and terrify him lost his bright vaudeville smile. Once, when he called out to Johnson during a round, the negro laughing across Jeffries shoulder, gave him as good as he sent. Once a man far up in the seats called down to Johnson. "Why don't you smile now?" and the negro, who seemed to know everything that was going on in an out of the ring without at any time paying close attention, deliberately turned his head and smiled, He looked fierce occasionally, but that was only when he feinted. When something real and dangerous was to be done, he was apparently dreaming placidly as the flowers of May.

A Mirage for the Multitude

The rest is an old story now—how the big man, bleeding, beaten, but glaring stubbornly out of his one good eye, bored steadily in as the bull charges the matador toward the end of his fight: how suddenly, the main drama about which had gathered such a curiously modern and top-heavy mountain of accessories, rushed to its swift and unexpected conclusion. In the thirteenth round the crafty black turned loose for a moment, and it was all over then but the shouting.

In the fourteenth and fifteenth rounds, however, the old champion came crouching back, groggy but willing: in the fifteenth there was a quick clash, and all at once his tree-like legs caved-in, and the great hairy-brown hulk, which had never been knocked down before nor beaten, sank close to the ropes. The crowd didn't cheer. It rose and stood and stared, as if the solid ground beneath it were turning to a mirage.

At the count of nine Jeffries got to his feet, only to be sent back again, this time between the ropes. His camp followers forgetting themselves in the desperation of the moment, pushed him to his feet, but it was only to stagger across the ring and go down again, and for the last time on the other side.

The lifted the fallen idol and slapped his big shoulders and led him away; men rushed down and hopped over the sputtering telegraph instruments to cut the ropes and floor canvas into souvenirs, and Mr. Jack Arthur Johnson, with only a slightly cut lip, rode back to camp in his automobile with a harder road ahead of him than any he ever yet has traveled—the gilded, beguiling pathway of him who is not climbing but has arrived.

The After-Effect

The white race, whose supremacy this contest was going to establish, must, naturally, have been as dead as the Aztecs or the Incas; but the representatives of it in Reno seemed to battle their way into the overflowing restaurants to-night with their usual interest to smoke their black cigars with their customary zest, and gaze out at the pink and lavender lights turning to purple and ashes in the distant mountains with the usual air of equanimity. They reasoned, I believe, that there hadn't been any fight, that Jeffries was only a shell of a man, and it wasn't certain that they were convinced that he even *had* any arms.

That was all very well after the event and for those who forget how things stood when the battle opened. But any one who happened to see, from Johnson's corner, the face of Jim Jeffries as he climbed into the ring, and felt the focused mind and heard the taunts and jeers of the hostile crowd, knows that it took something more than boxing skill for that black man to go out and meet his fate; that he had concentration right enough if it didn't show on the outside, and stood on his own feet and thought for himself, and fought and vanquished a brave opponent cleanly and like a brave man.

CHAPTER 4
TWENTIETH-CENTURY AMERICAN SPORT

Whether as an activity that ostensibly built character, provided an entertaining way to spend leisure time, or even, for some, an opportunity to make a fortune, by the turn of the century few Americans could doubt the increasing presence and significance of sport in American life. Today, none of us would question that fact. Attention to sport as business, as amusement, and as an arena that both mirrors and at times anticipates major issues in American society—be it the development of a capitalist economy, race relations, feminism, and even domestic and international political controversy—is commonplace. The expansion of the American marketplace and the development of a consumer-oriented society; a communications revolution encompassing radio, television, and even outer space; two world wars, and the rise of communism; dramatic changes in American race relations and a sexual revolution are just some of the major factors that have influenced the place and shape of sport in twentieth century America.

Without attempting to be comprehensive or chronological, the following selections reflect the belief that sport in the twentieth century is an integral part of the fabric of American life—a multifaceted social institution of human interaction that illuminates a whole range of experiences, hopes, problems, limitations, and even fantasies of Americans.

THE BUSINESS OF SPORT

Late nineteenth and early twentieth century entrepreneurs and athletes recognized the economic possibilities inherent in sport. Yet even men as bold as A. G. Spalding or Babe Ruth would be astonished by contemporary developments. Today, in one form or another, sport has become an integral part of American capitalism and a major form of business enterprise. Every time we open a newspaper or turn on a radio or television we are bombarded with evidence to this effect. Prominent athletes selling everything from breakfast cereals to cars, stories reporting the sale of sports franchises for millions, negotiations of television contracts for college and professional sport for billions, the strike demands of millionaire professional football players, or the corruption and exploitation of college athletes by football coaches and universities in quest of financial contributions and prestige are commonplace. Although many of these phenomena have been around since the turn of the century, they have reached new dimensions since the 1920s. The following selections suggest why this is so while offering a sense of both the problems and the promise that are part of the commercialization of sport.

COHEN AT THE BAT

On September 22, 1927, Bernard Baruch, Charlie Chaplin, Douglas Fairbanks, Ty Cobb, George M. Cohan, and Jack Johnson crowded into Chicago's Soldier Field to watch Jack Dempsey try to regain his heavyweight crown from Gene Tunney in what promoter Tex Rickard billed as the second "Fight of the Century." Known in boxing history for its legendary "long count," the fight is no less important for what it suggests about the popularity of sport in what many commentators have characterized as its "golden age."

Over 104,000 people paid $2,658,660 to watch Tunney's victory while an estimated fifty million boxing fans listened to Graham McNamee's radio broadcast carried by 73 stations on the NBC network. Although Dempsey failed to regain the title that he had first won in 1919, he had the satisfaction of knowing that during his eight year reign he had fought before some 500,000 people, earned over $10 million and had been regaled by a new generation of sports writers including Grantland Rice, Paul Gallico, Damon Runyon and Ring Lardner as the "Manassa Mauler," a new American hero whose popularity rivaled that of Charles Lindbergh and Babe Ruth.

The factors that accounted for boxing's success were the same ones that made the 20's the so-called Golden Age of American sport. The role of the radio and newspapers in reaching millions of people and in shaping a national cultural experience, the positive response of mass spectatorship to athletic spectacle, the popularity of heroes who embodied individual strength and sensational feats in a society becoming more bureaucratic and less tolerant of idiosyncracy, the willingness of people to spend money as means of self-gratification and the ability of capitalists of leisure to exploit these opportunities and needs encouraged unprecedented development of sport as commercial venture that set the tone for the twentieth century. In a post war consumer hysteria that saw the automobile and electrical power come of age, Americans with discretionary income spent it on all kinds of things, from labor-saving devices like washing machines to golf and tennis equipment and to tickets to athletic contests like the Dempsey-Tunney fight in a mad rush to enjoy the good life. In 1929 alone Americans spent over $17 million on golf equipment and some $3.4 million on tennis gear while elevating those sport's best practitioners like Bobby Jones, Helen Wills, and Big Bill Tilden to hero status. The birth of the National Hockey League, The National Football League, the continuing expansion and growth of big-time college football and the resurrection of professional baseball after the debacle of the 1919 Black sox scandal offer additional evidence of a 20s' sports explosion fuelled by the possibility of profit.

Although the exploits of Babe Ruth and the New York Yankees provide the best known example of both the popularity of America's "national game" and its commercial possibilities in these years, the story of John McGraw and Andy Cohen deserves notice. Anxious to find a drawing card to counter the commercial success of the Bronx Bombers and the Sultan of Swat, McGraw, manager of the New York Giants, came up with a novel way to attract new fans to the Polo Grounds. In 1923, he brought up Moses Solomon, a Jewish ballplayer who he nicknamed the "Rabbi of Swat" with hope that his appearance in the Giant lineup would bring out large numbers of Jewish East European immigrants who had settled in New York's lower East Side and the Bronx. Although Solomon lasted only two games, five years later McGraw tried again. After trading the legendary Rogers Hornsby to Boston, the Giant skipper replaced him with Andy Cohen, a Baltimore born, El Paso bred ballplayer, Jewish by name if not by practice. On the opening day of the 1928 season, over 30,000 spectators, many of them working-class Jewish immigrants, crowded into the Polo Grounds to see the Giants play Boston. New York won 5–2. Cohen scored twice, had two RBI's, and knocked in the winning run.

The enthusiastic response to Cohen's debut is captured in the following parody of "Casey at the Bat." Although Cohen's major league career was a short one, his story underlines the growing popularity of professional spectator sport to an expanding market, something that sports entrepreneurs were to be increasingly aware of in the future. The overt anti-Semitism apparent in the poem was no less a part of American society and culture in the 1920s.

Cohen at the Bat

The outlook wasn't cheerful for the Giants yesterday
They were trailing by a run with but four innings left to play.
When Lindstrom flied to Richbourg and Terry weakly popped,
It looked as though those Bostons had the game as good as copped.
But Jackson smacked a single over Eddie Farrell's pate,
And from the stands and bleachers the cry of 'Oy, Oy' rose.
For up came Andy Cohen half a foot behind his nose.
There was ease in Bob Smith's manner and a smile on Hornsby's face,
For they figured they had Andy in the tightest sort of place.
It was make or break for Andy, while the fans cried 'Oy, Oy, Oy,'
And it wasn't any soft spot for a little Jewish boy.
And now the pitcher has the ball and now he let's it go,
And now the air is shattered by the force of Casey's blow.
Well nothing like that happened, but what do you suppose,
Why little Andy Cohen socked the ball upon the nose.
Then from the stands and bleachers the fans in triumph roared.
And Andy raced to second and the other runner scored.
Soon they took him home in triumph amidst the blare of auto honks,
There may be no joy in Mudville, but there's plenty in the Bronx.

Television and Sport

In 1871, a franchise in baseball's first professional league, the National Association of Professional Baseball Players, cost $10.00. In 1983 the going price for the Detroit Tigers was $50 million. Many observers agree that television's ability to reach an ever-expanding national marketplace has been the single most important factor in the commercialization of sport. So powerful is television's influence that the rules of particular sports, the expansion of sports franchises and even the creation of new sports leagues have been governed by the dictates of those who control the medium. Examples abound. In 1959, the American Football League came into being only because the ABC television network agreed to broadcast its games for five years at a cost of $2 million. The continued existence of the floundering league in the early 1960s, before its eventual merger with the NFL, depended on NBC's offer of $42 million over five years after the network had failed to outbid CBS for the rights to televise National Football League games. In 1958, the Professional Golf Association switched most of its tournaments from match to medal play because golf officials believed the new format would be more exciting and attract a larger television audience. Baseball's restructuring into four divisions and the introduction of a playoff system was dictated by the lure of extended television coverage and the increased revenues that went with it. And in 1986, the Super Bowl, watched by 115 million Americans, cost NBC $17 million for the broadcast rights, a figure easily recouped by the network that offered its 50 commercial spots on the telecast at a rate of $550,000 per thirty seconds.

Television has made mass spectator sports out of unlikely prospects and made all sports more accessible to a national, even global, viewing public. Nor is it likely that the number of American cities able to enjoy professional sports franchises would have more than doubled since 1961 if it weren't for the revenues television executives guaranteed sports leagues in anticipation of making their own money because of new markets. At the same time, astronomical player salaries that turn off many fans who wonder what happened to participation based on the love of sport, overexposure of particular sports like college football, and the negative consequences the lure of T.V. money has had on college athletics are just some of the problems associated with television's impact on sport.

Some measure of television's role is offered by the following *New York Times* report of March 23, 1982, which details the National Football League's television contract. What do you make of the reporter's reference to professional football as show business? Aside from the discussion of incredible amounts of money, what other matters concerning the NFL hinted at in the article suggest the "business" side of the game? Why would a sports league seek exemption from Federal antitrust legislation? What happens to the interests of ticket-holding fans in a situation where television revenue guarantees some NFL teams a profit whether or not a single person enters the stadium?

N.F.L. TV PACT $2 BILLION

PHOENIX, March 22—With a show of hands on the first day of their spring meetings, the owners of the National Football League's 28 teams unanimously approved today network television contract that will enrich each club by more than $70 million over the next five seasons.

The pact's total value is about $2 billion, which makes it by far the richest in show-business history and caused Marv Levy of the Kansas City Chiefs, one of the coaches in town for the meetings, to describe it as "mind-boggling."

Commissioner Pete Rozelle would not disclose specific figures, but sources within the three major networks confirmed that each team would average $14.2 million a year for the duration of the agreement. The payments will start at about $12 million for next season and escalate yearly.

The $14.2 million average means, for example, that the Denver Broncos, who were sold in 1980 for $20 million, will earn about two-thirds that amount in television income alone for one season. The average is also about three times what each team received from the league's last deal with the network, which was worth a total of $640 million over four years, ending last season, and was until now the richest pact ever in show business.

CBS, which televises more games than ABC and has higher ratings in the Sunday afternoon market than NBC, reportedly paid the highest price in the new contract: $700 million to $750 million. But it failed during the negotiations to win the right to move into the prime-time market, which was retained exclusively by ABC.

The sources said that NBC and ABC had each paid $600 million to $650 million.

In return, this is what the networks received:

CBS and NBC each won the rights to an extra preseason game, raising the number to three each.

All three networks were permitted to sell another minute's advertising per game, raising the time for commercials to 24 minutes.

ABC won the rights to the Super Bowl of January 1985, breaking the hold of the two other networks, which had televised all 16 previous Super Bowls. For the four other years of the contract, NBC and CBS will rotate Super Bowl coverage, as they have in the past. That means NBC will televise the games in 1983 and 1986, and CBS in 1984 and 1987.

ABC picked up an extra prime-time night game to televise, in addition to its regular "Monday Night Football." It will televise a total of five times on Thursday or Sunday night.

Jim Spence, the senior vice president of ABC Sports, would not confirm the financial details of the agreement, but said he was pleased by the package, particularly since "we kept prime time for ourselves."

"We paid enough to keep CBS out," he said.

In addition, another potential source of competition was kept at bay for the next five years. A key factor in the contract's being so expensive was a guarantee to the networks that there would be no cable television contracts for the duration of the deal.

But on a day when the owners were approving a contract whose negotiations had gone smoothly, they were also hearing about vexing problems, including the stalled negotiations for a new contract with the players association.

Another subject of discussion was legislation pending in Congress to exempt the league from Federal antitrust statutes. Such legislation has a bearing on the celebrated retrial, for which jurors are now being selected in Los Angeles, of the Oakland Raiders' suit against the league.

The Legacy of Curt Flood

When A. G. Spalding and William Hulbert organized the National League in 1876, they were intent on creating monopoly control over the business of professional baseball in terms of players and markets. Over the years, by instituting a reserve rule that bound players to their original club of contract for life and by controlling when and where new franchises could be added, they were able to achieve such ends, despite very real challenges to their authority by players and by competing groups of capitalists.

In the twentieth century, those involved in organized professional team sports successfully formalized the monopoly control that Hubert and Spalding struggled after, thanks, in part, to the help of the federal government. In 1915 and 1933, in cases brought by competing baseball leagues and individual ballplayers aimed at gaining a share of the professional baseball market and in ending the reserve rule, the Supreme Court ruled in effect that baseball was not a business and therefore was not bound by federal antitrust laws that would have limited their power to control markets and labor.

In 1970, Curt Flood, one of professional baseball's premier outfielders, challenged the reserve rule in the Supreme Court. Although Flood lost in his bid to have the clause and baseball's exemption from antitrust legislation invalidated, his attempt set in motion a series of challenges that ultimately led to the end of the reserve rule in 1975. The era of free agency, high salaries, and moving franchises that now dominate discussions of all professional sports dates from Flood's efforts.

The individual struggles of athletes like Flood and the concerted actions of player's unions in professional team sports has dramatically changed the rules of the capitalist game of sport in this country. Many commentators seriously question whether or not sport stories belong in the sport or business section of the newspaper. The following account by Curt Flood that appeared in *Sport*, tells his version of his struggle with baseball's establishment. What were his reasons for challenging organized baseball? What do you think of his arguments in favor of high baseball salaries? How does Flood's story compare to the relationships between capitalists and workers in American society?

THE LEGACY OF CURT FLOOD

It is an important moment in the 1977 preseason, the first meeting between the coach and his baseball team. In a soft voice, but firmly, quite firmly, he begins talking about what he expects of his players. They face him in a row along the third-base line, silent, attentive. Clearly, he has not only their command, but also their respect. They know that he was one of the most accomplished players of his time.

His time was the late '50s and the '60s. He batted .293 in a 15-year major-league career and appeared on the cover of *Sports Illustrated* in 1968 under the billing, "Baseball's Best Centerfielder." He was known, too, for his intelligence and broad interests. He earned money by hitting baseballs, but also by taking photographs and painting portraits. He brought mental agility as well as physical skills to sport, over all perspective as well as concentration on his craft. It is no surprise, thus to see him now, at 39, teaching, coaching.

Except. Except these are not professional ballplayers, but sandlotters, American Legion players. Their coach, Curt Flood, cannot get a job in "organized baseball." He has tried, but he has the reputation, after all, as "the man who started it all," the man whose 1969 lawsuit paved the way for the freedom and large salaries major-league baseball players have today.

To validate his case, Curt Flood had to stay out of baseball a full season, sacrificing a salary of more than $100,000. And when he lost in the courts and tried to come back as a player, he was physically spent and emotionally beleaguered. Very quickly, he left baseball permanently and for seven years sought a new life in places like Denmark, mainland Spain, and the island of Majorca. Now he is back in the States, in Oakland, standing out here with his American Legion team, dedicated, happy to be involved again with his game.

Partly because of what he did in 1969, ballplayers today are making those millions. Curt Flood did not get a cent. The noted sports attorney, Bob Woolf, wrote in a recent book that "the legacy of Curt Flood will live on. The years ahead may prove that Flood left a greater imprint on sports than any Hall of Famer." Here, Flood tells the story behind that legacy. At a time when it has become reflex to criticize athletes in their fight for higher and higher pay, it is instructive to examine, through Flood's story, some of the very valid roots of those fights. His is the story of a battle for rights, and its aftermath, the story of what can happen to someone who dares challenge wealth, authority and tradition.

* * * * * *

I guess the thing I like most about major-league baseball today is that finally, we, the athletes, are getting what we deserve. For 100 years the

Buschs, the Ewing Kauffmans, the O'Malleys and the George Steinbrenners have been making all the money. I don't mean petty cash either. Millions. Babe Ruth made $80,000. Willie Mays made $100,000. They were two of the greatest athletes of all time, but the only reason their salaries stood out was because everyone else's was so low. Today, a guy like Chris Speier is able to swing a deal for $2 million. What the hell is wrong with that? The athlete is the show so why shouldn't he make a compensatory wage? I hear people today saying that these kids today are all spoiled silly. I tell these people to sit down and shut up. You know what Johnny Carson makes a night? Eighteen thousand dollars a night to sit and interview people. Nobody complains about that. But they complained when I played and made $90,000 for six months.

Understand, money wasn't the reason I sued baseball. I sued because I'm a person, not a chattel and not owned by anyone. I sued for my freedom. How'd you like to think of yourself as owned? How'd you like to be controlled by a "reserve clause," to have no choice at all for the rest of your life in where you can work within your profession. For the rest of your life. Literally. That's the way it was. In an attempt to work out some settlement before I brought my case to court, the major-league player representatives and I met with a number of owners and their aides. After a lot of haggling, one of the player reps, Jim Bouton of the New York Yankees, laughed and said, "Okay, we can resolve this thing right now. Let's make a man a free agent when he's 65." All of us on our side of the table laughed. The owners didn't laugh. In fact, they said no. We couldn't believe it. So Bouton asked them why not. And John Gaherin, their chief negotiator, said, "Because you'll get your foot in the door, then you'll want to be free agents at 55." He was serious.

I was 17 when I signed my first baseball contract and 14 years later I was still bound by terms in it. So I fought back. And I'm still paying a price for that fight. Several months ago I wrote a letter, asking for a job in baseball. My sister sent a copy of that letter and a copy of my resume to every major-league club, and I still haven't received even one reply. A reporter from CBS recently asked me if I thought I was being blackballed. Well, with the credentials I have, I certainly should have been offered some job in baseball, someplace, a job coaching in some capacity. I'd rather not travel continously again, but I think I know enough about hitting and fielding where I could really help someone during spring training; let me stay on a kid's butt for six weeks and I'll either make a great fielder out of him or he'll end up hating my guts. Then the rest of the year I could scout the Oakland area, where I live.

But that's nothing more than a dream I guess. And I've certainly learned, during my battle and its aftermath, about hard reality.

It was October, 1969, when Jim Toomey of the St. Louis Cardinals' front office called to tell me I'd been traded to the Phillies. I couldn't believe it. Twelve years with the team and I'd just been told I was fired. Really, being traded and being fired are synonymous. "We no longer want you" is what they're saying. Ego trip, right? I thought I was the greatest centerfielder who ever lived and they didn't want me.

I sat down and thought about it for a while. I was supposed to forget 12 years of my life and just move to Philadelphia. Difficult to do. The next day I received an index card in the mail. On it was my name, Flood, Curtis," then my contract number, then the words, "You have been" followed by a list of possible means of dispensation—"waived, sold, released, traded." Next to each was a square, to be checked off where appropriate. On my card the square next to "traded" had been checked. They had sent me a form. Twelve years was worth more than a form.

I started to think, "What the hell am I, a used car?" In the next couple of days I talked to a friend of mine, Allan Zerman, an attorney. Allan said I had three options: Either retire, go to Philadelphia or challenge the right of one man to own another. He said the reserve clause was illegal, but that I'd probably lose a court fight anyway, that baseball was too powerful to be damaged by someone like me. I guess I realized that, but I didn't care.

Now, when I decided to fight, a few people in the media, like Howard Cosell, gave me a fair hearing. Most, however, were like Bob Burnes, a St. Louis newspaper columnist, who wrote that here's Flood making all this money and bellyaching, a little spoiled brat; without baseball, Flood would be mopping floors someplace; what the hell does Flood want? What Flood wanted was not to be owned, not to be a slave. I said something like, "Being owned by a baseball team is like being a slave 100 years ago. No matter how much money you make, they just trade you from one plantation to another, depending on how they want the cotton chopped." The word "slave" really brought on ridicule. My adversaries thought it was hilariously funny. They never seemed to understand the philosophical point I was trying to make.

People always ask me if I have a history of being a rebel. The answer is no. I can't think of a time before the reserve clause fight when I stood up against authority. And I wasn't moved by any psychological resentments toward the game, either. I've always loved baseball. I started playing when I was eight or nine, in Oakland. It was a mixed community, about 50-50 black and white, a working-class neighborhood. There was a park right across from my house and I played baseball there all the time. Frank Robinson and Vada Pinson played there, too. And Tommy Harper, although he was a little younger than us. And Bill Russell, the great basketball player. We had good times.

I still love the game of baseball. I have nothing but fond memories of the guys I played with. So many of them were wonderful companions and unique men. A few of them were geniuses and expressed themselves in that wacky way geniuses often do. Bob Gibson, who was my roommate for ten years, had his own view of pitching. "I pitch like I make love," he used to say. "I go for as long as I can as hard as I can and I don't want any relief." And I once asked Stan Musial his thoughts on hitting. I figured that was like hearing the Ten Commandments from Moses. Stan said, "Hitting is easy. When you get a ball in the strike zone, hit the shit out of it."

We not only had a great time together on the Cardinals, we were a helluva great team. We won pennants in 1964, 1967 and 1968, and two World Series. We were 25 high-strung athletes who would stay on each other. At that time Steve Carlton was with us and back then he had no idea what a great pitcher he was. We would tell him to go out there and just throw strikes, that they couldn't hit him, but he couldn't believe he was that good. One night, I think it was in Los Angeles, he pitched a fabulous game, but was beaten in the ninth when someone hit a ball out. He'd pitched such a great game that the radio guy had him on the postgame show anyway. The first question Steve got asked was, "What kind of pitch did the guy hit," and Steve, still in that pitcher's-intensity fog, said, "It was a fastball about cock high." I could imagine those cats in the control room turning knobs and shouting, "Cut that off." We were listening to it in the clubhouse and couldn't believe what we heard. We laughed like crazy and when Steve got back, we demanded an instant replay of the question, and especially the answer. For the next two weeks, we always picked Steve as our "star of the game" and wanted him on the postgame show. Whether he pitched or not.

Because of my love for the guys, and the great relationships I had with them, I was disappointed, I guess, that not one ballplayer came to court when my reserve-clause case went to trial. But I understood the reason. It was the same reason that made athletes accept the status quo for so long. Management could do anything it wanted to you.

Look, I was afraid to challenge management for years, too. From 1956 until 1958, when I was sent to the Cardinals, I was in the Cincinnati organization. My first year in organized ball I played in High Point, N.C. and led the league in batting with a .340 average, hit 29 homers, knocked in 128 runs, scored 133. Since I'd earned peanuts, I thought I'd surely get a raise. Wrong, I met with Gabe Paul, the Cincinnati general manager, and he said that while they'd like to give me more money, he couldn't. What you really ought to do he advised, is go to Savannah, Ga, have a good year, come back next year, and we'll talk about giving you more money. Right then, under any kind of logical circumstances, you would just say, "I'm going to work for someone else. Someone who will pay me some money now that I've proved some worth." But the reserve clause said I couldn't do that.

I was 19 years old when Gabe Paul told me to come back next year, a kid up against a man whose whole life had been sitting behind a desk and dealing with ball players. But in 1969, when the Cardinals traded me to the Phillies, I was 31, a man with numerous business ventures in St. Louis, who had a sense not only of his own individuality, but his worth. I called Marvin

Miller, the executive director of the Major League Players Association, and told him I wasn't reporting to Philadelphia. I said I had discussed this at length with my attorney and had decided to sue in order to test the legality of the reserve clause. I said I wanted and needed the help of the association. Miller asked if I were sure I wanted to do this. He said it could end my career and bring me permanent enemies. I told him I didn't care, I knew what I wanted to do.

My attorney friend, Al Zerman, and I went to New York and met with Miller and Richard Moss, the Players Association's chief counsel. After we had talked long and hard, Miller said, "Go home and think about it some more. When you have, if you still want to sue, we'll talk about it again."

So I did that. I went back to St. Louis, thought about it, and decided it had to be done. Some guy making $10,000 a year wasn't going to do it. So two weeks later I went back to New York, alone, and convinced Miller that this was what I really wanted to do. When Miller was finally sure that I was sure, he invited me to the player representatives' meeting in Puerto Rico.

At the meeting, I answered questions from the player reps. They weren't sure what I really wanted. Hell, I was making $90,000 and they thought I might be trying to raise it to $125,000.

They questioned me for about an hour. Giants catcher Tom Haller asked if my suit was tied to black militancy. I told him it was related to the Constitution of this country. When the guys were convinced that I was sincere, they unanimously voted to support me and agreed to pay all the costs of a trial.

When I got back home I heard from John Quinn, the Phillies general manager. He wanted to meet with me. I knew no amount of money could get me to play, but decided he deserved the courtesy of a meeting. And when we got together, it was a funny feeling. It was the first time I'd been with a baseball executive and felt I had options.

I started by telling Quinn that I had decided to go to litigation, but he still thought he could talk me out of it by offering a contract for over $100,000 a year. Every time I said, "No, money is not what I'm after," he would raise his offer. Then he began offering me automobiles. In his frame of reference ballplayers were only interested in shiny cars, cocktail bars and movie stars. I met with him several more times, out of respect for him, but we were talking different things. The only offer I could have possibly accepted would have been a contract without a reserve clause.

I made a number of attempts to reach an accord with baseball before a trial. In a civil series of telegrams and letters to Bowie Kuhn I said I was a human being and a free agent, not a piece of property. Kuhn, in a nice, friendly letter, agreed I was a human being and not a piece of property, but said I was owned by the Philadelphia team.

Soon after that exchange, the player representatives and I met with the owners to see if a court case could be avoided. For the first two hours, management people talked only about how long a player's sideburns should be. The argument grew hot and heavy over whether the hair should be allowed to come below the earlobe or whether it should remain above it. Someone actually pulled out a ruler. After the decision was put off, to be resolved in the future by a committee, we finally got to talk about the reserve clause. That's when Bouton laughingly suggested they let us become free agents at 65, and they let us know that they were't backing off, that a trial was inevitable.

The trial was a blur. But some of the things that happened at it will always stay with me. I guess memory number one is that of Jackie Robinson coming to testify for me. Jackie wasn't just anybody. He had freed another group of slaves 80 years after Lincoln. He had taken an enormous amount of garbage for every black athlete who followed him. And there he was talking about me, saying, "It takes a great amount of courage for any individual—and that's why I admire Mr. Flood so much for what he's doing—to stand up against something that is appalling to him." That was worth everything to me.

I have other strong memories. Hank Greenberg testified on my behalf. And Bill Veeck. Their support, and Robinson's, was very important to me because you always wonder if you've done the right thing. They were saying I had. Miller said that, too, and so did Moss, and our chief attorney, Arthur Goldberg, the former justice of the Supreme Court. Goldberg and Miller had been collegues at the Steelworkers union and because of their association and his personal interest in the case, Goldberg took on my case for no fee, only an agreement that expenses and his associates' time—which came to $200,000—would be paid.

I kept thinking, "Isn't this something, a former Supreme Court justice representing me." Because he was running for governor of New York, Goldberg could not spend as much time on the case as he would have liked, but he was around often enough to make an impression on me. I remember one tactic of his as particularly brilliant. He would hold a blank piece of paper in his hand while cross-examining a witness. He would say to the witness, "Didn't you say," then pause, refer to the paper and continue the alleged quote. The witness who never knew the page was empty, would invariably be disoriented.

I remember another of our attorneys, Jay Topkis, confronting Joe Cronin, then the president of the American League. Cronin had testified strongly in favor of the reserve clause, insisting it preserved the sanctity of the game. He said he had learned this from his uncle-in-law, Clark Griffith, an old time player who later owned the Washington Senators. When Topkis opened his cross-examination, he asked if Cronin knew that Griffith had jumped his own reserve clause in 1901 and had become the center of a furor back then. Cronin's answer was a barely audible no.

With the exception of those who were now in management, only one ballplayer or former ballplayer testified against me. Joe Garagiola. First he told the judge, "I wish you were on a bubblegum card." Then he said that baseball, just the way it was, had the best system anyone could devise.

More than the specifics of the trial, I remember the pressure. Insane. For months I'd been in a pressure cooker. I was constantly being badgered for interviews. I had no time for myself. I was so preoccupied I couldn't keep a close watch on the photography business I owned in St. Louis and while the trial was going on, the business went under. Talk about irony. Here I was in New York City, involved in the biggest court case in sports history, being defended by a former associate justice of the U.S. Supreme Court, and at the same time I'm being sued in some small claims court in St. Louis because my photography business went bust. I'm hearing major legal brains talking strategy during the day and talking to people back in St. Louis at night about paying the lightbulb bill. I felt warped. I had to get away. When the trial ended, I was told it could take months before a decision was handed down, before I'd know if I won. I needed to escape. I left the country.

I went to Denmark, a place I'd visited before. I knew no one cared about baseball there, that I would be left alone and could do absolutely nothing if I wished. When I got there I checked into a Copenhagen hotel and discovered that the Rolling Stones were staying there, too. By watching what was happening to them, I got a view of my own life. People beating on their door and calling them on the phone constantly. It was nuts.

Copenhagen was too hectic for me. I needed more quiet and privacy. I moved to a beautiful little town, Vaethbeck, 15 miles north of Copenhagen. I painted a little. I chased girls. I tried to sort out my thoughts.

About six months after I arrived in Denmark, I read the international Herald Tribune that a decision had been reached in my case. I'd lost. I wasn't surprised. Not really. I'd thought all along—and I've never said this to anyone before, not even privately—that there was no way a black man was going to win that suit. Listen, it eventually took two white guys—Andy Messersmith and Dave McNally—to destroy the reserve clause. Their battles were appreciably the same as mine. I know that a main reason I lost was because I was too far ahead of my time, that before you change a tradition, you need a groundbreaker, need to make people think about the situation, understand it. Okay, I was the groundbreaker. But I don't think I'm being paranoid in also feeling that my color hurt me. You don't think they were going to allow a little black kid to walk away with two million dollars, do you? That was the amount I'd sued for.

We appealed the decision and soon after that I got a call from Robert Short, the owner of the Washington Senators, who had bought the rights to talk to me about playing ball. Short said he wanted to talk about a contract.

I told him no, the case was still in litigation, that we had an appeal going and I couldn't do anything until I consulted my lawyer. Short said he'd like to come up and see me. I thought, "Sonofabitch, he's in the lobby, he's downstairs." I said, "Come on up." He said no, he's still in Washington, but why don't we meet in New York? I felt tingly all over. I really wanted to play baseball again. It was December 1970, and I hadn't played baseball in a year and a half.

I phoned Marvin Miller and told him about Short's call. Miller said that he had been the one who suggested that Short make the call. Miller had discussed the situation with Goldberg and they'd decided that because I had missed the 1970 season I had suffered enough damage to make my case viable whether I played the next year or not. Both Miller and Goldberg suggested I come to New York to meet with Short.

Short offered me a contract for well over $100,000. I accepted, but wanted an understanding: If I felt I couldn't make it, I could quit and go back to Denmark. He said, "Okay, that's a deal," and shook my hand.

Short is a first-class person. He assigned a man to spend a month with me in Florida before spring training. The guy's only duties were to help me get ready. He ran with me, pitched to me, hit fly balls to me, gave me as much work as I could handle in a month. Then, when the team came in, Ted Williams, the manager wanted me to take over and act as sort of team captain, a link between him and the kids on the squad. It was difficult to do because I was in awe of Ted Williams, too; he was such a perfectionist, worked so hard.

Except for Short, no one in baseball—not umpires, players, managers, general managers or owners—ever brought up the lawsuit to me. It was as if 1,000 people had sworn an oath of silence on the subject. But while I heard nothing from the people in my business, I heard plenty from the fans. They really got on me, saying I was greedy. But what the fan doesn't understand is all the athlete wants is a fair share of the tremendous amounts of money people make of sports. When I sued baseball, I sued for modifications in the structure, so that the owner could still make a fair profit without owning a man's body. That's all I ever wanted.

I lasted eight weeks in the spring of '71. That's all. I saw that I couldn't keep up with the kids. I just didn't have the ability to play anymore. I was drained. I wasn't going to take money under those circumstances, so the day I reached my decision, I sent Short a telegram from the Washington airport, telling him I was leaving. Then I flew to New York to connect with a flight to Denmark. To show you how fast Short moves, he had two people waiting for me at the New York airport. They tried to talk me out of getting on the plane to Denmark. But I was gone.

I stayed in Vaethbeck for six months, then moved to Spain, where it was warmer. There I met a woman named Ann and we soon opened a bar in Majorca. We called it "The Rustic Inn" and catered to U.S. sailors from the Sixth Fleet. We did a fantastic business for a number of years. It was an American oasis, an American sports hangout. We had a videotape player in the bar and we showed major-league baseball games, Muhammad Ali fights and other sports events. Howard Cosell would send me the tapes.

The Spanish police never understood what was happening. No one had ever heard of baseball in Spain, except the kids off the Sixth Fleet. When the Majorcan cops saw all those black people coming into my bar, they assumed I had to be doing something wrong. Selling dope or something. So they were on us from the time we opened until we closed. They would search the place like you wouldn't believe. I got sick and tired of being rousted three nights a week. And after a few years I left Spain.

I went to Andorra, but only for a little while. I realized I was bloody homesick. I had long ago lost my case and the appeal, and—remember—I hadn't left the United States because I didn't think it was a great country, I had left because I needed peace of mind and couldn't get the privacy I needed here. My children are here. People understand what you're saying here. I speak Spanish, but I'm never sure people really get the point of what I'm saying. I knew that for sure when I said to some girl, "Would you like to go to bed with me?" and she said, "I'm really not sleepy."

So I'm back. I've been back since early 1976. Back in Oakland, where I grew up. My mother is still living in the house I bought for her 15 years ago. And Sam Bercovich, whom I consider the world's finest human being, is still sponsoring an American Legion baseball team—the same team that Frank Robinson, Vade Pinson and I played on 25 years ago. Now I'm coaching that team and also coaching a Connie Mack League team that Sam sponsors. I'm working for Sam, too, doing public relations work and commercial lettering for his furniture store. And I'm also making money painting portraits for people.

I love coaching kids, working with them on mechanical skills and teaching them mental agility, teaching them, for example, to always think two plays ahead. I especially make them concentrate on their attitude about winning. All my life people have been telling me it's not whether you win or lose. Well, shoot, if you teach a kid how to lose, he'll be a loser for the rest of his life. You have to have an attitude about losing. You have to know where you made your mistakes, correct them, then kick youself in the butt and try again.

I'm nearly 40 years old now, and I'd like to try again—in baseball. I hope they'll give me the chance. I did something I thought was right, but at the same time, over the past seven years I've not made that much money. I've been stripped of my security. You always have a little selfish thing in the back of your mind which asks, "Did I give up too much to do this?" I'll never know.

* * * * * *

Curt Flood is sitting in the home he owns in Oakland, sipping beer and answering questions. Near him, tacked on a wall of the living room, is the 1968 Sports Illustrated cover billing him as "Baseball's Best Centerfielder." It is a large living room and a pleasant house. He lives here alone, next door to his mother. His five children live in Los Angeles with his former wife and occasionally come up for visits.

"Have you ever been given any award or any kind of recognition for what you did?" Flood is asked. "By say, the Players Association?"

"No."

"No one has ever acknowledged that you did something?"

"Only my closest friends."

"When you go to major league games, do the players recognize you?"

"It is not like that. These kids don't have the slightest idea who I am."

"Doesn't anyone come up to you, acknowledge you at the games?"

"Fans, yeah. But the players . . ." Curt Flood pauses. "The players couldn't care less who I am."

The Corruption of Intercollegiate Athletics

Ever since the 1890s, when college alumni and university presidents realized the possibility of using successful athletic programs to build a university's reputation and to increase revenues, charges have been raised about illegal recruiting, transcript tampering, game fixing, and the prostitution of higher education and amateur sport. For example, reviewing the history of intercollegiate athletics, an investigative study undertaken by the Carnegie Foundation for the Advancement of Teaching in 1929 concluded that college football was primarily a commercial enterprise where athletes were paid to play by wealthy alumni and grades were changed to keep athletes eligible. The emphasis on winning rather than on participation, the report concluded, was polluting the very concept of higher education.

Periodic cries for reform like the Carnegie Report have encouraged colleges and universities, working through their own athletic conferences and the NCAA, to undertake efforts at stopping these abuses. Success, however, has been uneven. In the early 1950s a rash of scandals including the point-shaving of CCNY's basketball team, the only team ever to win both the NIT and NCAA basketball championships in the same year, and the involvement of a number of West Point football players in a cheating scandal that caused their dismissal from the academy, shocked the sports world. Ten years later college basketball was rocked once again by a point-shaving scandal. More recently, due to the lucrative money afforded by television and the dramatic impact of revenue-producing sports like football and basketball on the economic welfare of universities and their communities, evidence of corruption and the exploitation of athletes by their coaches and by their universities have noticeably increased. Sports columnist John Underwood, in a 1980 essay on college sport for *Sports Illustrated* cited twelve incidents alone reported in the press between November 15, 1979, and April 30, 1980, ranging from the suspension of college basketball coaches for tampering with student transcripts to players receiving credit for courses they never attended. The following selections reflect part of the reality of contemporary intercollegiate athletics, shaped by its increasing commercialization.

Until his death in 1982, Red Smith was America's premier sports journalist. The following column appeared in the *New York Times* on November 12, 1979. In it Smith voices strong criticism of the exploitation of student athletes and of what he saw as the corruption of American higher education. Why does Smith see the so-called student athlete as the victim of the system?

THE STUDENT ATHLETE

Some edifying words about student athletes were heard on the air over the weekend. Whenever a college football game is on radio or television, it is accompanied by edifying words about student athletes, about the importance of intercollegiate athletics in a rounded educational program and about the vital role played by the National Collegiate Athletic Association. The edifying words are composed by writers for the N.C.A.A.

Student athlete is a term susceptible to various definitions. It can mean a biochemistry major who participates in sports, or a Heisman trophy candidate who is not necessarily a candidate for a bachelor's degree. Some student athletes are more studious than athletic, and vice versa.

There is at hand a piece written by a student athlete in his senior year at a major university that has been polishing young intellects for more than a century. He is an attractive young man, short months away from graduation, the best wide receiver in the school. One of his professors, who happens to be a football buff, asked him why his teammate, John Doe, never played first string although he was a better passer than Richard Spelvin, the starting quarterback. The Young man said he would write the answer "like it was a quiz."

What follows is an exact copy of the young man's answer. That is, it is exact except for the names. The quarterbacks are not really named John Doe and Richard Spelvin and the university's athletic teams are not known as the Yankees.

* * *

"People (Some) feel that Doe did not have the ability to run the type of offense that the yankys ran. He also made some mistakes with the ball like fumbling.

"As a wide receiver it didnt make me any different who quarterback. But I feel he has the best arm I ever saw or play with on a team. Only why I feel the I do about the quarterback position is because I am a receiver who came from J.C. out of state I caught a lot of pass over 80 and I did not care a damn thing but about 24 in one year.

"Spelvin is my best friend and quarterback at my J.C. school. Spelvin has an arm but when you don't thrown lot of half the time I dont care who you are you will not perform as best you can. Spelvin can run, run the team and most of all he makes little mistakes.

"So since they didn't pass Spelvin was our quarterback. But if we did pass I feel Spelvin still should of start but Doe should have play a lot. Tell you the truth the yanky's in the pass two years had the best combintion of receivers in a season that they will ever have. More—ask too talk about politics alum Doe problems just before the season coaches hate?"

The last appears to be a suggestion that alumni politics may have played a part in the coaches' decision on which quarterback would play first string. However, the professor who forwarded this material did so without comment or explanation.

* * *

The importance of disguising the names of these student athletes and the identity of the university is obvious. It would be unforgivable to hold a kid up to public ridicule because his grip on a flying football was surer than his grasp of the mother tongue. He is only a victim. The culprit is the college, and the system.

The young man's prose makes it achingly clear how some institutions of learning use some athletes. Recruiters besiege a high school senior with bulging muscles and sloping neck who can run 40 yards in 4.3 seconds. The fact that he cannot read without facial contortions may be regrettable, but if his presence would help make a team a winner, then they want his body and are not deeply concerned about his mind.

Some colleges recruit scholar athletes in the hope that the scholar can spare enough time from the classroom to help the team. Others recruit athletes and permit them to attend class if they can spare the time from the playing field. If the boy was unprepared for college when he arrived, he will be unqualified for a degree four years later, but some culture foundries give him a degree as final payment for his services.

One widely accepted definition of the role of a college is "to prepare the student for life after he leaves the campus." If the young man quoted above gets a job as wide receiver for the Green Bay Packers, then perhaps the university will have fulfilled its purpose. However, only a fraction of college players can make a living in the National Football League. Opportunities are even more limited for college basketball player, for pro basketball employs fewer players.

Where outside of pro football can our wide receiver go? He can pump gas. He can drive a truck. He has seen his name in headlines, has heard crowds cheering him, has enjoyed the friendship and admiration of his peers and he has a diploma from a famous university. It is unconscionable.

Efforts at Reform

In the wake of an NCAA investigation of its football program for illegal recruiting practices in 1973, and faced with new financial problems raised by the growth of women's sports and federal mandates calling for equitable support, Michigan State University examined the purpose and operation of its intercollegiate athletic programs that operate at a cost today of $10 million a year. The following statement on The Mission, Goals and Organization of Intercollegiate Athletics at Michigan State University was considered by its Athletic Council, the faculty committee responsible for reviewing the school's athletic program, in April, 1979. How does it describe the purpose of intercollegiate athletics today? What steps does it recommend to insure that the abuses described by Red Smith will diminish? Note the document's concern for financial considerations and for the ability to market its product. Does it successfully define a place for big-time college sport in an institution of higher learning?

THE MISSION, GOALS AND ORGANIZATION OF INTERCOLLEGIATE ATHLETICS AT MICHIGAN STATE UNIVERSITY

The following statement on the mission, goals, and organization of inter-collegiate athletics at Michigan State University has been prepared by the Athletic Council in accordance with its mandated responsibility to exercise faculty control over the athletic programs of the University. It recognizes the fact that intercollegiate athletics at Michigan State, as at all American universities, is clearly entering a period of transition and change resulting from the need to provide equitable opportunity and support for both men's and women's sports programs. These changes are occurring at a time of economic constraint whose pressures are likely to increase in the foreseeable future. As a result, it seems clear that athletic programs at institutions like Michigan State will be forced to rely heavily on those financial resources that they themselves are able to generate, and that in order to maximize those resources, priorities will have to be established and sound fiscal, organizational, and management policies put in place.

Athletics and Institutional Mission:

The argument over the pros and cons of intercollegiate athletics, and their place upon a college or university campus, has been with us for most of the present century, and there would seem little point to rehashing them here. What is clear, however, is that successful and well-operated programs of intercollegiate athletics do allow midwestern, state-supported universities like Michigan State to achieve their larger goals and purposes, and in ways that can be readily enough documented. Intercollegiate athletics serve:

1. To call attention to the rest of the University and its programs.
2. To focus the attention and enlist the financial support of University alumni. For institutions with a large and heterogeneous alumni constituency, many of whom live at great geographical distances from the University, success in athletics—particularly at the national level—serves as a source of pride, identification, interest, and financial support for the University at large. For many alumni, in fact, the only sustained contact they have with the University is through the intercollegiate sports program.
3. To enlist the interest and support of the general public throughout Michigan who are not alumni. The support of such individuals is crucially important for institutions like MSU which are heavily dependent upon tax dollars.
4. To provide economic stimulus for local business. Studies at the University of Wisconsin, a comparable Big-10 institution, have demonstrated that athletic events do have a direct rather significant impact upon the local business economy.[1]

There are, of course, dangers, which if not recognized and controlled can do serious, if not irreparable, damage to the institution's larger role. The greater the size and complexity of the athletic program, the greater the potential danger. There is, for example, the danger that athletics zealously pursued will dominate academics in terms of the status and recognition accorded the University. There is the constant danger too that abuses within the athletic program—abuses which raise serious fundamental questions about moral integrity, trust, and judgment—will, in turn, raise serious

---

[1]The Greater Madison, Wisconsin, Chamber of Commerce estimated that in 1975 Wisconsin football fans spent some $4,680,000 in Dane County over six home game weekends, *excluding* revenues brought to the University through ticket sales, parking, concessions, etc.

questions about the integrity and standards of the institution as a whole. To fail in setting and adhering to such standards is to fail the very values in which universities have long prided themselves, quite apart from whatever penalties and loss of revenue follow from their disclosure. The maintenance of standards and integrity rest, in the final analysis, upon individuals and the relationships which they establish. One of the basic trusts of this document is to suggest the establishments of clear lines of authority, accountability, and control whose effective and efficient functioning will contribute to decisions and judgements which constantly reflect the highest standards of the total institution.

Goals:

The goals of an intercollegiate athletic program can properly be considered from two perspectives: the perspective of the student-athlete and the perspective of the institution that the student-athlete attends. Rightly considered and emphasized these two perspectives support and enrich one another to the benefit of both the student-athlete and his or her university.

In return for their participation in the intercollegiate sports program of Michigan State University student-athletes have the right to expect the following:

1. That they will receive a total undergraduate educational experience, within a comparable time-frame, which is consistent with the quality of the educational experience offered to the non-athlete, including academic and non-academic support services.
2. That their talents as athletes will not be exploited at the expense of their educational and personal development as young adults.
3. That their athletic careers will be conducted under conditions that foster and contribute to the highest level of personal and institutional integrity.
4. That the University will provide quality of coaching appropriate to the level of competition and skill determined by the policies and fiscal resources of the Athletic Department and the University.
5. That the Univsersity will provide those support services unique to sport's competition at a level appropriate to the level of competition and skill determined by the policies and fiscal resources of the Athletic Department and the University.

Because intercollegiate athletics exists within the total program of the University, the University, on its part, has every right to expect the following:

1. That the policies and procedures which govern the athletic program (and the Athletic Department) will reflect both the academic purposes and functions of the institution and the broad principle of faculty control of intercollegiate athletics.
2. That the athletic program will be governed by the principles of equality of opportunity and maximum particiation for MSU students at a level of competition

appropriate to their skills and abilities consistent with the policies and fiscal resources of the Athletic Department and the University.

3. That there will be full compliance with both the spirit and the letter of the regulations governing the conferences and athletic organizations to which the University belongs, as well as with all state and federal regulations.

4. That the Athletic Department will adopt policies reflecting sound fiscal and management practices together with organizational procedures, policies, and levels of responsibility which are clearly defined and articulated.

Implementation:

The effective establishment and maintenance of such standards and goals will require that the Athletic Department be willing and able to marshall effectively its existing resources, both human and fiscal. A better, more productive use of existing resources is essential, and to that end a number of concrete recommendations regarding internal reorganization follow below. The aim of such reorganization is to provide a day to day operating structure within the Athletic Department that provides maximum communication, efficiency, and accountability in carrying out the Department's activities and responsibilities.[2]

It can be expected that more efficient organization will also lead to a better use of existing dollars, thus making available what are, in effect, new dollars for current programs. Such a policy of internal reallocation through reorganization, besides reflecting sound fiscal and management policy, will in all likelihood prove essential in building any case for new support from the University's General Fund. The question of financial resources is clearly a pressing one, given inflation, the general economic climate of higher education, the emergence of women's athletics and the need for full Title IX compliance. A more efficient internal organization should place the Athletic Department in a better position to generate those additional dollars that will become so important during the next few years.

Reorganization is imperative as well if the Athletic Department is to place itself in a position to deal equitably with women's athletics and the requirements of Title IX legislation. As the recent basketball suit illustrates so well, an institution which fails to anticipate and take charge of its own destiny in effect risks abdicating institutional control in favor of judicial or government directives. Such an alternative is unthinkable for a university which desires to maintain its institutional autonomy.

---

[2]The chain of accountability extends, of course, to the highest levels of University administration. As Edwin H. Cady observes, "The president who does not steadily face the realities of his intercollegiate athletics situation puts himself in jeopardy . . . . If he does not keep it under control, if he tries to ignore its realities, it will come and get him." Edwin H. Cady, *The Big Game: College Sports and American Life* (Knoxville, Tennessee, 1978), p. 143.

Organization:

The Department of Intercollegiate Athletics at Michigan Sate University exists in order to provide an efficient and just translation of university and department goals into daily activities. Accordingly, the mission of intercollegiate athletics has as its foci three levels of activities: (1) policy making and overall guidance; (2) operations and administration; (3) coaching and its related support activities, i.e., sports medicine, academic counseling, etc.

Each of these three levels is necessary to a successful program of intercollegiate athletics, but none is sufficient in and of itself to insure success. Each level must work actively to augment and to support efforts at other levels in the organization, and must do so in a manner which orchestrates both human and financial resources in order to derive maximum benefit for the University. This demands a *structure of organization which is highly visible, and protects the integrity of operations by having unambigious loci of critical skills, responsibility and accountability at each level.* It is the intention of the Athletic Council that such a structure be implemented before the current President terminates his service with the University.

Policy-making and Guidance Function:

The policy-making function in the area of athletics lies with the Athletic Council. The President has the ultimate administrative responsibility and duty for providing a statement of clear, concise, meaningful goals and objectives of the program of Intercollegiate Athletics at Michigan State University. The President has the responsibility to deal openly in all athletic matters with and through the Athletic Council. While the Athletic Council must share with the President the burden of developing clear concise statements of policies and objectives and of making certain that they are implemented and carried through at the appropriate organizational level, the Athletic Council maintains the separate responsibility of keeping the President advised of all developments which affect the attainment of those policies and objectives. The President is also responsible for maintaining clear and open communications with the Athletic Director and with the Athletic Council; though neither the President nor the Athletic Council can or should be expected to or shall play a role in the day to day operations of the Department of Intercollegiate Athletics. Should the President choose to delegate portions of his/her responsibilites to others, those individuals are then charged with that portion of presidential responsibility appropriate to the degree of delegation and pursuant to the Athletic Council bylaws.

Operations and Administration:

The role of the Athletic Director is to provide leadership consistent with administrative accountability in accord with sound fiscal and human resources management. The Athletic Director shall in no case render a decision in violation with the letter or spirit of the larger presidential statement of policy and objectives. So long as the Athletic Director conforms to the intent of policy and objectives he/she can reasonably expect to be allowed maximum freedom in the administration of the program. The level of support provided the Athletic Director shall consist of: (1) appropriate authority to manage Intercollegiate Athletic operations; (2) both human and fiscal resources commensurate with the statement of policy goals.

The duties of the Athletic Director center on the development of operational decisions and implementation of those decisions in a manner assuring the accomplishment of university objectives in compliance with policy. As the responsibility for success or failure of the integrated collegiate sports program of Michigan State rests with the Athletic Director, so does the authority for the establishment of an enforcement of operational policy and objectives. Thus while the Athletic Director is free to delegate authority for particular planning or operating activities to his/her administrative and coaching staff, he/she cannot delegate the responsibilty for successful achievement of university goals. The Athletic Director is responsible for the clear and open communication of his/her operational policies throughout the Department of Intercollegiate Athletics; is responsible for informing the President and Athletic Council of developments which affect the accomplishment of organizational policy and objectives; and is responsible for insuring that all activities of the Department of Intercollegiate Athletics are in compliance with appropriate judicial, legislative, executive, athletic governing body, or university mandates.

Coaching and Competition:

Coaches and athletic support service personnel are charged with the accomplishment of objectives set out by the Athletic Director. These individuals (in the performance of their delegated duties) shall in no case violate the letter or spirit of university policy or the policies established by the Athletic Director.

Priority Issues Within the Athletic Department:

The recent resurgence of Michigan State athletics has, ironically enough, been a phenomenon of mixed values. National reputation and ranking have brought fame, dollars, pride, increased recruiting potential, and other benefits. Paradoxically, however, this very success has served to divert attention from the redress of serious chronic problems within the Department of Athletics. The Athletic Council feels that it has become imperative that solutions for these problems be forthcoming now, during a period of relative strength. These problems must be addressed if a strong and effective program of intercollegiate athletics is to be established on a permanent basis.

There is a critical need for the development of written policy and objective statement so that the resources of the Athletic Department may be marshalled effectively. Among the current problems are the following:

- At the policy-making level, neither the Athletic Council nor the President has developed a statement of policy or objectives which provide guidance for the program as a whole. Without such a statement the Athletic Director is placed in a weakened and relatively dangerous posture. At the Athletic Director's level, there seem to be no statements of policy for ongoing operations of critical importance, e.g., ticket assignment priority, responsibility for public information releases, job descriptions and responsibilites, etc.
- Compliance with Title IX requirements is the administrative responsibility of the President through the Athletic Director, not the judicial system through the University attorney.
- In spite of the approaching dollar crunch, there is no mechanism for formal marketing or market planning, nor are those skills present in the Department of Athletics as constituted. This condition exists in spite of the stated goal of increasing the number of "revenue" sports through wider and more effective market appeal.
- Within the Department there has been a long history of mistrust and confusion among staff members. A strong well-ordered organization structure which insures maximum participation without the abdication of responsibility is required to replace petty gamesmanship and self-interest.

RACE AND SPORT

The prominence of Muhammad Ali, Edwin Moses, Earvin "Magic" Johnson, Kareem Abdul Jabbar, Hank Aaron, and Walter Payton underline the prominence of black athletes in contemporary American sport. Annual college and professional all-star teams in sports like football, basketball, and baseball are dominated by black athletes, many of whom earn huge amounts of money for their athletic ability. Only in the last quarter century, however, has the black athlete achieved such visibility. Until recently, although blacks participated in most sports, whether on the amateur or the professional level, they usually competed with each other, segregated in their pursuit of athletics as they were in other phases of American life. When certain individuals did compete successfully against whites, their experiences, from Jack Johnson to Joe Louis, were limited by the fact of their race and by the ways in which white society responded to them.

Regardless of white attitudes towards them, black athletes served as important symbols of black pride and success among a people proud of their own heritage, denied access by law, custom, and violence to the opportunities of American society, and determined to seek out their own destiny. For all the discrimination successful black athletes experienced before 1947, few of them would deny that their own lives provided more opportunity for freedom, self-expression, and relative economic security than other members of the American black community. Although gains have been made by blacks because of the Civil Rights movement, it is not clear that the recent success of black athletes accurately reflects the general improvement of the economic, social, and political situation of American blacks or the lessening of racism and discrimination in American society. The accounts of Maya Angelou, Jackie Robinson, Harry Edwards, and Walt Frazier offer provocative commentaries on these issues.

Joe Louis and Black Pride

Joe Louis was one of the greatest heavyweight champions of all time. The "Brown Bomber" won the crown from James Braddock in 1937 and defended it successfully twenty-five times until his retirement twelve years later in 1949—both records for any weight division. When Louis fought for the title in 1937, he was the first black to do so since Jack Johnson. His opportunity, however, did not represent any dramatic change in race relations or of the unequal treatment of blacks in American society. Consciously promoted by his managers as a clean-living, modest man who knew his place in a white-dominated world, Louis did not appear as threatening to whites as Johnson had twenty-five years earlier. Louis's victory over the Italian Primo Carnera in 1935, coinciding with Mussolini's successful Ethiopian campaign, established him as a symbol of American freedom against oppressive fascism and increased his stature among all Americans. His defeat by and subsequent victory over Max Schmeling, the great German and world heavyweight champion regaled as evidence of Nazi Aryan superiority, further enhanced his status as the defender of the American way, an ironic twist for a black man whose own people suffered discrimination and indignities throughout the era of his reign.

Regardless of Louis's meaning to white Americans, he became an important person in the black community. Maya Angelou is a prominent black poet and writer, not an athlete. Yet this brief excerpt from her autobiography, I Know Why The Caged Bird Sings (1970), offers a powerful statement about the pride black people took and the meaning they placed on the success of prominent black athletes such as Joe Louis. Set in rural Arkansas in the mid-1930s when she was a young girl, Angelou recreates the experience of listening to a Joe Louis fight on the radio. What does her account suggest about race relations in the South? What does Joe Louis represent for her?

MAYA ANGELOU REMEMBERS JOE LOUIS

The last inch of space was filled, yet people continued to wedge themselves along the walls of the Store. Uncle Willie had turned the radio up to its last notch so that youngsters on the porch wouldn't miss a word. Women sat on kitchen chairs, dining room chairs, stools and upturned wooden boxes. Small children and men leaned on the shelves or on each other.

The apprehensive mood was shot through with shafts of gaiety, as a black sky is streaked with lightning.

"I ain't worried 'bout this fight. Joe's gonna whip that cracker like it's open season."

"He gone whip him till that white boy call him Momma."

At last the talking was finished and the string-along about razor blades were over and the fight began.

"A quick jab to the head." In the Store the crowd grunted. "A left to the head and a right and another left." One of the listeners cackled like a hen and was quieted.

"They're in a clench, Louis is trying to fight his way out."

Some bitter comedian on the porch said, "That white man don' mind hugging that niggah now, I betcha."

"The referee is moving in to break them up, but Louis finally pushed the contender away and it's an uppercut to the chin. The contender is hanging on, now he's backing away. Louis catches him with a short left to the jaw."

A tide of murmuring assent poured out the doors and into the yard.

"Another left and another left. Louis is saving that mighty right . . ." The mutter in the Store had grown into a baby roar and it was pierced by the clang of a bell and the announcer's "That's the bell for round three, ladies and gentlemen."

As I pushed my way into the Store I wondered if the announcer gave any thought to the fact that he was addressing as "ladies and gentlemen" all the Negroes around the world who sat sweating and praying, glued to their "master's voice."

There were only a few calls for R.C. Colas, Dr. Peppers, and Hire's root beer. The real festivities would begin after the fight. Then even the old Christian ladies who taught their children and tried themselves to practice turning the other cheek would buy soft drinks, and if the Brown Bomber's victory was a particularly bloody one they would order peanut patties and Baby Ruths also.

Bailey and I lay the coins on top of the cash register. Uncle Willie didn't allow us to ring up sales during a fight. It was too noisy and might shake up the atmosphere. When the gong rang for the next round we pushed through the near-sacred quiet to the herd of children outside.

"He's got Louis against the ropes and now it's a left to the body and a right to the ribs. Another right to the body, it looks like it was low . . . Yes, ladies and gentlemen, the referee is signaling but the contender keeps raining the blows on Louis. It's another to the body, and it looks like Louis is going down."

My race groaned. It was our people falling. It was another lynching, yet another Black man hanging on a tree. One more woman ambushed and raped. A black boy whipped and maimed. It was hounds on the trail of a man running through slimy swamps. It was a white woman slapping her maid for being forgetful.

The men in the Store stood away from the walls and at attention. Women greedily clutched the babes on their laps while on the porch the shufflings and smiles, flirtings and pinching of a few minutes before were gone. This might be the end of the world. If Joe lost we were back in slavery and beyond help. It would all be true, the accusations that we were lower types of human beings. Only a little higher than apes. True that we were stupid and ugly and lazy and dirty and, unlucky and worst of all, that God Himself hated us and ordained us to be hewers of wood and drawers of water, forever and ever, world without end.

We didn't breathe. We didn't hope. We waited.

"He's off the ropes, ladies and gentlemen. He's moving towards the center of the ring." There was no time to be relieved. The worst might still happen.

"And now it looks like Joe is mad. He's caught Carnera with a left hook to the head and right to the head. It's a left jab to the body and another left to the head. There's a left cross and a right to the head. The contender's right eye is bleeding and he can't seem to keep his block up. Louis is penetrating every block. The referee is moving in, but Louis sends a left to the body and it's the uppercut to the chin and the contender is dropping. He's on the canvas, ladies and gentlemen."

Babies slid to the floor as women stood up and men leaned toward the radio.

"Here's the referee. He's counting. One, two, three, four, five, six, seven . . . Is the contender trying to get up again?"

All the men in the store shouted, "NO."

"—eight, nine, ten." There were a few sounds from the audience, but they seemed to be holding themselves in against tremendous pressure.

"The fight is all over, ladies and gentlemen. Let's get the microphone over to the referee . . . Here he is. He's got the Brown Bomber's hand, he's holding it up . . . Here he is . . ."

Then the voice, husky and familiar, came to wash over us— "The winnah, and still heavyweight champeen of the world . . . Joe Louis."

Champion of the world. A Black boy. Some Black mother's son. He was the strongest man in the world. People drank Coca-Colas like ambrosia and ate candy bars like Christmas. Some of the men went behind the Store and poured white lightning in their soft-drink bottles, and a few of the bigger boys followed them. Those who were not chased away came back blowing their breath in front of themselves like proud smokers.

It would take an hour or more before the people would leave the Store and head for home. Those who lived too far had made arrangements to stay in town. It wouldn't do for a Black man and his family to be caught on a lonely country road on a night when Joe Louis had proved that we were the strongest people in the world.

Should Black Athletes Be Role Models?

Walt Frazier was a basketball star for the New York Knickerbockers of the 1970s. Drafted out of Southern Illinois in 1967, he led the Knicks to world championships in 1970 and 1973. A fine ballhandler, scorer, and tenacious defender, Frazier was known as much for his appearance off the court as on. Dressed in fur coats, the latest styles, and visible even in New York in his Rolls Royce, "Clyde," as the media tabbed him, was known for his "cool" image and glamorous lifestyle. In this May 1, 1977, column, "Talk About Doctors Instead of Athletes," written for the *New York Times*, Frazier comments on the problems of being a folk hero for black youth of today. What does he have to say about the situation of black Americans in the 1970s compared to the 1930s of Maya Angelou's Arkansas? What dangers does he see in promoting people like himself as role models?

TALK ABOUT DOCTORS INSTEAD OF ATHLETES

As Arthur Ashe said, all black parents should get their kids to read, should get them to go to school. But it's easier said than done.

For too many black kids, their idols aren't even athletes. Their idols are pimps—the guys they see with the big cars, the flashy clothes and women. Go up to this kid and say, hey, read a book. It's hard to convince him after what he's seen in his environment.

Whose fault is it? One major factor is the media—TV, newspapers, magazines. The people the media talk about are the athletes, the movie stars. Their lifestyles are glamorized.

I've been one of those glamorized. I have had money, and I've enjoyed it. I have led the good life, and I've enjoyed it. I've had the adulation that comes with being a sports celebrity, and I've liked that, too.

But that's not all I'm about. I care about people. I care about the environment. And I care about myself: I've developed an interest in the tranquil life—in yoga and meditation—and I take pride in keeping my body clean. I like being the master of my body, instead of being a slave to my body, so I stay away from drugs.

I think the media should change their focus. Instead of talking about Walt Frazier, talk about a black banker, a black doctor, a black teacher. Put these people in the limelight. Maybe then the kids can begin to relate to them.

Well, if the media aren't steering the kids right, who should? The parents, of course. But here we run into the basic problem. Parents should be the dominating influence on children. They're with kids a lot more than I am or some other celebrity is, in many cases they aren't with them enough.

Someone Has to Start

Black parents, because of their economic situation, sometimes have to work two jobs. The kids run wild. The family doesn't eat meals together. The kids don't eat the proper foods. Not enough supervision.

Parents have to stress reading and education to their kids. If it helps, tell them that Walt Frazier had to go to college to get into the pros. He went to school. He read. You've got to get an education before you can become a pro basketball player.

Now, a lot of black parents have never gone to college. So this is a big handicap, too. Kids can't relate to college because of it. But there's got to come a break. As in my family, where I was the first to go to college.

In my freshman year at Southern Illinois University, I found college very hard. I was from Atlanta and I had never been in an integrated situation before. My public school education in the South was inferior to that in the North, and I was behind in my college studies from the start. It was frustrating, and I was very unhappy. I called home and told my mother I was leaving school. She said, "Over my dead body."

When I came home for spring break I was ready to quit again. But now I saw the same guys on the street corner doing the same things they were doing when I left—gambling, fooling with drugs, acting tough. They were an inspiration for me: I didn't want to be like them. I used them like stepping stones, and I stuck it out in college.

I got better as a student as I learned study habits. Before, I'd read every word and try to memorize the whole thing. Then, in a test, my mind would go blank. After awhile I learned the ropes. I learned to read for essence as well as for facts.

I was fortunate that I was a good athlete and got a college scholarship for basketball. But blacks now have opportunities to get academic scholarships, too. I didn't finish college because I got a good pro contract. I have no regrets about that. But I was very, very lucky. I had the talent and I used my talent.

But when I talk to kids, I tell them that they might not have the talent to become a pro athlete. But they have other talents. They should make the most of what they have. And school is the best place to develop those talents. School, not the streets.

I tell them that they should go to school and try to be somebody, not just a basketball player.

Jackie Robinson and the Integration of Professional Baseball

When Jackie Robinson signed with the Brooklyn Dodgers in 1946, he broke the "color line" in American professional baseball that had been firmly in place since the 1890s. Although men like Josh Gibson, Satchel Paige, Cool Papa Bell, and Buck Leonard displayed incredible baseball talent playing for all black teams like the Homestead Greys, the Cuban Giants, and the Pittsburgh Crawfords in the Negro Leagues, they were denied access to the white world of professional baseball until Robinson's historic signing.

A controversial figure both on and off the diamond, Robinson, like Joe Louis, became a black folk hero and a symbol of race pride. Robinson was playing for the Kansas City Monarchs of the Negro National League when Branch Rickey, the Dodgers' president, offered him a contract with the team's Montreal farm club. Although most baseball experts agree that he was hardly the best ballplayer in the Negro Leagues, Rickey picked Robinson not only for his baseball talent but because of his background. Jackie had been a star athlete at UCLA and had served in the Army. He was known as a strong individual who stood up for his rights. In Rickey's mind, Robinson's experiences in the white world and his character were crucial to bringing blacks into the major leagues. The ability of Robinson and a whole host of other blacks who soon joined him in the majors— men like Don Newcombe, Larry Doby, and Roy Campenella—to intergrate baseball have been credited by some as setting the style, tone, and tactics of the Civil Rights movement.

The following selections are from Robinson's autobiography, *I Never Had it Made* (1972). The first excerpt recounts his interview with Branch Rickey that set the stage for his signing with the club. The second excerpt served as a foreword for the book and reflects his attitudes about his own experience, the role of the black community in his success, and implicitly, his views about race relations in American society in 1972. What does Robinson have to say about these issues? What do his comments suggest about the situation of American blacks in the 1940s and in the 1970s?

BRANCH RICKEY AND
JACKIE ROBINSON

But Sukeforth (Clyde Sukeforth was a scout for the Dodger organization) looked like a sincere person and I thought I might as well listen. I agreed to meet him that night. When we met, Sukeforth got right to the point. Mr. Rickey wanted to talk to me about the possibility of becoming a Brown Dodger. If I could get a few days off and go to Brooklyn, my fare and expenses would be paid. At first I said that I couldn't leave my team and go to Brooklyn just like that. Sukeforth wouldn't take no for an answer. He pointed out that I couldn't play for a few days anyhow, because of my bum arm. Why should my team object?

I continued to hold out and demanded to know what would happen if the Monarchs fired me. The Dodger scout replied quietly that he didn't believe that would happen.

I shrugged and said I'd make the trip. I figured I had nothing to lose.

Branch Rickey was an impressive-looking man. He had a classic face, an air of command, a deep, booming voice, and a way of cutting through red tape and getting down to basics. He shook my hand vigorously and, after a brief conversation, sprang the first question.

"You got a girl?" he demanded.

It was a hell of a question. I had two reactions: why should he be concerned about my relationship with a girl; and, second, while I thought, hoped, and prayed I had a girl, the way things had been going, I was afraid she might have begun to consider me a hopeless case. I explained this to Mr. Rickey and Clyde.

Mr. Rickey wanted to know all about Rachel. I told him of our hopes and plans.

"You know, you have a girl," he said heartily. "When we get through today you may want to call her up because there are times when a man needs a woman by his side."

My heart began racing a little faster again as I sat there speculating. First he asked me if I really understood why he had sent for me. I told him what Clyde Sukeforth had told me.

"That's what he was supposed to tell you," Mr. Rickey said. "The truth is you are not a candidate for the Brooklyn Brown Dodgers. I've sent for you because I'm interested in you as a candidate for the Brooklyn National League Club. I think you can play in the major leagues. How do you feel about it?"

My reactions seemed like some kind of weird mixture churning in a blender. I was thrilled, scared, and excited. I was incredulous. Most of all, I was speechless.

"You think you can play for Montreal?" he demanded.

I got my tongue back. "Yes," I answered.

Montreal was the Brooklyn Dodgers' top farm club. The players who went there and made it had an excellent chance at the big time.

I was busy reorganizing my thoughts while Mr. Rickey and Clyde Sukeforth discussed me briefly, almost as if I weren't there. Mr. Rickey was questioning Clyde. Could I make the grade?

Abruptly, Mr. Rickey swung his swivel chair in my direction. He was a man who conducted himself with great drama. He pointed a finger at me.

"I know you're a good ballplayer," he barked. "What I don't know is whether you have the guts."

I knew it was all too good to be true. Here was a guy questioning my courage. That virtually amounted to him asking me if I was a coward. Mr. Rickey or no Mr. Rickey, that was an insinuation hard to take. I felt the heat coming into my cheeks.

Before I could react to what he had said, he leaned forward in his chair and explained.

I wasn't just another athlete being hired by a ball club. We were playing for big stakes. This was the reason Branch Rickey's search had been so exhaustive. The search had spanned the globe and narrowed down to a few candidates, then finally to me. When it looked as though I might be the number-one choice, the investigation of my life, my habits, my reputation, and my character had become an intensified study.

"I've investigated you thoroughly, Robinson," Mr. Rickey said.

One of the results of this thorough screening were reports from California athletic circles that I had been a "racial agitator" at UCLA. Mr. Rickey had not accepted these criticism on face value. He had demanded and received more information and came to the conclusion that, if I had been white, people would have said, "Here's a guy who's a contender, a competitor."

After that he had some grim words of warning. "We can't fight our way through this, Robinson. We've got no army. There's virtually nobody on our side. No owners, no umpires, very few newspapermen. And I'm afraid that many fans will be hostile. We'll be in a tough position. We can win only if we can convince the world that I'm doing this because you're a great ballplayer and a fine gentleman."

He had me transfixed as he spoke. I could feel his sincerity, and I began to get a sense of how much this major step meant to him. Because of his nature and his passion for justice, he had to do what he was doing. He continued. The rumbling voice, the theatrical gestures, were gone. He was speaking from a deep quiet strength.

"So there's more than just playing," he said. "I wish it meant only hits, runs, and errors—only the things they put in the box score. Because you know—yes, you would know, Robinson, that a baseball box score is a democratic thing. It doesn't tell how big you are, what church you attend, what color you are, or how your father voted in the last election. It just tells what kind of baseball player you were on that particular day."

I interrupted. "But it's the box score that really counts—that and that alone, isn't it?"

"It's all that ought to count," he replied. "But it isn't. Maybe one of these days it will be all that counts. That is one of the reasons I've got you here, Robinson. If you're a good enough man, we can make this a start in the right direction. But let me tell you, it's going to take an awful lot of courage."

He was back to the crossroads question that made me start to get angry minutes earlier. He asked it slowly and with great care.

"Have you got the guts to play the game no matter what happens?"

"I think I can play the game, Mr. Rickey," I said.

The next few minutes were tough. Branch Rickey had to make absolutely sure that I knew what I would face. Beanballs would be thrown at me. I would be called the kind of names which would hurt and infuriate any man. I would be physically attacked. Could I take all of this and control my temper, remain steadfastly loyal to our ultimate aim?

He knew I would have terrible problems and wanted me to know the extent of them before I agreed to the plan. I was twenty-six years old, and all my life back to the age of eight when a little neighbor girl called me a nigger—I had believed in payback, retaliation. The most luxurious possession, the richest treasure anybody has, is his personal dignity. I looked at Mr. Rickey guardedly, and in that second I was looking at him not as a partner in a great experiment, but as the enemy—a white man. I had a question and it was the age-old one about whether or not you sell your birthright.

"Mr. Rickey," I asked, "are you looking for a Negro who is afraid to fight back?"

I never will forget the way he exploded.

Robinson," he said, "I'm looking for a ballplayer with guts enough not to fight back."

After that, Mr. Rickey continued his lecture on the kind of thing I'd be facing.

He not only told me about it, but he acted out the part of a white player charging into me, blaming me for the "accident" and calling me all kinds of foul racial names. He talked about my race, my parents, in language that was almost unendurable.

"They'll taunt and goad you," Mr. Rickey said. "They'll do anything to make you react. They'll try to provoke a race riot in the ball park. This is the way to prove to the public that a Negro should not be allowed in the major league. This is the way to frighten the fans and make them afraid to attend the games."

If hundreds of black people wanted to come to the ball park to watch me play and Mr. Rickey tried to discourage them, would I understand that he was doing it because the emotional enthusiasm of my people could harm the experiment? That kind of enthusiasm would be as bad as the emotional opposition of prejudiced white fans.

Suppose I was at shortstop. Another player comes down from first, stealing, flying in with spikes high, and cuts me on the leg. As I feel the blood running down my leg, the white player laughs in my face.

"How do you like that, nigger boy?" he sneers.

Could I turn the other cheek? I didn't know how I would do it. Yet I knew that I must. I had to do it for so many reasons. For black youth, for my mother, for Rae, for myself. I had already begun to feel I had to do it for Branch Rickey.

"I NEVER HAD IT MADE."

I guess if I could choose one of the most important moments in my life, I would go back to 1947, in the Yankee Stadium in New York City. It was the opening day of the world series and I was for the first time playing in the series as a member of the Brooklyn Dodgers team. It was a history-making day. It would be the first time that a black man would be allowed to participate in a world series. I had become the first black player in the major leagues.

I was proud of that and yet I was uneasy. I was proud to be in the hurricane eye of a significant breakthrough and to be used to prove that a sport can't be called national if blacks are barred from it. Branch Rickey, the president of the Brooklyn Dodgers, had rudely awakened America. He was a man with high ideals, and he was also a shrewd businessman. Mr. Rickey had shocked some of his fellow baseball tycoons and angered others by deciding to smash the unwritten law that kept blacks out of the big leagues. He had chosen me as the person to lead the way.

It hadn't been easy. Some of my own teammates refused to accept me because I was black. I had been forced to live with snubs and rebuffs and rejections. Within the club, Mr. Rickey had put down rebellion by letting my teammates know that anyone who didn't want to accept me could leave. But the problems within the Dodgers club had been minor compared to the opposition outside. It hadn't been that easy to fight the resentment expressed by players on other teams, by the team owners, or by bigoted fans screaming "nigger." The hate mail piled up. There were threats against me and my family and even out-and-out attempts at physical harm to me.

Some things counterbalanced this ugliness. Black people supported me with total loyalty. They supported me morally; they came to sit in a hostile audience in unprecedented numbers to make the turnstiles hum as they never had before at ball parks all over the nation. Money is America's God and business people can dig black power if it coincides with green power, so these fans were important to the success of Mr. Rickey's "Noble Experiment."

Some of the Dodgers who swore they would never play with a black man had a change of mind, when they realized I was a good ballplayer who could be helpful in their earning a few thousand more dollars in world series money. After the initial resistance to me had been crushed, my teammates started to give me tips on how to improve my game. They hadn't changed because they liked me any better; they had changed because I could help fill their wallets.

My fellow Dodgers were not decent out of self-interest alone. There were heart-warming experiences with some teammates; there was South-ern-born Pee Wee Reese who turned into a staunch friend. And there were others.

Mr. Rickey stands out as the man who inspired me the most. He will always have my admiration and respect. Critics had said, "Don't you know that your precious Mr. Rickey didn't bring you up out of the black leagues because he loved you? Are you stupid enough not to understand that the Brooklyn club profited hugely because of what your Mr. Rickey did?"

Yes, I know that. But I also know what a big gamble he took. A bond developed between us that lasted long after I had left the game. In a way I feel I was the son he had lost and he was the father I had lost.

There was more than just making money at stake in Mr. Rickey's decision. I learned that his family was afraid that his health was being underminded by the resulting pressures and that they pleaded with him to abandon the plan. His peers and fellow baseball moguls exerted all kinds of influence to get him to change his mind. Some of the press condemned him as a fool and a demagogue. But he didn't give in.

In a very real sense, black people helped make the experiment suc-ceed. Many who came to the ball park had not been baseball fans before I began to play in the big leagues. Suppressed and repressed for so many years, they needed a victorious black man as a symbol. It would help them believe in themselves. But black support of the first black man in the majors was a complicated matter. The breakthrough created as much danger as it did hope. It was one thing for me out there on the playing field to be able to keep my cool in the face of insults. But it was another for all those black people sitting in the stands to keep from overreacting when they sensed a racial slur or an unjust decision. They could have blown the whole bit to hell by acting belligerently and touching off a race riot. That would have been all the bigots needed to set back the cause of progress of black men in sports another hundred years. I knew this. Mr. Rickey knew this. But this never happened. I learned from Rachel who had spent hours in the stands that clergymen and laymen had held meetings in the black community to spread the word. We all knew about the help of the black press. Mr. Rickey and I owed them a great deal.

Children from all races came to the stands. The very young seemed to have no hang-up at all about my being black. They just wanted me to be good, to deliver, to win. The inspiration of their innocence is amazing. I don't think I'll ever forget the small, shrill voice of a tiny white kid who, in the midst of a racially tense atmosphere during an early game in a Dixie town, cried out, "Attaboy, Jackie." It broke the tension and it made me feel I had to succeed.

The black and the young were my cheering squads. But also there were people—neither black nor young—people of all races and faiths and in all parts of this country, people who couldn't care less about my race.

Rachel was even more important to my success. I know that every successful man is supposed to say that without his wife he could never have accomplished success. It is gospel in my case. Rachel shared those difficult years that led to this moment and helped me through all the days thereafter. She has been strong, loving, gentle, and brave, never afraid to either criticize or comfort me.

There I was the black grandson of a slave, the son of a black sharecropper, part of a historic occasion, a symbolic hero to my people. The air was sparkling. The sunlight was warm. The band struck up the national anthem. The flag billowed in the wind. It should have been a glorious moment for me as the stirring words of the national anthem poured from the stands. Perhaps it was, but then again perhaps the anthem could be called the theme song for a drama called THE NOBLE EXPERIMENT. Today as I look back on that opening game of my first world series, I must tell you that it was Mr. Rickey's drama and that I was only a principal actor. As I write this twenty years later, I cannot stand and sing the anthem. I cannot salute the flag; I know that I am a black man in a white world. In 1972, at my birth in 1919, I know that I never had it made.

Sport and Black Protest

On July 18, 1949, Jackie Robinson, the National League's Rookie of the Year in 1947 and the Brooklyn Dodger second baseman in the midst of a season that would make him the league's most valuable player, testified before the United

States House of Representatives UnAmerican Activities Committee to rebut public statements by Paul Robeson. Robeson, an articulate black activist, was born in New Jersey in 1898, two years after the historic Supreme Court decision known as Plessy vs. Ferguson had legalized segregation in the United States. The son of a minister, he attended Rutgers University and became that school's first all-American football player while amassing twelve varsity letters in four sports. Called by Walter Camp in 1918 as the "greatest defensive end ever," Robeson graduated from Columbia University's law school and became a prominent singer and Shakespearean actor. Through it all, he remained an outspoken black activist who traveled widely throughout the world and who increasingly came to believe that American blacks had been systematically denied opportunity and freedom by a racist America. In the midst of a Cold War hysteria that swept across the United States in the late 1940s and 1950s Robeson questioned why American blacks should rally behind the flag for a country that had oppressed them for generations. White political leaders, anxious to discredit Robeson and to offer an alternative view for American blacks to consider chose Robinson to do it, and for the most part, he complied. In later years, Robinson himself recognized publically that Robeson, who was accused of Communist sympathies and harassed out of the United States, had only been trying to help his own kind in their quest for freedom and equality.

Some twenty years later, Harry Edwards, a former shotputter, a black sociology professor at the University of California, and an outspoken critic of American sport and society, attempted to organize a boycott of American black athletes at the 1968 Olympics as part of an overall effort to protest black inequality in the United States. For him, the cause that Robeson espoused was still vital.

Despite the support of a number of black civil rights leaders, most American black athletes did not join the boycott. Karem Abdul Jabbar, then playing under his given name of Lew Alcindor at UCLA, chose to stay home. Tommie Smith and John Carlos, gold and bronze medalists in the 200 meter race focused attention on Edwards' concern when they offered the clench fist salute of the Black Power movement on the victory stand while the Star Spangled Banner played in the background. Both were immediately suspended from the American team by the United States Olympic Committee and ordered to leave Mexico City.

In the following selection from *The Black Scholar*, written ten years after the boycott effort, Harry Edwards evaluates the Olympic Project for Human Rights that he initiated while also offering an analysis of racism and oppression that he sees as endemic in American society. What was the purpose of the O.P.H.R.? How successful was it? What evidence does Edwards offer for his argument that sport in America masks the real problems faced by blacks in achieving true equality? How would Edwards respond to Walt Frazier's views about the black athlete as role model? Can you think of evidence since 1978 that could be offered to either rebut or support Edwards' position?

THE OLYMPIC PROJECT FOR HUMAN RIGHTS: AN ASSESSMENT TEN YEARS LATER

The "Olympic Project for Human Rights" was launched in November of 1987 to advocate a black boycott of the 1968 Mexico City Olympic Games. Its major aims were: (1) to stage an international protest of the persistent and systematic violation of black people's human rights in the United States; (2) to expose America's historical exploitation of black athletes as political propaganda tools in both the national and international arenas; (3) to establish a standard of political responsibility among black athletes vis-a-vis the needs and interests of the *black* community, and to devise effective and acceptable ways by which athletes could accommodate the demands of such responsibilities; and (4) to make the black community aware of the substantial "hidden" dynamics and consequences of their sports involvement.

Suffice it to say that the obstacles threatening achievement of these goals were immense. But of all the problems confronted, by far the most difficult was black America's highly illusionary perspective on sports. Black people had been brainwashed so long and so completely about sport's supposed uniquely beneficent role in their lives that the very idea of either using sport as a protest vehicle or protesting the character and circumstances of Afro-American involvement in sport—particularly in connection with their Olympic Games participation—seemed to most as quite mystifying, to some ludicrous, and to yet others criminal, or worse, treasonous. That sport could ever amount to a political and cultural malignancy whose growth and influence had tragically contributed to choking and stifling personal and institutional development in black society was literally *unthinkable*.

Nonetheless, the benefits of the O.P.H.R. were not long in coming, even to some of the project's most vocal critics—and in many cases *especially* to its critics. It was due largely to the athletic revolts that the O.P.H.R. set in motion that such organizations as the United States Olympic Committee began to appoint black head coaches to United States Olympic Teams and to name blacks to the Committee itself. In permanently closing the prestigious and racist New York Athletic Club Indoor Track Classic at Madison Square Garden in 1967, the O.P.H.R. put all such organizations on notice that a new day had dawned. If they wanted black athletic talent on the field, there must be black input at the front office and a black presence in the coaching ranks. Blacks must be accorded the dignity and respect accorded all others involved in the sports of this country.

Further, the O.P.H.R. and its student-athlete revolts contributed greatly to the struggle for black faculty, coaches and athletic administrators on predominantly white campuses. Starting in 1967 with the forced cancellation of a football game at San Jose State University in protest of racism in its sports program and the lack of minority student and faculty recruitment generally, O.P.H.R. established a model by which black athletes, black students and the larger black community could effectively collaborate for the achievement of mutually advantageous ends. There are black coaches and faculty today who will deny this and say they were hired because they were "qualified." We agree. Most of them are as qualified as their white counterparts. Some are more qualified. But that is not the reason they received positions at predominantly white campuses.

Of course, the climax of the O.P.H.R. was Tommie Smith and John Carlos' brilliant and courageous protest at the victory podium of the 1968 Mexico City Olympic Games. With this stunningly dramatic and inspiring gesture, the illusion of sport's inherently insular and apolitical character was shattered for all time. The first and the most difficult link in the chain shackling black people's minds relative to sport has been irreparably smashed. "The very reaction of the sports establishment, the United States police intelligence community and conservative elements in American society as a whole demonstrated beyond any doubt that sport was far removed from the "toy department" of human affairs. Not only was sport revealed to be *serious business* (in both a figurative and a literal sense) but also an important component in this nations's domestic social control machinery and its international political propaganda program.

Dramatic revelation, however, is one thing; delineating through systematic investigation, the precise dynamics of sport's relationship to society—and to the black community in particular—is quite another. And if the sacrifices made and the insights gained were to be of any lasting consequence, the latter had to be accomplished. The whole phenomenon of sport's relationship to society had to be removed from the fiery, but shallow and ephemeral rhetoric of activist politics and incorporated within a body of theoretical concepts and empirical frameworks that would allow for systematic investigation and the accumulation of accurate and dependable knowledge.

As the principal architect of the O.P.H.R. and as one with substantial training in sociology, I felt a fundamental responsibility to undertake the task, even though my basic scholarly interest since completing my Master's degree in 1966 had been "The Black Family" and even though there was no established sociological field focusing upon sport I returned to Cornell University in 1968 and was fortunate enough to have on the faculty there people who allowed advanced graduate students the broadest possible latitude in sociological investigation. The end product of my two years of research was a book entitled *The Sociology of Sport* which is regarded by many as the first systematic sociological analysis of the relationship between sport and society. Thus, the O.P.H.R. spurred creation and development of an entirely new sub-discipline in sociology—the "sociology of sport."

And what have research efforts uncovered since 1968 relative to the dynamics and consequences of black sports involvement? In sum, even given broad areas of conflicting and inconclusive evidence, sport for blacks must be viewed as an institutional minefield, traditionally shrouded in naivete and ignorance, and even further obscured by decades of calculated, selectively accumulated myth. For from the much fabled "escalator" out of the degradations of the "ghetto," sport is revealed to be a "treadmill" for all but the few—and more often than not, even for the "successful" black athlete, life in sport comes to approximate a racist nightmare more so than the "dream come true" it is purported to be. A brief profile on the circumstances of blacks in sport will demonstrate this point.

Item: Despite the tremendous visibility of the black collegiate athlete, less than five percent (5%) of the athletic scholarships awarded in this country go to blacks. In order to receive one of these, the black athlete (more so than his white counterpart) must be demonstrably "blue chip" (all-state, all-American, state or national champion, or perceived to be of superior athletic potential).

Not only do more than ninety-five percent of all collegiate scholarships go to white athletes, but a disproportionately high number of blacks are given athletic scholarships out of junior college rather than high school. This means that the athletic departments adopting this tact are getting a superior athlete *cheaper*—for the price of a two-year rather than a four-year scholarship. In short, they can get two proven black athletes for the price of one athletic scholarship. This situation, of course, contributes to the disproportionately high number of blacks who achieve "star" status. The traffic in black athletes between two-year and four-year colleges is appropriately called the "slave trade."

Item: On the average, fifty-five to sixty-five percent of all black athletes on scholarship major in physical education. On some campuses it runs as high as seventy-five percent. Only twenty-five to thirty percent of white scholarship athletes major in P.E.

It is also quite typically the case that most black athletes never graduate from college. Thus, at the University of Illinois, a 1975 research study reports sixty-five percent (65%) of the black athletes failed to graduate *although* sixty-six percent (66%) of them were majoring in P.E. In other words, they remained eligible from two to four years, but they left college without a degree and completely unscathed by education. Blacks, then, under these circumstances merely become Twentieth Century Gladiators in the service of white institutions.

In the Southwest Conference, a 1976 study indicates that over seventy-five percent (75%) of the white scholarship athletes graduated in four years. On the other hand, sixty-seven percent (67%) of black scholarship athletes *failed* to graduate. Over fifty percent (50%) of the blacks on scholarship in that conference were P.E. majors. Only twenty-five percent (25%) of the white athletes majored in P.E. White coaches have traditionally tracked black athletes into P.E. in order to protect the school's scholarship investment under the assumption that the black athlete was incapable of academic success outside of P.E. where he can be *given* grades. Of course, the classic case highlighting the institutionalized rip-off of black athletes is that of the 1965 University of Texas at El Paso NCAA Champion basketball team. Not one of the five black starters for UTEP graduated. All five of the defeated University of Kentucky white players graduated on time and two with honors.

Item: Between 1954 and 1971 more than 2000 black coaches lost their jobs due to the integration of jobs at heretofore all black schools. With the decline in the protest movements of the 1960s, few predominantly white schools are actually seeking black coaches today and few of the black coaches who leave predominantly white institutions will be replaced with other black coaching prospects.

Further, inflation, the increasing cost of college for all students, the rising cost of athletic programs and National Collegiate Athletic Association restrictions on the number of athletic scholarships that can be awarded each year are factors which place a premium on athletic scholarship awards. In the future we can expect fewer, but more athletically talented black athletes to receive athletic scholarships to major universities. As a result, there will be less need for black coaches at predominantly white schools since they were hired at the outset principally as "race men"— "Head niggers in charge of nigger affairs" whose first responsibilities were to sit by the door, be visible and to "cool out" any discontent among black athletes. Under the circumstances, the proportion of black athletes majoring in P.E. would be unjustifiable—even if most graduated.

Item: In all of professional sports, there are just over 1500 blacks. If a black athlete is to make it in professional sport, his best chances lie in basketball, football or baseball. In these three sports combined, there are less than 900 professional black athletes. If to this 900 were added all blacks participating in all other professional sports, all the black managers, black coaches, trainers and doctors active in professional sports, plus all black minor league baseball players and semi-professional football players, *there would be just over 1500 all total.*

Typically, most blacks are blinded to this fact by the dazzling performances of Afro-American super-stars and by blacks' disporportionately high representation and visibility in four of five major sports—boxing, baseball, basketball, football and track. And lest we forget, it should be remembered that despite blacks' proven athletic abilities, most American sports—eighty to ninety percent of them—remain for the most part *lily-white*.

Item: Just as the black collegiate has to be superior to his white counterpart to achieve the same rewards, *the black professional must likewise be better and sign cheaper*. Studies indicate that the cumulative average performance for black professional athletes is substantially superior to that for whites in every major sport, but that blacks will make substantially less money than whites of comparable abilities.

Further, there are disproportionately few front office jobs waiting after retirement for black athletes. Likewise with lucrative product endorsement opportunities during their active careers.

Item: Racism severely restricts opportunity even within the four sports offering blacks professional advancements. What is more, the positions typically filled by blacks are those having the highest injury rates in many instances. Thus in football, wide receiver, running back, and defensive back are "black," positions whose incumbents have an average playing career of three and a half years. The average career in the league is four and a half years long and incumbents to positions such as center and quarterback—"white" positions—might last a career average of seven to nine years.

Item: Proportionately fewer blacks than whites qualify for post-career pension benefits. Blacks are simply released from athletic squads more readily than whites and they are frequently injured more severely and in disproportionately high numbers because of the nature of their position responsibilities.

Item: And, rather akin to the final insult, blacks are less likely than whites of comparable ability to be named to a sport's "Hall of Fame," and if blacks are so named, on the average it takes longer to be enshrined. This classic case of racism in this regard, of course, occurred when major league baseball established a "special" section in its "Hall of Fame" for players from the All Negro League. Whites who played on segregated teams are enshrined along with modern era baseball stars—even though Negro league all-stars defeated white all-stars in 60% of the games they played.

But the circumstances of the black athlete are far from an individual tragedy. Because of sport's disproportionately high visibility in black society, literally millions of black youth are influenced to imbibe career aspirations in sport, aspirations which for the overwhelming majority are futile and foredoomed to frustration and failure.

Compounding the problem is the fact that serious involvement in sport frequently results in the neglect of other vitally important areas of development—particularly so for those who are ill-prepared for the challenges of educational and alternative occupational achievement from the outset. And because so many who achieve some advancement through sport major disproportionately in P.E. and fail to graduate even in that, black society loses the potential contributions of *successful and failing* athletes alike.

And so the disproportionate influence of sport in black society not only misleads a substantial majority of aspirant black youth on to a "treadmill" going nowhere, but it results in increased numbers of non-contributors, under-contributors and, not infrequently, mal-contributors in the black community.

The white media's propagation of the myth of race-based black athletic superiority is a key link in the chain placed around black people's minds relative to sport. It plants firmly in the heads of millions of black youth that they are by racial heritage *natural athletes*. In combination with the myth of sport's "unique beneficent" role relative to black people, a very subtle trap is laid which ultimately contributes towards retarding both personal and institutional development in black society. For in their concentration on sport, substantial numbers of black people are put at an extreme disadvantage in competing with whites for skills attainment and occupational positions outside of sport but nonetheless vital to the future of black people and black institutional development (e.g. law, science, economics, education, medicine, technology, etc.). But, then, if the notion of race-linked black physical superiority is accepted, race-linked white intellectual superiority becomes at least plausible *in a world where intellect-generated technology has reduced physical superiority to irrelevance beyond the sports realm.* So when white coaches, sports commentators, and sports-writers such as Martin Kane (senior editor at *Sports Illustrated Magazine*) state the blacks are by racial heritage physically superior to whites, what they are implying is that today the only legitimate role remaining for blacks in a highly industrialized, modern, technologically sophisticated society is that of a *Twentieth Century Gladiator. And, thus, this society is justified in denying black people all human rights in every other realm of life.*

Why encourage us to strive for achievement outside of sport if we are, *by race*, not equipped to either compete successfully or contribute?

As Martin Kane states in his 1971 *Sports Illustrated* article (a view reiterated by scores of writers since):

> Every Black male child, however he might be discouraged from a career with a Wall Street brokerage firm or other occupational choices, knows he has a sporting chance in baseball, basketball, football, boxing or track. The Black youngster has something real to aspire to when he picks up a bat or dribbles a ball . . .

And, apparently, even in sport our involvement must be strictly controlled since we participate for the most part in only *five* American sports, and even in these there is extensive positional segregation by race. But, like gorilla, we are regarded as physically superior to whites—the corollary presumption being the traditional racist American stereotype that we are little advanced beyond the apes in our cultural and intellectual evolution.

Further, black women, more than half the black people in the United States, are ignored completely insofar as they enjoy high prestige occupational opportunities neither *inside* nor *outside* of sport.

We must understand that a racist, oppressive society can only have a racist, oppressive sport institution regardless of any appearances to the contrary. Just as the "Jim Crow" laws and traditions that existed prior to 1954 have been replaced today by more intricate, subtle but no less effective social and political mechanisms for accomplishing the same ends as Jim Crow—"keeping the niggers in their place"—in sport too, the segregation of the pre-modern era has been replaced by infinitely more subtle and effective methods that are part of modern America's machinery for systematically denying black people their human rights.

Not only must Afro-Americans perpetually analyze the shifting character of these methods but we must constantly work at devising effective means of combating them. And, we must start right now by adjusting our own priorities. For through the very "success" of black involvement in sports—as shallow as it is—we have contributed to the perpetuation of widespread retardation in personal and institutional development in our own society. We must understand that undeniable black superiority in a few sports results from white manipulation of what is at best a tragically brutal selection process in sport, and the fact that disproportionately high numbers of blacks are channeled into sport by racist discrimination limiting black role models and opportunities in vital alternative high prestige occupations outside of sport. When black people themselves place an unrealistically high value on sports careers to the virtual neglect of all other spheres of development, we expose our political backwardness and contribute to our own oppression.

If we are to realize the goals of our human rights struggle in this society, not only must we *de-emphasize* the priority placed upon athletic achievement in black society, but we must re-double our efforts to reopen and expand opportunities for blacks beyond the sports realm—particularly in the wake of Bakke-type judicial decisions, increasing white assaults on affirmative action, and the general collapse of the "Second Reconstruction" that was forged over the 1950s and 1960s.

Sport reflects the structure of human relations and the ideological value emphasis of American society as a whole. Thus the fortunes and futures of blacks in sport and those of the black masses are not only intricately intertwined but *inter-dependent*. And there is no escape from this reality via sport or any other route. In recognition of the implications and consequences of this fact, it becomes imperative that all concerned *under-*

stand that *sport for Afro-Americans is no game—and to act accordingly*—for as Stevie Wonder states in his song "Superstition":
   "When you believe in things you don't *understand—you suffer!"*

THE POLITICS OF SPORT

The 1968 Olympic boycott was not the first time that this major international event became a focus of political protest nor was it last. Moreover, demonstrations either in celebration of or in protest against particular political regimes or policies at sporting events have not been the only ways that sport in the twentieth century, both in the United States and elsewhere, manifests its connection to larger questions of politics and ideology. Although sport is hardly the most significant arena in which differences over policy or ideology are displayed or resolved, the commercialization of sport and its increasing visibility due to the revolution in communications technology in the last seventy-five years, makes it an especially attractive and accessible avenue for such activity. The selections in this section about the Olympic games and the observations of a prominent sports journalist on the connection between sport and American values in contemporary America suggest how integral a part of our politics and our lives sport has become.

The Nazi Olympics

The 1936 Olympic Games held in Berlin, Germany, marked a watershed in the political use of sport. Anxious to display to the world the rise of Germany from the ashes of World War I and the new German character that he hoped would soon dominate the world, Adolph Hitler expended over $30 million to build facilities, train German athletes, and display his Third Reich to what he hoped would be an admiring and eventually subservient world. The elaborate Olympic stadiums, the festivities and pageantry, medal counts by countries, worldwide media attention, and even the torch run that we accept today as part and parcel of this quadrennial event were all innovations of these games.

Hitler clearly intended the Olympics as a means of demonstrating Aryan superiority and of celebrating the political system that produced it. Most Americans, however, remember the Nazi Olympics because of the exploits of one black American runner, Jesse Owens, who won an unprecedented four gold medals. For many, Owens' achievements offer demonstrable proof that American democracy, even if displayed by a man whose color in the United States of his time denied him and his race equal opportunity, was superior to German fascism.

Some Americans at the time, however, questioned whether American athletes should participate at all in competition organized by a fascist country with professed racist policies that included open hatred and overt discrimination of Jews and other "non-Aryan" people. Between 1933 and 1936, despite the assurances of Charles Sherill, an American member of the International Olympic Committee, that the German government would allow German Jews to participate in German Olympic tryouts, and Avery Brundage, the president of the American Olympic Committee who had traveled to Germany to investigate conditions, a number of prominent Jewish and Catholic officials, newspaper columnists, congresspeople and other politicians rightly questioned Nazi intentions. Together they organized what turned out to be an unsuccessful effort to convince the American athletic establishment and American athletes to boycott the 1936 Olympics.

The following selection comes from *Preserve the Olympic Ideal: A Statement of the Case Against American Participation in the Olympic Games at Berlin*, a pamphlet published in 1936 in support of the boycott movement. In what specific ways is Germany accused of using the Olympics for political purposes? Can you think of comparable examples practiced by the United States or the Soviet Union in recent Olympic competition? According to the pamphlet, how is sport and Nazi ideology tied together? Are there any parallel connections in the development of organized sport in the United States?

IN SUPPORT OF THE BOYCOTT MOVEMENT

The question whether America should participate in the Eleventh Olympiad, if it is held in Nazi Germany, is now being debated throughout the length and breadth of the country. In the last analysis this question will have to be and will be decided by American athletes themselves. If we know them correctly, they will not permit it to be decided for them either by the International Olympic Committee or by the American Olympic Committee which, in order to obtain the high prerogative of making up the American athlete's mind for him, represent him as the forgotten man, themselves as his only friend, and everyone else as his betrayer.

In all the history of American sport American athletes have never had to decide a more momentous question. It is not too much to say that upon their decision rest the future and the integrity of amateur athletics throughout the world. For as America goes on this question the world will go, the American Olympic Committee to the contrary, notwithstanding. In view of the importance of the question, it is highly desirable that it should be debated thoroughly and dispassionately and that all the relevant facts should be made known. Only in this way will it be possible to answer the question wisely and in the best interests of athletics and athletes. The American Olympic Committee has issued a pamphlet presenting the case for American participation. The purpose of this booklet is to present the case against American participation. . . .

The issue is not whether America should take part in the Eleventh Olympiad, but whether America should participate in it if it is held in Germany; and these are two entirely different questions.

In 1932 the International Olympic Committee awarded the Games to Berlin which was then in Republican Germany. Republican Germany no longer exists; and if the Games are held in Germany, they will be held in a Berlin and a Germany which are Nazi. In sports, as in almost every other way, Nazi Germany is a very different country from Republican Germany.

Sports in Republican Germany were democratically organized and privately conducted, just as they are in America. Sports in Hitler's Germany, including all activities in connection with the Olympics, are dominated and controlled by the Nazi Government and the Nazi Party and have entirely lost their private, their democratic and their independent character.

The issue is rather whether Nazi policies and activities in the realm of sports and in connection with the Olympic Games themselves are of such a character as to make it impossible for the Games to be held in Nazi Germany in the true spirit of sportsmanship and of the Olympics. If that is the case, American athletes ought to refuse to participate in the Games in Nazi Germany and the International Olympic Committee ought to remove the Games from Nazi Germany.

In the pages that follow we shall show that that is the case; that Nazi Germany has violated her pledge not to exclude German Jews from the German team solely because they are Jews, by denying them the opportunity to train and compete for the German team; and has violated her pledge to observe the Olympic Code not only by her treatment of her Jewish athletes, but by her treatment of her Catholic and Protestant athletes and by her misuse of the Games to serve the interests of the Nazi régime rather than the interests of sport.

If the International Olympic Committee should now consider the matter of removing the Games from Germany, it would not be for the first time. The Committee found it necessary to consider that question on June 6, 1933, when it met in Vienna after the Nazi régime had been in existence for only three months. In order to understand why the International Olympic Committee then found it necessary to consider the matter, it is necessary to recall some of the events which had occurred in Germany in that brief period, events which were utterly inconsistent with the tradition and ideals of the Olympics.

Long prior to their accession to full power on March 5, 1933, the Nazi party had formulated a program which called for the complete elimination of German Jews from all aspects of German life and, eventually, for their complete extermination; and this program they began to execute with relentless ferocity as soon as they came into power.

Jews were subjected to brutal physical violence and many of them were killed or maimed, not in fair combat but in cowardly attack. On March 28, 1933, a national boycott of Jews in business and the professions was proclaimed and on April 1 was put into effect, although, because of the protests of a world horrified by Nazi brutality, for only one day. On April 7 of that year the Nazi Government promulgated the first of a series of laws and decrees which are directed against all non-Aryans, meaning Jews and Christians descended from a Jewish parent or grandparent, and which culminated in the law enacted at Nuremberg on September 15, 1935, by which Germans of Jewish blood were deprived of their German citizenship. This series of laws and decrees is designed ultimately to make it impossible for Jews or for those Christians who have as much as one-fourth part of Jewish blood to exist in Germany. These laws therefore affect more than 2,000,000 people.

Almost immediately upon the institution of the Nazi régime, steps were also taken to exclude non-Aryans from sports as well as from other phases of German life, merely because of their race. Thus, on April 1, 1933, the German Boxing Federation forbade Jewish boxers or referees to take part or officiate in German championship contests, and as early as April 26, 1933, Jews were barred from membership in German sports associations. On June 2, 1933, the German Minister of Education issued instructions that Jews were to be excluded from youth, welfare and gymnastic organizations and that the facilities of these organizations were to be closed to them. Moreover, Dr. Theodore Lewald, a Christian, who was then the President of the German Olympic Committee, was threatened with removal from his office because one of his grandparents was a Jew.

International Olympic Committee Acts

Disturbed by these and similar events, the International Olympic Committee on June 6, 1933, threatened to remove the Games from Germany unless the German representatives on the Committee guaranteed that Dr. Lewald would be permitted to retain his office and that Germany would not discriminate against her Jewish citizens in the realm of sports. The demand for these guaranties was made largely at the instigation of General Charles H. Sherrill, Colonel William May Garland and Commodore Ernest Lee Jahncke, the American representatives on the Committee.

Whatever his present opinions may be, General Sherrill was not then of the opinion that Germany could comply with the Olympic code at the eleventh hour by the gesture of inviting one or two Jews to compete for or to become members of her team, or that obstacles to train and compete placed in the way of German athletes of Jewish blood were none of his business, or that it was enough to justify and excuse German violation of the Olympic code that some American clubs do not admit Jews to membership and that Negroes do not engage in sports with white persons in our southern states.

Evidently, General Sherrill's opinions have, in the meantime, undergone radical alteration.

At this point athletes should ask themselves these questions, which the American Olympic Committee do not attempt to answer:

If it was not meddling in Germany's domestic affairs for the International Olympic Committee to demand these pledges, why is it meddling in those affairs for America to withdraw from the Games because these very same pledges have been broken?

If it was not telling Germany how her team should be chosen for the International Olympic Committee to demand these pledges, why is it telling Germany how to manage her own affairs for America to withdraw from the Games because these very same pledges have been broken?

The Spirit of Sports in Nazi Germany

In order to understand how Nazi Germany has gone about excluding Jewish athletes from the German team, solely because they are Jews, it is necessary to understand the spirit in which sports are conducted and the manner in which they are organized in Nazi Germany. It is also necessary to realize that sports like all activities of the German people are required to conform to Nazi ideology, an ideology which regards chivalry and sportsmanship and fair play as the vices of the weak rather than as the virtues of the strong, and which rejects Christianity for paganism and repudiates the principle of equality, upon which both political democracy and the democracy of sport are based, for the dogma of the superiority of the Aryans to all other peoples.

Some indication of the spirit in which sports are conducted in Nazi Germany can be gotten from a book, entitled "The Spirit of Sports in the National Socialistic Ideology," which Bruno Malitz, Sports Leader of the Berlin Storm Troops, published in 1934. That Herr Malitz is an authoritative interpreter of the Nazi sporting spirit is indicated by the fact that the Nazi Party sent a copy of his book to every sports club in Germany and that the German Minister of Enlightenment and Propaganda placed it on the list of books which all Nazis should read. This is the Nazi conception of the spirit of sport as interpreted by this great Nazi sportsman:

"Frenchmen, Polaks and 'Jew Niggers' have competed on German tracks, have played on German football fields, have swum in German swimming pools. Whether the international relations of our beloved Germany with our enemies have thereby improved, no one can say, aside, naturally, from these traitors to the German cause who spread pacifism and atrocity propaganda in Paris, Geneva and Prague. We National Socialists can see no positive value for our people in permitting 'Niggers' to travel through our country and compete in athletics with our best." . . .

As we have seen, the German Olympic Committee not only pledged itself specifically not to exclude Jewish athletes from the German team solely because they are Jews, but also pledged itself generally to observe all laws regulating the Olympic Games. The violation of the first of these pledges necessarily constitutes a violation of the second, but the failure of the Germans to observe the Olympic Code has gone far beyond their discrimination against Jewish athletes.

Even the American Olympic Committee admit, and quite correctly, that the Olympic Code requires that race, religion and creed be kept out of the Olympics; and it is precisely this requirement which, in addition to the requirement of fair play, Germany has violated in her treatment not only of Jewish athletes but also Catholic and Protestant athletes.

Germany Has Introduced Race into the Olympics

It must be clearly understood that German discrimination against her Jewish athletes is not an expression of the kind of prejudice against the Jew which unfortunately exists in this and other countries and which manifests itself principally in private social relations. It is, on the contrary, the expression of a fundamental principle of Nazi ideology, of German political theory and of German law. This principle is the dogma of racial inequality, of the superiority of the Aryans not only to the Jews but to all peoples whom the Germans do not regard as members of their own race. It has become embodied in German law in the now famous Aryan paragraph by which non-Aryans are excluded from the civil service, the professions, large sections of business, the educational system and from other phases of German life. In short, the treatment of German athletes is nothing more or less than the application of a fundamental principle of Nazi law to the realm of sport; and it is this fact which at one and the same time distinguishes German discrimination against non-Aryan athletes from the exclusion of Jews and negroes and other groups from private clubs in other countries. It is this fact which makes that discrimination a violation of the

Olympic Code, for the Code recognizes in the realm of sports the absolute equality of all races and faiths.

Germany Has Introduced Politics Into the Olympics

The Nazis have also violated their pledges by introducing politics into the Olympics. In the first place, as we have seen, the Nazi Government directs and controls all preparations and arrangements for the Games through the Reichssport-Kommissar, a government official, who is a member of and who dominates the Berlin Organizing Committee to which the German Olympic Committee has abdicated its prerogatives. How completely the German Government controls the arrangements for the Olympics and how it is using its control to further its own policies is indicated by its recent announcement that "no arrangements for the housing of visitors and Olympic teams will be made in the homes of Jews."

Olympic Reform

In one way or another, virtually every Olympic Games since Berlin has been subject to political manipulation or confrontation. The Helsinki Olympics of 1952 marked the first of successive games where the ideological conflict between communism and capitalism spilled over into international athletic competition. The boycott imposed by President Carter of United States athletes in 1980 as a means of protesting the Soviet invasion of Afghanistan and Russian refusal to participate in the 1984 Los Angeles Games are the most recent examples of sport's involvement in this continuing ideological struggle. The massacre of Israeli Olympic athletes by Arab terrorists at the 1972 Munich Olympics and the protests of African athletes at recent games as a challenge to South African apartheid policies offer other examples of the increasing connection of politics and sport.

Bill Bradley played on the United States Olympic basketball team that competed in Tokyo in 1964. An All-American at Princeton University, Bradley was also a Rhodes Scholar and a teammate of Walt Frazier's on the championship New York Knickerbocker basketball teams of the early 1970s. Today he is a United States Senator from New Jersey and a prominent Democrat often spoken of as a potential presidential candidate. In the following *New York Times* piece of July 21, 1976, Bradley offers a plan to reform the Olympics and to de-politicize it. What emphasis does Bradley place on returning the games to the athletes? Do his suggestions reflect an appreciation of the technological and commercial forces that have transformed sport in the twentieth century? What kind of political goals does Bradley have in mind in restructuring the Olympics?

FIVE WAYS TO REFORM THE OLYMPICS

Maybe the Olympics won't end exactly that way, but many people have called for their abolition on the grounds that they have been too expensive and too political. I believe the United States should discontinue its participation in the Games unless the promotion of mutual understanding among nations becomes a more central focus of the quadrennial festival.

First, the Olympics should be open to everyone. An athlete's skill should be the only requirement for eligibility. Amateurism is impossible to interpret or to enforce with uniformity in a world with disparate political and economic values. In 1974, I played on the United States Olympic basketball team in Tokyo. We beat the Soviet Union for a gold medal. Two years later I was playing for the team of an Italian meatpacking firm in the European Cup championship. We met (and defeated) the Soviet team in the semi-final. Man for man they were the same as the Soviet national team in Tokyo, except now they were called the Soviet Army Club Team. They were professionals paid for playing basketball, yet by international standards they were amateurs.

Second, team sports should be eliminated from the Olympics. They too easily simulate war games. One has only to consider the Soviet-Hungarian water polo game in 1956, the Soviet-Czechoslovak ice hockey match in 1968, or any time the Indians and Pakistanis meet in the field hockey final, in order to see that the "friendly combat" of the playing field whips up national passions. Even participants in team sports frequently feel they represent their countries more than themselves and compete for national prestige rather than for the joy of collective fulfillment that a team's quest for excellence can uniquely provide. If the public demands world champions, each sport can sponsor a separate world tournament, but not in the Olympics.

Third, everyone in the Olympics should get a participant's medal. Silver and bronze medals should be eliminated and the gold medal should go only to someone who breaks an Olympic record. Then an athlete would compete against a standard, not against another athletes or another country.

Fourth, the Olympics should be situated permanently in Greece, the country of their origin. All nations who compete in the Games should help underwrite the expense of a permanent facility that ultimately might become self-sustaining. Every four years, the world's youth would return to Mount Olympus in a spirit of friendship to compete in the finest athletic installation in the world.

The present system of financing the Olympics promotes the incursion of the festival into the politics of the host nation. Furthermore, the quadrennial expenditure of vast sums of money ($600 million in Mexico City,

$800 million in Munich, $1.5 billion in Montreal) for capital projects that are little used after the Games is incredibly wasteful.

If the appeal of a purified Olympics could be parlayed into a sharing of the financial risks and rewards by all nations, each Olympiad could be made a time to focus on the oneness of the world instead of a time to champion the nationalistic grandeur of increasingly expensive physical facilities.

Fifth, the Olympics should be more participant-oriented. The athlete has gotten lost amid the site competitions, the multi-million-dollar construction projects, the TV cameras and the hordes of tourists. I would like to see the Games become more of a festival.

Everything should be aimed toward providing the participant with a unique experience. By lengthening the Games to two months, events could take place at a less feverish pace. Athletes could spend more time in the Olympic Village getting to know each other. The normal diversions of the village might be expanded to include cultural and artistic expressions from various parts of the world. Though the emphasis would still be athletic, the presence of other disciplines would recognize the value of the whole person. In such an environment the stress would lie not on the rewards to be taken home but the experience of living for two months in a microcosm of the world. Such an Olympics might even contribute to mutual understanding among nations.

The Varsity Syndrome

The coincidence of the Civil Rights movement, protests against the war in Vietnam, and the reawakening of the feminist movement in the 1960s triggered critical appraisal of the place and operation of sport in American society. A host of journalists, athletes, and sports activists commented on the manipulation of sports for political purposes, the excessive violence in organized team sport, and the control commercial forces have had on the way in which Americans participate in sport. One of the most perceptive commentators has been Robert Lipsyte. From 1957 to 1971, Lipsyte covered sports for the *New York Times*. In 1975 he published an influential critique of American sport titled *Sportsworld: An American Dreamland*. Currently he is a sports journalist for NBC. The following selection, "Varsity Syndrome: The Unkindest Cut," first appeared in *The Annals of the American Academy of Political and Social Science* in September, 1979. What does Lipsyte mean by the "varsity syndrome" and by "sportsworld?" Do you agree with his assessment that values learned in "sportsworld" spill over into our daily life in detrimental ways? What connections do you see between these values and those espoused in less critical ways by such people as Theodore Roosevelt or A.G. Spalding? What hope for the future does Lipsyte offer?

VARSITY SYNDROME: THE UNKINDEST CUT

Americans must win back the natural birthright of their bodies, a birthright which has been distorted and manipulated by political and commercial forces that have used sports and physical education for purposes that often negate the incredible potential for individual and community progress that is inherent in sports—the one human activity that offers health, fun, and cooperation with the chance to combine physical, mental, and emotional energy.

Sports is the single most influential currency of mass communication in the world. Unlike so many other activities—music, art, literature—sports easily hurdles the barriers of age, education, language, gender, social and economic status that tend to divide a population.

Sports has the potential to bring us together but the evidence suggests it rarely does. In fact, it often further divides communities by promoting overzealous competition, violence, specialization, professionalization and an attitude of "win at all costs" that spills over into other aspects of daily life.

Over the years there have been changes, hopeful changes, in sport. The emergence of the black athlete, the emergence of the woman athlete, the proliferation of serious academic studies of athletes and of their impact on our culture are examples. Yet, there has been no real breakthrough in the attempt to reduce the effects of a pervasive pattern of emphasis and expectations which keeps us from realizing the intensive pleasures of sport. I call that pattern the "varsity syndrome."

We experience the effects of the varsity syndrome in childhood and its influence is lifelong. It begins in kindergarten with "organized games" and culminates each year when more than eighty million Americans watch perhaps eighty men act out our fantasies—The Super Bowl, a celebration, we are conditioned to believe, of manliness, courage, fruitful labor, pain, endurance, strength and achievement, all characteristics to which every man would aspire to hold to some degree.

Confrontation with the varsity syndrome starts early for boys in any neighborhood, the killer word is "fag." Call a boy a fag and he will have to fight or slink away. The homosexual connotation of the word is implicit, though not primary. Since we were taught that homosexuals were unmanly, somehow "feminine," the word really meant to us that a boy was "girlish," unfit for the company of men. We all "knew" that girls were smaller, weaker, less physically skilled. They had no place or future in the big leagues of life. Sports taught us that.

A boy tried very hard to avoid being labeled a fag. He might play games in which he found no pleasure; he might root for teams that bored him; he paid constant lip service to sports. In my day it was, "Who you like better, fella, Mantle or Mays?" You could answer anyway you wanted to, you could even say "Duke Snider," just so long as you didn't say, "who cares?" The schoolyard—that no-womans land—was a male sanctuary, and the first of many arenas in which a man would be tested for his ability to perform under stress, with skill and with the ruthlessness that passes for pragmatism.

Sports was the first great separator of the sexes. Sometime after kindergarten, a girl was handed (symbolically or literally) the majorette's baton and told to go in the corner and twirl. Her athletic moment was over. She now existed only as an encourager of males. There were, of course, girls who dropped the baton and picked up the bat and beat males at their own games. However, the culture had prepared a way to combat this seeming inconsistency. Athletically superior boys might be considered supermen, but athletically superior women were something less than real women. They were locker-room jokes. Boys would tell each other, she's playing because she can't get a date; she's a tomboy; or, most devastatingly, she's a dyke. And if she turned out to be world-class, the world was quick to suspect her chromosomes.

Reading about Babe Didrikson in Paul Gallico's popular 1938 book, "Farewell to Sport," I had no reason to disbelieve his statement that she became one of the greatest of all American athletes merely as an "escape, a compensation."[1] Galico wrote that Didrikson "Would not or could not compete with women at their own best game . . . man-snatching."[2] Most sportswriters, observers, and participants accepted Gallico's statement as fact, or at the least as a manifestation of routine sexism. After all, women were barred from press boxes, locker rooms, and anything other than cheerleader positions in sport. Only recently, while researching a book, I came across an even simpler explanation for Gallico's slur. A fine and vain athlete himself, Gallico once raced Didrikson across a golf course. She ran him into the ground. And he never again wrote about her without mentioning her prominent adam's apple, or the down on her upper lip. I assume his rationalization was traditional: a woman can't beat a man unless he's a fag or she's not really a woman.

The usual justification for restricting women from sports competition—the very first manifestation of the varsity syndrome—was that their delicate bodies needed protection from physical harm. More realistically, I believe, women were rejected to protect the delicate egos of men who have been taught that their manhood depends on the presence of an underclass. James Michener, a respected writer and an avid sports fan and participant, recently published a book called *Sports in America*, which contained a concept that I feel is very dangerous because it is so widely held.[3] Michener

---

[1]Paul Gallico, *Farewell to Sports* (New York: Alfred A. Knopf, 1945), p. 229.

[2]*Farewell to Sports*, p. 229.

[3]James Michener, *Sports in America* (Chicago: Random House, 1976).

wrote that between the ages of about eleven and twenty-two men and women should not compete against each other in sports because of the possible damage to the male's ego should he lose.[4] No consideration is given to the ego of the young female who is striving to exhibit and stretch to the outer limits her own talents and skills.

The sexism of the varsity syndrome transcends sports. Athletics give youngsters an opportunity to learn the positive values of leadership, of cooperation and dedication and sacrifice for a goal. Games are a source of skill development, whether it be physical, mental, or social. Many women have been stunted in their growth toward full citizenship because they were denied an opportunity routinely afforded to every male. The woman who does succeed in American sports does so at a certain cost. I recall one afternoon in the middle sixties, coming off a tennis court after a victory, sweaty, rackets under her arm, Billie Jean King was intercepted by a male spectator from the stands who asked, "Hey, Billie Jean, when are you going to have children?" Billie Jean answered, "I'm not ready yet." The man continued, "Why aren't you at home?" Billie Jean snapped right back "Why don't you go ask Rod Laver why *he* isn't at home?"

Varsity Syndrome—Elite Deference

Another component of the varsity syndrome, learned on the streets and reinforced throughout school, is elitism. Special privileges are afforded athletes, including a special psychological aura or deference that ultimately proves to harm the athlete as well as the non-athlete. This aspect of the varsity syndrome is so pernicious it finds its supporters at both poles of the playing field, from neanderthal coaches on the right, whose authoritarian methods squeeze out joy of sports, to so-called sports revolutionaries on the left who see athletes as a higher order of human beings.

Traditionally, soon after fifty-one percent of the potential athletes—the women—were cut from the team, the process of winnowing the boys begins. This process, which George Sauer, the former New York Jets wide receiver, has called a form of social darwinism, has many ramifications.[5] First of all, it separates boys into worthy and unworthy classes just at a time in their lives when they are most confused about their bodies and their relationships with their peers. Those annointed as athletes often drop away from other social and intellectual pursuits, and it becomes harder and harder for them to catch up when they, too, are eventually cut from the team. It happens to everyone eventually, and no matter the age or level of competition, the cut is hard to take. Those who are marked as failures at critical times in their lives often seem to spend the rest of their lives measuring up. Those who measure up early and last for awhile become jocks.

---

[4]*Sports in America*, p. 129.
[5]Robert Lipsyte, *Sports World* (New York: Quadrangle, 1975), p. 51.

In our society the jock is often the male equivalent of the stereotyped female, the broad.

The jock and the broad are selected and rewarded for beauty and performing skills. They are used to satisfy others and to define themselves by the quantity and quality of that satisfaction whether it be as a Heisman Trophy winner or Miss America, rookie of the year or starlet, all-America or prom queen. When they grow too old to please they are discarded.

One of the cruelest ramifications of the elitist component of the varsity syndrome is the way it has been used to turn black athletes into a gladiator legion in American sports. Contrary to prevailing opinion, sports success has probably been detrimental to black progress. By publicizing the material success of a few hundred athletes, thousands, perhaps millions of bright young blacks have been swept toward sports when they should have been guided toward careers in medicine or engineering or business. For every black who escaped the ghetto behind his jump shot, a thousand of his little brothers were neutralized, kept busy shooting baskets, until it was too late for them to qualify beyond marginal work.[6]

Those who do make it big, white or black, male or female, are generally lionized out of all proportion to their intrinsic worth, or to their importance to society. The athlete is damaged by the exaggerated adulation and the rest of us are given a pantheon of heroes on a nest of false laurels. An example from my own experience illustrates this point. When I was about twenty-one, a brand-new reporter at *The New York Times*, I was sent to Yankee Stadium to interview Mickey Mantle. Several nights earlier, a fan jumped out of the stands and traded some punches with Mantle. This was years before the advent of what psychiatrists' now call "recreational violence," and it was quite unusual. Apparently Mantle had gotten the worst of the scuffle; he couldn't chew very well for a day or two. No one had dared interview him about the incident. I was sent because I was expendable as a cub reporter and I asked him about it because I didn't know any better. So, in my most polite reportorial tones I asked Mickey if his jaw still hurt. Mickey looked at me contemptuously and made an obscene and physically impossible suggestion. Somehow, after years of reading about Mantle in newspapers and magazines and books, I was not exactly prepared for his answer. So I rephrased it and tried again. He then signalled to Yogi Berra, another all-star charmer, and they began throwing a baseball back and forth an inch over my head. I sensed that the interview was over.

I don't want to make too much of this because I think a celebrity has the right (within limits that apply to us all) to act any way he or she wants. But, I also think the rest of us have a right not to be deceived. That little incident at Yankee Stadium was a real consciousness-raiser for me. If this was the real Mickey Mantle, I thought, then we haven't been getting the

[6]Rick Telander, *Heaven is a Playground* (New York: Grosset and Dunlap, 1976).

right information. Like so many athletes in our culture, Mantle had been isolated early by virtue of the varsity syndrome, given privileges denied the rest of us. Those privileges begin with favors and gifts in grade school, little presents in high school such as an unearned diploma, perhaps a college scholarship. Athletes are waved, as it were, through the toll booths of life. And then, as celebrities, they are given a whole new identity as heroes.

Of course, to publicize any frailties in athletic character structure is to bring down a wave of criticism and often categorical rejection. When Jim Bouton's book, *Ball Four*, came out a few years ago, the big rap against the book wasn't its stories or that major league shenanigans were untrue, but that kids shouldn't hear them—that the false image of athletes as somehow a super race apart, must be retained, even at the price of truth.[7] Why is it so important that kids look up to false heroes as models of behavior? Why not know the truth and learn to separate what people do from what they are; to appreciate athletes as dedicated specialists, as entertainers, but not as gods.

Varsity syndrome—Athletes as Salesmen

There are, of course, so many components of the varsity syndrome we could never even touch them all in this limited space. But there is one other significant dimension that deserves mention—the use of athletics and athletes to sell a product. At its lowest form, athletes sell shoes or panty hose, breakfast cereals or underarm deodorant. They sell colleges that have four books in the library but a multi-million dollar fieldhouse. Athletes sell cities which mortgage their futures to build ball-parks in order to be plunged into a national entertainment network which is valuable for tourism and investment. And, on the highest and perhaps most grotesque level, athletes are used to sell ways of life, ideologies.

This is the most distorted level, not only because world class athletic competitions, like the Olympic Games, are such major events, but because they would not be possible without the varsity syndrome, that careful and calculated selection process that starts in kindergarten. This narrow elitism makes most of us failed athletes long before we've had the chance to really feel the sensous delights of the wind in our hair while running, or the water lapping at our bodies while swimming, or the almost orgasmic pleasures of that one perfect shot or catch or leap that comes to everyone involved in sport. Sport is the best thing you can do with your body in public.

The Olympic Games are grotesque within themselves. As is probably known, the modern Olympics were the brainstorm of a French baron from a military family who never got over France's defeat in the Franco-Prussian War. Baron DeCoubertin wanted a rematch and he thought French youth could get in shape for the rematch through sports. That kind of

[7]Jim Bouton, *Ball Four* (New York: World, 1970).

nationalistic taint has never been removed from the games. In 1968 we saw the spectacle of black athletes, who raised their fists in protest against racism in America, thrown off the team even though theirs was an individual gesture in a context that is supposed to exist for individualistic expression. In 1972 the hideous extension of Decoubertin's nationalism— the use of the Olympics as a showcase for the strength of democracy or the goodness of socialism or the love of the Junta—resulted in the murder of a team of competitors from Israel. In 1976, the various machinations over China and South Africa reenforced the Olympics as *Politics in a Sweatshirt.*

The Olympics not only represents a major political event, it also is a significant entertainment and commercial event. The most poignant lesson, to me, came at a press conference prior to the 1976 games. The president of ABC sports at the time, Roone Arledge, a very powerful man in international sports, was asked by an idealistic journalist why the opening event of the Games, the ceremonial parade of athletes, couldn't be run for its full hour or more without commercial interuptions. Arledge replied quite amiably that it wouldn't be commercially feasible . . . "after all, sponsors pay for telecasts."

But the questioner continued . . . "Many countries which use the Olympics as a showcase or as a statement of identity, might never be seen except in that opening parade. After all, many countries win no medals at all. And some sports, like field hockey, water polo, and volleyball, are not well covered. So some countries, lost in a commercial, might never get on the world television feed at all."

"That's true," said Arledge.

"How do you pick candidates for obscurity?" asked the journalist.

"Well," said Arledge, "we have to make judgements. Suppose we've just had two little South American countries, and its time for a commercial, and here comes a third South American country . . . sooooooo, sorry about that Chile."

That third little South American country, or that little midwestern college, betting its identity on the ephemeral possibility of national or international exposure, is putting a kind of graffiti on the windows of the world, shouting, "I'm here, we're alive."

They are in the trap of the varsity syndrome. The payoff can be great, but the price to pay is also great and, for most, rarely worth the gain. The struggle to success may be stalmated prematurely by the whim of a television producer or the vargaries of the system itself. Win or lose, the country and the college invariably sell their souls cheap to a system that uses them up and moves on.

This is a system in which, for the past one hundred years or so, most Americans have been taught to believe that playing and watching competitive games are not only healthful activities, but exert a positive force on our national psyche. Though sports, they have been led to believe, children will learn courage and self-control; old people will find blissful nostalgia; families will discover non-threatening way to communicate among themselves, immigrants will find shortcuts to recognition as Americans, and, rich and poor, black and white, educated and unskilled, we will all find a unifying language with democratization the result: The melting pot may be a myth in real life, but in the ballpark or on the playing field we are one community, unified in common purpose. Even for ballgames, these values, with their implicit definitions of courage and success and manhood, are not necessarily in the individual's best interests. But for daily life they tend to support a web of ethics and attitudes, part of that amorphous infrastructure called *SportsWorld* . . . that acts to contain our energies, divert our passions, and socialize us for work or war or depression.

In 1928, a Columbia University historian named John Krout wrote: "During depressions, with thousands out of work, sports helps refocus our attention on the great American values and ideals and also helps us to remember that life does not begin and end with the dollar."[8] This infrastructure, SportsWorld, is neither an American nor a modern phenomenon. The Olympics of ancient Greece were manipulated for political and commercial purposes. SportsWorld is no classic conspiracy, but rather an expression of a community of interest. In the Soviet Union and East Germany, for example, where world-class athletes are the diplomat-soldiers of ideology, and where factory workers exercise to reduce fatigue and increase production, it is simple to see that the entire athletic apparatus is part of government.

In this country, SportsWorld's power is less visible, but no less real. In America, banks decide which arenas and recreational facilities will be built; television networks decide which sports shall be sponsored and viewed; the press decides which individuals and teams will be celebrated; municipal governments decide which clubs will be subsidized through the building of stadiums; state legislatures decide which universities and which aspects of their athletic programs, will prosper; and the federal government, through favorable tax rulings and exemptions from law, helps develop and maintain sports entertainment as a currency of communication that surpasses patriotism and piety while exploiting them both.

Conclusion

Educators and journalists are at fault for their support of this system. And we are often in the position of being the fall guys. It sometimes seems as though we are in what the play-by-play announcers call a no-win situa-

---

[8]John Krout, "Some Reflections on the Rise of American Sport," *Proceedings of the Association of History*, #26 1929. Reprinted in *The Sporting Set*, ed. Leon Stern, (New York: Arno Press, 1975), pp. 84–93.

tion. By working within the rules of the system, preparing athletes and teachers to function smoothly in SportsWorld, and to prosper with the varsity syndrome, we are perpetuating a pattern that is basically anti-sports, that deprives the joy of healthy play and competition to the society as a whole. By trying to beat the system by de-emphasizing big-time sports and cutting back on the massive construction of arenas that are wasteful in terms of human use, in favor of some broad-based physical education programs, we are often in danger of jeopardizing the financial health of our institutions and discriminating against the really talented athletes who deserve the chance to develop to their limits just as surely as do the young poets in the English Department or the student engineers. Educators and journalists are the fall guys because when things go wrong they are often blamed, and sometimes fired—even though the ultimate decisionmaking power in SportsWorld is never theirs.

Sports is, has always been, and will always be, a reflection of the mainstream culture of the society. Those who claim that we could or should keep sports free of politics, or free of commercialism, or free of ideology are fools. If sports were not such a reflection, it would be nothing more than an isolated sanctuary, an irrelevant little circus hardly worth considering. But sports is, as I firmly believe it should be, a critical part of the lives of every man, woman, and child in the country and in the world. Furthermore, it should be accessible, inexpensive, and fun.

Activists have always seen sports as a tool to change or direct society, and they have been criticized for it. Yet when establishment politicians and coaches talk about sports as preparation for life or about football as a way of training young men for war or for corporate positions, they are using sports as a tool just as surely as is anyone who calls for a boycott of an all-white South African rugby team. The answer, of course, is that society must be changed before sports can be changed. But that, too, can sometimes be a self-defeating answer. It allows too many of us to sit back and throw up our hands. Changing society seems like an incomprehensible, much less possible task.

However, things are happening in sports, exciting things, some progressive, some reactionary, some scary. First, there's a growing awareness of the importance of sports in our lives. Second, the increasing academic interest in sports is a hopeful sign. Institutes, both independent and on campuses, are being created with the explicit goal of investigating, analyzing, and understanding the role of sport and society. Third, there are new laws to help end the systematic exclusion of women. (But care must be taken that the varsity syndrome does not permeate the organization of womens' sport.) Fourth, there's a growing body of work exposing the so-called Lombardi ethic of "Winning isn't the Most Important Thing, its the Only Thing" (A phrase, by the way, which Lombardi didn't invent) as appropriate for the professional Green Bay Packers, but a crippler, physically and psychologically, when applied to youngsters just starting in sports.

Despite the enormous amount to be accomplished, there are little contests each of us can engage in that will win for us all: one little community recreation program for older people; one totally non-sexist grade school sports program; one high school program which involves every student regardless of skill level; a girls team that doesn't use the JV's leftover shoes and the gym at dinner time; a college pool that doesn't discriminate against non-varsity swimmers; a little league that defuses the pressures of joyless competition; and a university classroom that openly approaches the possibility of new games, new methods, and fresh concepts in sport studies. Each victory will shed some light on sports and will help shape our lives through its cultural impact. Each victory will help dispel the darkness of SportWorld, the varsity syndrome, and a system that separates people by calling some athletes and some non-athletes. When this beautiful and good thing we call sports allows each person to be an athlete forever, then it will have been true to its original purposes.

WOMEN AND SPORT

Martina Navratilova and Nancy Lieberman, millionaire professional tennis and basketball stars, are a far cry from the country club and college women of the late nineteenth century who first began participating in sport in large numbers. Indeed, today there is ample evidence—from the success of professional athletes to the increase in participation of women in high school and intercollegiate sport, even to the way in which clothing, perfume, and feminine hygiene products are advertised—that a sports revolution for women has taken place in the last twenty-five years.

In important respects, the history of women's participation in sport parallels the ebb and flow of the women's rights movement—especially in terms of the arguments used to justify female involvement and in terms of the intensity with which women pursued their freedom. Opportunities for women in sport in the twentieth century have also reflected the broader situation of women's role and place in society. As with men, class and race have been critical factors in defining and limiting possibilities for particular groups. Whatever the experience, women involved in sport constantly confronted a sexist framework which forced organized participation to develop in different ways than men's sport, presumably to serve the different biological, emotional, and social needs of the sexes. For those individuals who challenged this framework, rewards often were colored by public ridicule and derision. The following selections illustrate the progress and the problems women's athletics has experienced.

Senda Berenson: The Mother of Basketball

In 1848, at Seneca Falls, New York, a small group of northern, white middle-class women held a convention on woman's rights that is generally hailed as the beginnings of the organized feminist movement in the United States. Although not all agreed on how far to challenge the notion of separate spheres and the philosophy on which it rested, at its outset, most of these early feminists demanded that the United States be true to the spirit of the Declaration of Independence and give women full equality and the freedom to pursue any endeavor.

By the turn of the century, after modest gains in some areas, especially the opportunity for women to become college-educated either at previously all male institutions or in newly formed women's colleges, the movement turned conservative. Accepting the long-held sexist beliefs that women were more moral and spiritual than men, that virtue and self-control were her necessary traits in the struggle to make society better, and that her place was in the home, feminists emphasized these positions in demanding suffrage—a philosophy and tactic that had much to do with the enactment of the nineteenth amendment to the U.S. Constitution in 1920 that gave women the right to vote.

Women's involvement in sport in the early decades of the twentieth century reflected these trends. The growth of women's colleges created a demand for a new profession, the woman physical educator. Although premised on traditional beliefs that women were less prepared than men to withstand the physical and emotional demands of college life, the opening of this new field of employment demonstrated increasing opportunities for women within a familiar, restrictive framework of gender first popularized earlier in the nineteenth century by Catherine Beecher and others.

Senda Berenson, a graduate of the Boston Normal School of Gymnastics and the director of physical education at Smith College from 1892 to 1922, was one of these women. Best known for introducing basketball for women, a game she learned from its originator, James Naismith, who invented the game in 1892 in the neighboring town of Springfield, Massachusetts, Berenson taught, lectured, and wrote about the benefits of organized sport for women in the spirit of her profession. She also modified the rules of the men's game in ways that reduced the potential for violent, physical contact and made basketball, in her mind, more suitable to the purposes and nature of women.

The following essay, "The Significance of Basketball for Women," appeared in several different editions of *Basket Ball for Women* between 1900 and 1913, a book in the Spalding Athletic Library edited by Berenson. Is Berenson talking to all women or to those of a particular class? How did she alter the rules of basketball to suit women? In what ways does she distinguish the purpose of athletics for men and women? How do her distinctions reflect her views on the larger roles that men and women play in society? What do you make of her criticism of "a win at all costs" philosophy associated with male sports? How do they differ or agree with Robert Lipsyte's earlier analysis of the same idea?

THE SIGNIFICANCE OF BASKETBALL FOR WOMEN

In competitive games one of two strong forces must become all-important. One will either abandon one's self to instinct and impulse in the quickness of action and intense desire for victory, and hence develop rough and vicious play; or, eliminating brute and unfair play, one's powers are put into developing expert playing, quickness of judgement and action, and physical and moral self-control.

Much of the element of rough play in games comes more from excitement and the desire to win at all and any cost than from inborn viciousness of character. Many players are ashamed of their conduct in games in their calmer moments. That is as it should be. The great danger lies in the fact that rough and unfair play, the results at first of impulse and carelessness, become strong forces in vitiating the characters of the players by developing another standard or morals for athletics than the one held for conduct in life.

Not only is this standard for athletics held by athletes, but a great number of the community at large seem to think certain elements in athletics perfectly fair, that from an ethical point of view are as bad as lying or stealing. "All is fair in love and war" we are told; certain games are mimic war; hence every action is justifiable in games. A young friend, apparently earnest, ambitious and honorable, told me with all seriousness that if you take all the objectionable features out of a game you take all the fun out of it—there is nothing left; that it really isn't so bad "to wind" or injure a man in football in order to weaken the other side. I heard a good old minister, who was preaching to a community of college men say, emphasizing his remarks with his fist on the reading desk, "When we play a game of football, what is our object? It is to win; nothing else counts; we go in to *win*." His very tones implied, "win at all hazards, by fair means or foul, do anything, but in the end win."

The greatest element of evil in the spirit of athletics in this country is the idea that one must win at any cost—that defeat is an unspeakable disgrace. Most of the brutality and unfairness come from this.

It is of course human nature to desire to win—to succeed in any undertaking. But I do believe that we need to cultivate the spirit that fair play comes first—defeat or victory afterwards. If victory is the result, we can congratulate ourselves on winning because of expert and clean work; if defeat, we can comfort ourselves with the thought that we did our best and were beaten fairly. Failure is as necessary in life as success, if those who fail profit by the experience. "We fall to rise, are baffled to fight better." I have no sympathy with narrow-minded people who see no good in athletics because of the few objectionable features in them. I would not be understood as believing that hard, earnest playing is objectionable. Just such playing is the best to bring out manliness and fearlessness in a youth. But it is because I believe that competitive games are such tremendous forces for good as well as for evil that I would have those elements in them encouraged which bring out the love of honor, courage and fair play, and eliminate those which encourage the taking advantage of laws, cruelty, brutality and unfairness.

All that precedes applies to athletics generally. I want to speak, however, on athletic sports for women in particular:

Within the last few years athletic games for women have made such wonderful strides in popularity that there are few directors of physical training who do not value them as an important part of their work. They have become popular, too, not as the outcome of a "fad" but because educators everywhere see the great value games may have in any scheme of education. Gymnastics and games for women are meeting less and less opposition, and gaining larger numbers of warm supporters because our younger generation of women are already showing the good results that may be obtained from them in better physiques and greater strength and endurance.

Now that the woman's sphere of usefulness is constantly widening, now that she is proving that her work in certain fields of labor is equal to man's work and hence should have equal reward, now that all fields of labor and all professions are opening their doors to her, she needs more than ever the physical strength to meet these ever increasing demands. And not only does she need a strong physique, but physical and moral courage as well.

Games are invaluable for women in that they bring out as nothing else just these elements that women find necessary today in their enlarged field of activities. Basket ball is the game above all others that has proved of the greatest value to them. Foot ball will never be played by women, and base ball is seldom entered into with spirit. Basket ball is played with deep earnestness and utter unconsciousness of self. Certain elements of false education for centuries have made woman self-conscious. She is becoming less so, but one finds women posing even in tennis and golf. It is impossible to pose in basket ball. The game is too quick, too vigorous, the action too continuous to allow any element to enter which is foreign to it. It develops quick perception and judgment—in one moment a person must judge space and time in order to run and catch the ball at the right place, must decide to whom it may best be thrown, and at the same time must remember not to "foul." It develops physical and moral courage, self-reliance and self-control, the ability to meet success and defeat with dignity.

It is said that one of woman's weakness is her inability to leave the personal element out of thought or action. If this is so—and there is some ground for such a supposition—a competitive game like basket ball does much to do away with it. Success in this game can be brought about only by good team-play. A team with a number of brilliant individual players lacking team-work will be beaten always by a team of conscientious players who play for each other. This develops traits of character which organization brings; fair play, impersonal interest, earnestness of purpose, the ability to give one's best not for one's own glorification but for the good of the team—the cause.

But just as basket ball may be made an influence for good so may it be made a strong influence for evil. The gravest objection to the game is the rough element it contains. Since athletics for women are still in their infancy, it is well to bring up the large and significant question: shall women blindly imitate the athletics of men without reference to their different organizations and purpose in life; or shall their athletics be such as shall develop those physical and moral elements that are particularly necessary for them? We can profit by the experience of our brothers and therefore save ourselves from allowing those objectionable features to creep into our athletics that many men are seriously working to eliminate from theirs. Since all new movements swing from the extreme of degeneracy or inertness to the extreme enthusiasm of newly acquired powers, unless we are most careful we shall allow that enthusiasm and power to run away with our reason. It is a well known fact that women abandon themselves more readily to an impulse than men. Lombroso tells us that women are more open to suggestion, more open to run to extremes than men. This shows us that unless we guard our athletics carefully in the beginning many objectionable elements will quickly come in. It also shows us that unless a game as exciting as basket ball is carefully guided by such rules as will eliminate roughness, the great desire to win and the excitement of the game will make our women do sadly unwomanly things.

This has already been proved. A basket ball match game was played several years ago between the teams of two of our normal schools. One team had been trained to play with the Y.M.C.A. rules; the other with modified rules. Since neither team wished to change its method of play, the first half was played by each team according to its own rules. The game was so rough that the second half was played by both teams with the modified rules. Let me quote from a paper commenting on this game:

"Probably no finer exhibition of basket ball playing by women has ever been seen in this country than the game played by these two teams during the *last* half of their contest. As a possibility of what women can show in the way of skill, alertness, accuracy, coolness and presence of mind under trying circumstances, and still be ladies, the game was a revelation to many present.

"To my mind the important lesson of this game, and the one that should make it a memorable one, is that a courteous consideration of an opponent, even in an antagonistic game, does not necessarily diminish a team's chances for victory."

Another instance; a basket ball team composed of refined women, in one of our New York cities, was challenged to play a game by a team just out of their town. The occasion was not only to be an athletic but a great social event. The visiting team had played with modified rules; the other with rules for men. The playing was not only rough to a degree, but the spirit shown toward the guests who were beating, by their opponents and their friends, was what one would think quite impossible in women who had any regard for the ordinary courtesies of life. Rough and vicious play seems worse in women than in men. A certain amount of roughness is deemed necessary to bring out manliness in our young men. Surely rough play can have no possible excuse in our young women.

Of course, these two cases and similar instances of which I have heard do not prove that many of our women who play basket ball do so in an undesirable way. They are sufficient, however, to make us pause and consider whether they are not enough to prove that we need to free the game from anything that might lead to objectionable play. And here a serious question may be raised as to whether it is for the best interest of women to go into inter-scholastic games.

However, just this fact that women are more open to suggestion is an encouraging one, for it shows us that they can the more easily be lead to right thought and action. This can be seen by the splendid results of clean sport and good spirit gained wherever basket ball has been guarded by careful rules and strict discipline.

But just here I must say that not only is it necessary to modify the game somewhat, but the physical director and umpire cannot appreciate too fully the responsibility of their positions. The best of rules will be no protection to one who does not insist on fair play and does not umpire most conscientiously. It is also important that the captain of the team shall not only be a good basket ball player, but one who represents the best athletic spirit. I may say that the spirit of athletics in our colleges and schools for women is what the director of the gymnasium makes it. The right spirit is not gained by autocratic methods, but by almost imperceptible suggestion and strong example. If the physical director takes it for granted that athletics can be no other than fair and honorable, her spirit will be imbibed unconsciously by her pupils.

The modifications in the rules contained in this pamphlet were carefully considered and are entirely the fruit of experience. The two important changes are the division of the playing field and the prohibiting of snatching or batting the ball from the hands of another player.

The division of the gymnasium or field into three equal parts, and the prohibiting of the players of one division from running into the domain of another seems an advantage for many reasons. It does away almost entirely with "star" playing, hence equalizes the importance of the players, and so encourages team work. This also encourages combination plays, for when a girl knows she cannot go over the division line to follow the ball, she is more careful to play as well as possible with the girls near her when the ball comes to her territory. The larger the gymnasium the greater is the tax on individual players when the game is played without lines. It has been found that a number of girls who play without division lines have developed hypertrophy of the heart. The lines prevent the players from running all over the gymnasium, thus doing away with unnecessary running, and also giving the heart moments of rest. On the other hand, the lines do not keep the players almost stationary, as some believe. A player has the right to run anywhere she may please in her own third of the gymnasium.

The divisions, then, concentrate energy, encourage combination plays, equalize team work and do away with undue physical exertion.

Allowing snatching or batting the ball from another person's hand seems the greatest element toward encouraging rough play in the game. It is apt to encourage personal contact; it has an intrinsic quality that goes against one's better nature; it has an element of insult in it. When a player gets the ball it should be hers by the laws of victory, ownership, courtesy, fair play. To prevent this rule, however, from making the game slow and spiritless, a rule was made that a player should not be allowed to hold the ball longer than three seconds under penalty of a foul. Preventing snatching or batting the ball has also developed superb jumping; for a player knows that since she cannot snatch the ball away from her opponent, by jumping in the air as high as possible she may catch the ball before it gets to her opponent.

When the game was first started many saw the danger of "dribbling." The objectionable element was done away with by not allowing the players to bounce the ball more than three consecutive times or lower than the knee. Since then the Y.M.C.A. rules have done away with dribbling together. It seems a good rule to eliminate it when the game is played without division lines—where a player by dribbling can easily get from one basket to the other—but that necessity is overcome with division lines. To allow a player to bounce the ball three times gives an opportunity for having possession of the ball longer than three seconds when she wishes to use a signal or combination play. On the the other hand, by demanding that the ball shall be bounced higher than the knee gives a quick opponent a fair opportunity to bat the ball away when it is between the floor and the player's hands.

Of course, if bouncing the ball becomes a nuisance—and one never knows what peculiar play will become popular—it can easily be remedied by doing away with it altogether until the team appreciates that it is a great advantage if used in moderation, a great hinderance if used to an extent.

The original rules allow only five on a team. We have changed the rules to allow any number from five to ten players on a team. My own conviction is that the smallest number of players should be six instead of five, for when the game is played with division lines the work in the centre is much too hard for one player. Some of the strongest and quickest work is done in the centre. The size of the gymnasium should decide the number of players on a team. If a gymnasium is 40×30 feet, it stands to reason that fewer players are necessary to meet all the hygienic and recreative requirements of the game than where the floor is 100×60. In one of our colleges ten play on a team because the players find they can bring about better combination plays with four centres. The dimension of their gymnasium is 108×60 feet—large enough to allow this increased number.

Should people imagine that these modifications take the fire and spirit out of the game, they can either try it with their own teams "without prejudice," or witness a game where such modifications are adopted to be convinced of their mistake. Perhaps it may not be out of place to quote some passages from an account which appeared in one of our leading newspapers with reference to a game played with modified rules at one of our colleges for women: "the playing was very rapid and extremely vigorous. From the time the ball went into play until a goal was tossed there was no respite. The playing could not properly be called rough. There was not an instance of slugging, but the ball was followed by the players with rushes, much the way it is on the gridiron. One who supposes it is a simple or weak game would be surprised to see the dash and vigor with which it is entered into. It is a whirl of excitement from start to finish, and yet, with all the desperate earnestness and determination with which the game is played, there is excellent control and much dexterity shown. There is splendid temper and true sportswomanlike spirit in the game. The services of a referee to end a dispute are seldom needed, and there are no delays on account of kicking. The amount of physical strength and endurance which is cultivated is readily apparent. One might suppose that it would be a namby pamby exhibition with much show, many hysterical shrieks and nothing of an athletic contest; but nothing could be more contrary to facts. True, there is no slugging or exhibition of roughness, but the play is extremely vigorous and spirited, and is characterized by a whirl and dash that is surprising to the uninitiated. The possession of self-control, both of temper and physical action, was clearly in evidence yesterday, even during the most exciting stages of the game."

The Competitive Woman Athlete

In 1923, the Women's division of the National Amateur Athletic Federation adopted a code of behavior for women's college sport that very much reflected the noncompetitive spirit of Berenson's ideas. Primarily comprised of professional women physical educators, this group, which represented the majority opinion about women and sport in America, led the fight to keep American women from competing in organized international competition such as the Olympic Games.

Not all women, however, subscribed to these views. Working-class women participated in AAU sponsored events in swimming, track and field, basketball, and gymnastics and in athletic competition sponsored by industrial teams. Most notable was Babe Didrickson, the daughter of a Norwegian immigrant family in Beaumont, Texas, who led her insurance company's women's basketball team to a national AAU championship in 1931 and who held five American Olympic or world records in track and field between 1930 and 1932. Although at times ridiculed by a male press as an oddity with too much of an Adam's apple and too much body hair to be a true woman, Didrickson demonstrated the potential women had as competitive athletes if they were willing to challenge conventional sexist views about woman's place and ability. Even more successful and less controversial in the 1920s and 1930s were tennis champion Helen Wills, ice-skating Olympic champion Sonja Hengy, and Olympic swimmer Esther Williams, all of whom demonstrated that women could be competitive champions while still retaining traditional feminine appearance and style.

World War II, which forced women into the workplace in new ways, and the feminist movement of the 1960s and 1970s that called for total equality, an end of sexism, and the right of women to have the opportunity of choice propelled women's involvement in sport to new levels. The fact that organized sport had long been seen as a visible bastion of male superiority and dichotomous sex roles for men and women made it an especially attractive arena for feminists who wanted to challenge traditional attitudes and practices.

Billie Jean King became a symbol of these developments by leading the demand for full equality in the world of professional women's tennis. A U.S. Open and Wimbledon singles champion several times over, she was a critical figure in establishing the Virginia Slims as a separate circuit for women in 1971. Her threats to lead a boycott of women stars at these prestigious tournaments was responsible for huge increases in prize money that brought women to equality with male professionals. In 1971, she became the first woman athlete to earn over $100,000. Two years later, before over 30,000 people at the Houston Astrodome and a national television audience, she smashed Bobby Riggs in a tennis match billed as "The Battle of the Sexes," further demonstrating the drawing power of professional women athletes. The following selection is from her autobiography, *Billie Jean,* published in 1974. What are King's views on the women's liberation movement? What is her definition of feminism? How does she see the connection of her own life to larger social and economic issues involving women?

BILLY JEAN KING AND FEMINISM

When the Women's Liberation Movement began to make a big splash in the late 1960s, my first reaction to it was pretty negative, I've got to admit. I thought it was a collection of fanatical, bra-burning women who hated men, and I really didn't have too much use for it. I'd never considered myself particularly radical about anything, burning bras was definitely out, and as far as men went, well, I sure didn't hate them and in a lot of ways I preferred their company. The men I knew usually had some kind of athletic background, or at least an interest in sports, and I found they generally had a better understanding of what I was all about than most women did. I was a little uneasy around women, especially those who weren't into a career the way I was. I didn't disapprove of women being wives and mothers, not at all, but that kind of life seemed to require the kind of social small talk and small outlook I just wasn't comfortable with. Although tennis was one of the few sports where men and women coexisted reasonably well, it was still a man's world, and I found it was pretty hard for me not to be caught up in that. Even several years later, after my thinking about Women's Lib had changed a lot, I remember standing up to give a speech to a practically all-women Lib audience and blurting out, "I'm sorry, but if you guys were all sportswriters I'd feel a lot more comfortable." The women broke up; because I think they understood what it had been like for me all those years to be in a profession dominated by men.

Women's Lib is a pretty personal thing in the end, I think. It's fine to talk about the history of the Movement and discuss Lib theory, and for the one or two percent of the women who can do that, great. But I know for a fact that the Movement has gotten hung up a lot of times on trivia in the interest of radical purity. Sometimes I think Libbers don't want to move three feet forward if they have to slide an inch to the side at the same time. *Ms.* magazine, I understand, once turned down a year's worth advertising and a neat five-figure deal from Virginia Slims because it didn't like the slogan "You've Come a Long Way, Baby." That's ridiculous. Virginia Slims was supporting women's tennis, which was certainly part of the Movement, so why lose all that good dough that could be used to spread the word? Libbers get down on me because I sometimes say "girls" instead of "women." Big deal. I sometimes say "boys" instead of "men," too. I occasionally feel the movement wants to create a new stereotype of the liberated woman almost as much as it wants to rid women of the old stereotypes. And one stereotype is just as false as the other.

When it comes to Women's Lib, I'm pretty much of a pragmatist, and I'd bet that most other women are too. Maybe you start comparing paychecks and find you're not making as much as the guy sitting next to you who's doing the same work. Or you apply to med school and find out you're going to the the only woman in a class of 200. Or you want to keep in shape when you're in college and learn there isn't any women's intramural sports program but that the university has just contracted for a $3.5 million basketball arena. Little things like that. Pretty soon you start thinking, "If I'm getting a lousy deal in my little world, I wonder what's going on with women in other places?" So you check around and find your experience isn't unique in the least. Then you decide to do something about it and all of a sudden you're part of the Movement. That's pretty much what happened with me.

To me, Women's Liberation means that every woman ought to be able to pursue whatever career or personal lifestyle she chooses as a full and equal member of society without fear of sexual discrimination. That's a pretty basic and simple statement, but, golly, it sure is hard sometimes to get people to accept it. And because of the way other people think, it's even harder to reach the point in your own life where you can live by it.

. . .

It's impossible for me to separate my tennis career from my personal life, or to separate either of them from Women's Lib. My personal awareness of the problems facing women came in bits and dribbles—once or twice in torrents—sometimes after the fact, and it's only been in the last three or four years, really, that anything has happened to me personally that I saw as a cut-and-dried Lib issue and could relate to the Movement as a whole.

For example, you might argue that the first bit of discrimination in my life came at that time when mom ended my football career and dad told me there were just those three sports—golf, swimming, and tennis—open to me as a woman. Could be. I realize now that my potential athletic career got chopped in half right then, but how many ten-year-old girls thought about sexism, especially in 1954?

Later, when I started speaking out against the shamateurism, hypocrisy, and nonprofessional attitudes of the USLTA and related organizations, I felt I was fighting for all tennis players, men and women. I felt we were all in the same boat, and if changes were made we'd all benefit. Sure, women were getting a lousy deal in tennis, but so were the men. It really wasn't until the early open-tennis years with the pretty obvious prize-money differences and the cutbacks in women's tournaments that I saw clearly that the women's deal was a whole lot lousier than the men's. That's when I started to look around and see what was happening to other women, especially women in sports.

It didn't take long to discover that my own experiences weren't very different at all. I once received a really sad letter from a mother whose daughter had been ridiculed by their local newspaper because she'd had the audacity to say she wanted to be a professional athlete. I don't even remember this girl's particular sport, but it killed me to read both her mother's letter and the newspaper clip. It was just something else that made me realize a double standard has always existed for women, even in sports, where you might figure there'd be a little more tolerance. I've since read about studies proving that women athletes have to be much more success-oriented than men because there's so much more social pressure for us to overcome, and I know for a fact that's true. For years, women who played sports full time into their late twenties, or, God forbid, their early thirties, were considered tough, overly aggressive, probably had too many male genes, and were for sure failures at love—and unfortunately, that kind of stereotyping still goes on. It works the other way too, of course. Male dancers, actors, musicians and the like have the opposite problem, but I don't think it begins to compare. The barriers are slowly falling, and I'd like to think our pro tennis tour has had something to do with it, but the barriers are still there.

· · ·

I like being a career woman and I love being an athlete. I *love* it. But I'm not the only one. More and more women are proud of themselves for having chosen a tennis career, and I wish some of the other players, especially the younger ones who still say to me, "You tell 'em how you fell, Billie, and we'll follow," would come out and tell 'em themselves. I think if they did, if they just came out and shouted, "It makes me happy to be a professional athlete," that maybe it would help to erase the sexist thinking that unfortunately still says it's wrong for a woman to be playing tennis when she could be off raising a family somewhere.

There's simply less and less reason for any woman to tie herself down with marriage and kids if she doesn't want to, and in sports, I think we tennis players might have one of the best deals going anywhere. On a per-tournament basis, our prize money—$50,000—is now equal to men's World Championship Tennis tour, and through the Women's Tennis Association we've been able to help set minimum prize-money standards for other tournaments throughout the world. Sure, there's more overall money available to the men, but there are more men players too. Even that's changing, however. In 1971 there were just those original sixteen women on the Virginia Slims tour; this year, including qualifiers, there are well over 150. That more women are making tennis their lifelong careers (athletically speaking) is also measured by the interesting fact that the average age of the world's top ten players had jumped from not quite twenty-three in 1962 to just over twenty-seven by 1971—the first year of our tour.

· · ·

I think in the back of their minds my parents always figured that I would quit tennis early—I know that's what they hoped—even after I'd been to places like Wimbledon and Forest Hills a few times, and that I'd settle down and get married to someone who would take care of me for the rest of my life. For a long time, so did I. Remember that essay I wrote about

Wimbledon when I was fourteen? Here's the rest of it, when I thought way ahead and imagined my life at the age of forty-five.

> . . . Here I am at home twenty-seven years later sitting at home with my four wonderful children. (At times they're wonderful.) After that summer of '61 I entered Pomona college, in California, spending five years, and graduated with a Masters Degree. I married Ramsey Earnhart, remember that boy I met on the way to the plane that day? Even though I never did achieve my ambition in tennis, I'm so glad I went ahead and received a higher education than high school instead of turning out to be a tennis bum. . . .

Incredible, that's what my expectations were—college, marriage, retirement, kids—just the way my parents wanted. They've really had to adjust a lot to accept what I've become. Years later, when Larry was in law school and I was helping out with my earnings from my "amateur" tennis and later from the National Tennis League, my mother still kept telling me she'd never raised me to be a breadwinner. And even now, they both think I should have started in on those four kids and forgotten about the tennis entirely.

I could have gone either way, really, up until 1966, when I started playing full time, and if I'd married somebody besides Larry King I might well have had a more conventional life. But Larry was cool. It's really strange. When we first met, Larry honestly didn't even know I was a tennis player. He thought I was just another friend of Marcos Carriedo, his bridge-playing buddy who'd introduced us at Los Angeles State. He found out in a hurry though, and in a lot of ways he sensed my needs and desires as a tennis player even more fully than I did. Larry was also quick to see the connection between women's tennis and Women's Lib—that the changes I was trying to bring about in my profession were exactly the same as the changes women in other professions had been fighting for in theirs for years. I'm fortunate to be married to a guy like Larry, because a lot of the demands of my career certainly haven't made his life any easier, and I'm sure he realized almost from the start of our marriage that if he'd wound up with somebody else his life might have been a little calmer too.

. . .

. . . I'm honestly amazed sometimes by the way people react to me. I mean like especially after the excitement of that perfect night in Houston when I beat Bobby Riggs and just plain went over the top, I think, as a public figure. You wouldn't believe the number of people who have got to tell me exactly what they did, wherever they were, as they watched the match.

Like the women at Mount Holyoke College who clustered around a dormitory television set shouting, "Right on!" after practically every point.

Or the magazine editor, a woman, who was supposed to have dinner ready on the table but wound up at a party at *Ms* magazine—where Bella Abzug waved her floppy hat almost the whole night—and finally called her husband: "Dear . . . darling . . . Billie Jean's ahead. I won't be home until after the match."

Or, the group at a country club bar in South Carolina, mostly men, who actually stood up and applauded the TV set, the *TV set*, when I was finished with Bobby.

Sure, the match grabbed everybody, but people had been reacting to me very strongly long before that. It began, really, about the end of 1971, after the Virginia Slims circuit had been under way for almost a year. Women especially really started to look up to me then, I think because they realized how much the tour and I had fought to get where we were.

Dick Butera, the president of the Philadelphia Freedoms of World Team Tennis, keeps telling me I have an effect on people without even thinking about it, and I guess he's right. I know I'm in a close to unique position and combined with my constitutional let's-change-the-world attitude, it makes for pretty powerful medicine, but boy, sometimes it really makes me nervous.

Sometimes I'm totally amazed by the things that happen. About two weeks after I played Riggs, I went to the Philadelphia *Bulletin* for a press conference. I must have met everybody in the building, and I talked to most of them—just small talk, nothing serious. I found out later, though, that the morning after the match with Bobby several of the women there had stormed into their bosses' offices, and demanded raises on the spot. I couldn't believe it, but I thought it was great.

It's a funny feeling to know that women look up to me, but that's one of the ways Women's Lib has changed things. Women aren't ashamed of identifying with other women. It's always been all right for a guy to look up to another guy, but it's hardly ever been okay for a woman to look up to another woman, because we were taught that men were the only successful and wonderful people in the world. The big reason was probably a lack of examples, but I think we're getting a bunch of our own now.

It' a two-way street. Maybe women look up to me, and that's fine, but in the last couple of years especially I've really tried to talk with other women too. I've tried to find out about their lives and their problems, and I think I've learned a lot.

The two basic things I've learned are these: We women are all the same, in the sense that somewhere along the line we've just about all of us encountered some kind of sexist discrimination either in our careers or in our personal lives, and probably in both. Some of us have been lucky and have had either the opportunity or some kind of inner strength to fight back and make a little niche for ourselves. Most of us haven't been so fortunate, however, and that's why mutual support among women is so important. Because although things are changing, they're changing slowly, and it's a pretty good bet we're not going to get too much help from anybody except ourselves.

The other thing I've learned is that we women are all different in our desires and our expectations. One of us might want a career, another a family life, and still a third might want both. We might want to swing or we might not want to swing at all. The important thing is for us to be able to do our thing with respect and dignity, to be able to lead the fullest possible lives we can, and to find the center of ourselves.

Liberalized abortion laws? Yes. An end to Job discrimination? Of course. Equal pay for equal work? No question. But those are details. What really counts is for us to be able to fulfill our potential in whatever way we choose. And the awareness of that possibility, that right, is only the beginning; the achievement is the end.

Title IX and the Visible Woman Athlete

The last twenty-five years have marked a virtual revolution in American women's sport. The exploits and achievements of American woman sports figures from Joan Benoit Samuelson to Chris Evert are common knowledge among today's sports aficiandoes of both sexes. Sports pages list with equal attention the huge earnings of professional golf and tennis players of both sexes and television offers broad coverage as well. Between 1970 and 1977 alone, the number of girls involved in organized high-school sport rose from 300,000 to 2 million. The NCAA regularly holds national championship competition in 17 women's sports and has almost 1,000 college women's sports programs as members. Although financial support for women's programs still lags behind that given to male programs, in 1977 alone 460 colleges awarded over 10,000 athletic scholarships with a total value of $7 million to aspiring female athletes. It is even possible to read of cheating scandals and grade tampering among female athletes that would make Senda Berenson turn over in her grave. In terms of visibility, numbers, variety, competition, and even commercialization, women's sports have come a long way.

An important factor in this revolution was the enactment by the U.S. Congress of the Educational Amendments Act of 1972. A specific provision in the bill, usually referred to as Title IX, said that "no person, on the basis of sex, should be excluded from participation in any educational program or activity receiving federal financial assistance." Vague in description, Title IX sent shivers through male-dominated college athletic departments who feared this potential challenge to their power and to the traditionally preeminent place of male sports. After public outcry from such prominent figures such as former president Gerald Ford and Alabama football coach Bear Bryant that strict enforcement of the policy would mean the end of college football and American manhood and following a number of legal battles between women athletes and university administrations, in

1979, the Department of Health, Education, and Welfare issued guidelines for compliance of the Title IX that have encouraged increased women's participation in sport. The following article by Cheryl Fields, "What Colleges Must Do to Avoid Sex Bias in Sports," summarizes the meaning of the 1979 ruling for college sport. It first appeared in the December 10, 1979 edition of the *Chronicle of Higher Education* along with the actual guidelines, a portion of which also appear below. How do the regulations treat male and female athletes? What exceptions are allowed for unequal allocation of funds? Could this article and the regulations themselves have been written in 1890?

WHAT COLLEGES MUST DO TO AVOID SEX BIAS IN SPORTS

Colleges and universities must provide "proportionately equal" scholarships for their men's and women's athletic programs. And they must offer "equivalent" benefits and opportunities in other aspects of intercollegiate sports.

Those are the key requirements of a new "policy interpretation" issued by the Department of Health, Education, and Welfare to clarify the responsibilities of institutions of higher education to provide equal athletic opportunities under Title IX of the Education Amendments of 1972.

A third section of the interpretation says that compliance with the law will also be measured by how effectively the institutions identify and accommodate the athletic interests and abilities of both male and female students.

Title IX bars sex bias in federally assisted educational programs and activities. The application of that law to intercollegiate athletics has long been the most controversial aspect of the statute.

Reaction to the interpretation was mixed. Representatives of women's organizations generally indicated that they could live with the interpretation and that, as one representative put it, the "proof of the pudding" would be in how vigorously federal officials enforced it.

A spokesman for the National Collegiate Athletic Association said his group was "very concerned" about the section of the interpretation stating that colleges and universities would be judged partly on whether they made "proportionately equal amounts of financial assistance" available to male and female athletes.

Regulations that H.E.W. issued in 1975 to carry out Title IX required that "reasonable opportunities" for such aid be provided to each sex, but did not require "proportionality of dollars," said William D. Kramer, a lawyer for the N.C.A.A.

The new interpretation says "the total amount of scholarship aid made available to men and women must be substantially proportionate to their participation rates" in intercollegiate sports. Institutions could justify disparities, however, by showing they resulted from "legitimate, non-discriminatory factors."

Opposition to Califano's Proposal

A proposed policy interpretation published last fall by former H.E.W. Secretary Joseph A. Califano, Jr., prompted outraged opposition from many universities with costly big-time college football programs. Their opposition centered on a proposal to judge institutions on whether or not they spent "substantially equal per-capita" amounts on certain "financially measurable" benefits such as scholarships, recruitment, equipment, travel, and publicity.

The per-capita standard was dropped in the final interpretation— replaced by sections indicating that the department would look for "proportional" spending on athletic scholarships and "equivalent" spending on 11 other factors affecting equal opportunity for athletes—including recruitment, travel, provision of facilities, and provision and compensation of coaches and tutors.

Patricia R. Harris, Secretary of H.E.W., said she believed that after weighing the 700 written comments received on the proposed interpretation and consulting extensively with academic administrators, coaches, and other groups, her agency had produced "a sensible, flexible policy that clearly provides colleges and universities with the guidance they requested on how to comply with the athletic provisions of Title IX."

Along with the yardsticks by which compliance with the law will be measured, she noted at a news conference, the interpretation also lists examples of exceptions that will be made and circumstances under which colleges and universities may justify disparate expenditures on aspects of their men's and women's programs.

Some of the exceptions note the large, and costly, role played by intercollegiate football.

Differences Will Favor Men

For example, in a section stating that the department will assess whether institutions are providing "equivalent" benefits and opportunities in such areas as coaching, equipment, and provision of facilities, the interpretation notes:

Some aspects of athletic programs may not be equivalent for men and women because of unique aspects of particular sports or athletic activities."

"For the most part, differences involving such factors will occur in programs offering football, and consequently these differences will favor men. If sport-specific needs are met equivalently in both men's and women's programs, however, differences in particular program components will be found to be justifiable."

Secretary Harris added that policy interpretation "is not writ in stone."

Sensitivity in Changes

"This department will watch very carefully to make certain that the policy serves the positive helpful function it is intended to serve. You may rest assured that if it does not serve this purpose, and proves in any way to be unworkable, I will be the first to admit it and to change the policy accordingly," she said.

She cautioned, however, that as institutions work to change their programs, the department will expect that "they would do so with sensitivity and with recognition that such changes should result in enhancing—not minimizing—the role of women coaches and athletic directors, as well as women athletes, in sports programs."

The Secretary noted that the Supreme Court had recently refused to review some cases in which lower courts had ruled that Title IX did not apply to employment practices. That, she said, did not affect the department's obligation under Title IX to look at practices—such as the availability of coaching—that could affect the athletic opportunities available to female students.

Mrs. Harris indicated that she hoped institutions would comply voluntarily with the policy statement, but noted that 120 persons in the Office for Civil Rights would be involved in enforcing its provisions. Investigators will concentrate on resolving nearly 100 athletic-bias complaints that the department now has on file, Mrs. Harris said, but the agency also plans to conduct compliance-reviews at other institutions.

Jack W. Peltason, president of the American Council on Education, said the council had some concerns about how the interpretation would be applied. He said his organization would work with institutions and with H.E.W. "to see to it that the progress which has been made toward equality of opportunity for women in athletic programs continues in a manner that preserves institutional integrity."

'Almost 100 Years Later'

Secretary Harris said she expected no problems with enforcement of the policy interpretation after the responsibility for enforcing Title IX shifts to the new Department of Education.

The Secretary closed her news conference by displaying a photograph of the 1885 Wellesley College rowing team. Pointing to the female team members, clad in long, tight-waisted dresses, Mrs. Harris said, "This proves that women's interest in sports is not new. Almost 100 years later the government has agreed that women are entitled to equal opportunity in athletics."

[Actual guidelines of the ruling follow.]

1. *The Regulation.* The Regulation requires that recipients that operate or sponsor interscholastic, intercollegiate, club, or intramural athletics, "provide equal athletic opportunities for members of both sexes." In determining whether an institution is providing equal opportunity in intercollegiate athletics, the regulation requires the Department to consider, among others, the following factors:

(1) 86.41(c)(1) on the accommodation of student interests and abilities, is covered in detail in the following Section C of this Policy Interpretation: (2) provision and maintenance of equipment and supplies; (3) scheduling of game and practice times; (4) travel and per diem expenses; (5) opportunity to receive coaching and academic tutoring; (6) assignment and compensation of coaches and tutors; (7) provision of locker rooms, practice, and competitive facilities; (8) provision of medical and training services and facilities; (9) provision of housing and dining services and facilities; and (10) publicity.

Section 86.41(c) also permits the Director of the Office for Civil Rights to consider other factors in the determination of equal opportunity. Accordingly, this Section also addresses recruitment of student athletes and provision of support services.

This list is not exhaustive. Under the regulation, it may be expanded as necessary at the discretion of the Director of the Office for Civil Rights.

2. *The Policy.* The Department will assess compliance with both the recruitment and the general athletic program requirements of the regulation by comparing the availability, quality, and kinds of benefits, opportunities, and treatment afforded members of both sexes. Institutions will be in compliance if the compared program components are equivalent, that is, equal or equal in effect. Under this standard, identical benefits, opportunities, or treatment are not required, provided the overall effect of any differences is negligible.

If comparisons of program components reveal that treatment, benefits, or opportunities are not equivalent in kind, quality, or availability, a finding of compliance may still be justified if the differences are the result of nondiscriminatory factors. Some of the factors that may justify these differences are as follows:

a. Some aspects of athletic programs may not be equivalent for men and women because of unique aspects of particular sports or athletic activities. This type of distinction was called for by the "Javits' Amendment" to Title IX, which instructed H.E.W. to make "reasonable [regulatory] provisions considering the nature of particular sports" in intercollegiate athletics.

Generally, these differences will be the result of factors that are inherent to the basic operation of specific sports. Such factors may include rules of play, nature/replacement of equipment, rates of injury resulting from participation, nature of facilities required for competition, and the maintenance/upkeep requirements of those facilities. For the most part, differences involving such factors will occur in programs offering football, and consequently these differences will favor men. If sport-specific needs are met equivalently in both men's and women's programs, however, differences in particular program components will be found to be justifiable.

b. Some aspects of athletic programs may not be equivalent for men and women because of legitimately sex-neutral factors related to special circumstances of a temporary nature. For example, large disparities in recruitment activity for any particular year may be the result of annual fluctuations in team needs for first-year athletes. Such differences are justifiable to the extent that they do not reduce overall equality of opportunity.

c. The activities directly associated with the operation of a competitive event in a single-sex sport may, under some circumstances, create unique demands or imbalances in particular program components. Provided any special demands associated with the activities of sports involving participants of the other sex are met to an equivalent degree, the resulting differences may be found nondiscriminatory. At many schools, for example, certain sports—notably football and men's basketball—traditionally draw large crowds. Since the costs of managing an athletic event increase with crowd size, the overall support made available for event management to men's and women's programs may differ in degree and kind. These differences would not violate Title IX if the recipient does not limit the potential for women's athletic events to rise in spectator appeal and if the levels of event management support available to both programs are based on sex-neutral criteria (e.g., facilities used, projected attendance, and staffing needs).

d. Some aspects of athletic programs may not be equivalent for men and women because institutions are undertaking voluntary affirmative actions to overcome effects of historical conditions that have limited participation in athletics by members of one sex. This is authorized by Section 86.3(b) of the regulation.

[They continue.]

C. *Travel and Per Diem Allowances* [Section 86.41(c)(4)]. Compliance will be assessed by examining, among other factors, the equivalence for men and women of: (1) modes of transportation; (2) housing furnished during travel; (3) length of stay before and after competitive events; (4) per diem allowances; and (5) dining arrangements.

D. *Opportunity To Receive Coaching and Academic Tutoring [Section 86.41(c)(5)].* (1) Coaching—Compliance will be assessed by examining, among other factors: (a) relative availability of full-time coaches; (b) relative availability of part-time and assistant coaches; and (c) relative availability of graduate assistants. (2) Academic tutoring—Compliance will be assessed by examining, among other factors, the equivalence for men and women of: (a) the availability of tutoring; and (b) procedures and criteria for obtaining tutorial assistance.

E. *Assignment and Compensation of Coaches and Tutors* [Section 86.41(c)(6)]. In general a violation of Section 86.41(c)(6) will be found only where compensation or assignment policies or practices deny male and female athletes coaching of equivalent quality, nature, or availability.

Nondiscriminatory factors can affect the compensation of coaches. In determining whether differences are caused by permissible factors, the range and nature of duties, the experience of individual coaches, the number of participants for particular sports, the number of assistant coaches supervised, and the level of competition will be considered.

Where these or similar factors represent valid differences in skill, effort, responsibility or working conditions they may, in specific circumstances, justify differences in compensation. Similarly, there may be unique situations in which a particular person may possess such an outstanding record of achievement as to justify an abnormally high salary. (1) Assignment of coaches—Compliance will be assessed by examining, among other factors, the equivalence for men's and women's coaches of: (a) training, experience, and other professional qualifications; (b) professional standing. (2) Assignment of tutors—compliance will be assessed by examining, among other factors, the equivalence for men's and women's tutors of: (a) tutor qualifications; (b) training, experience, and other qualifications. (3) Compensation of coaches—Compliance will be assessed by examining, among other factors, the equivalence for men's and women's coaches of: ((a) rate of compensation (per sport, per season); (b) duration of contracts; (c) conditions relating to contract renewal; (d) experience; (c) nature of coaching duties performed; (f) working conditions; and (g) other terms and conditions of employment. (4) Compensation of tutors—Compliance will be assessed by examining, among other factors, the equivalance for men's and women's tutors of: (a) hourly rate of payment by nature of subjects tutored; (b) pupil loads per tutoring season; (c) tutor qualifications; (d) experience; (e) other terms and conditions of employment.

F. *Provision of Locker Rooms, Practice, and Competitive Facilities* [Section 86.41(c)(7)]. Compliance will be assessed by examining, among other factors, the equivalence for men and women of: (1) quality and availability of the facilities provided for practice and competitive events; (2) exclusivity of use of facilities provided for practice and competitive events; (3) availability of locker rooms; (4) quality of locker rooms; (5) maintenance of practice and competitive facilities; (6) preparation of facilities for practice and competitive events.

G. *Provision of Medical and Training Facilities and Services* [Section 86.41(c)(8)]. Compliance will be assessed by examining, among other factors, the equivalence for men and women of: (1) availability of medical personnel and assistance; (2) health, accident, and injury assistance coverage; (3) availability and quality of weight and training facilities; (4) availability and quality of conditioning facilities; and (5) availability and qualifications of athletic trainers.

H. *Provision of Housing and Dining Facilities and Services* [Section 86.41(c)(9)]. Compliance will be assessed by examining, among other factors, the equivalence for men and women of: (1) housing provided; (2) special services as part of housing arrangements (*e.g.*, laundry facilities, parking space, maid service).

I. *Publicity* [Section 86.41(c)(10)]. Compliance will be assessed by examining, among other factors, the equivalence for men and women of: (1) availability and quality of sports information personnel; (2) access to other publicity resources for men's and women's programs; and (3) quantity and quality of publications and other promotional devices featuring men's and women's programs.

4. *Application of the Policy—Other Factors [Section 86.41(c)]*

A. *Recruitment of Student Athletes.* The athletic recruitment practices of institutions often affect the overall provision of opportunity to male and female athletes. Accordingly, where equal athletic opportunities are not present for male and female students, compliance will be assessed by examining the recruitment practices of the athletic programs for both sexes to determine whether the provision of equal opportunity will require modification of those practices.

An Incomplete Revolution

Despite the real gains made by women since World War II, many people would argue that full equality still remains to be achieved. The failure to gain ratification of the Equal Rights Amendment is an obvious example of this point.

Disagreement among women themselves about their role and place underline as well that the process of achieving full equality is still incomplete. The following selection on women athletes from philosopher Paul Weiss' *Sport: A Philosophical Inquiry* (1969), indicates the persistence of certain attitudes about men and women that help explain why women's access to the world of sports and to the larger society is still at issue. What arguments and evidence does Weiss use to show that women athletes are different than their male counterparts in terms of physical attributes, athletic capabilities, and emotional and motivational impulses? Do you agree with his analysis as to why fewer women than men become athletes? In what ways, according to Weiss, is athletics good for women? How different are Weiss' views from those expressed by Berenson or King?

WOMEN AND MEN: A PHILOSOPHICAL INQUIRY

Amateurs and professionals differ in prospect and objective, and usually in experience and skill. They are to be sharply distinguished, without being prevented from playing together or against one another under controlled conditions. Women are not always so readily distinguishable from men, particularly when they are clothed, or when sex differences are not determined by an examination of their sexual organs, but by a microscopic study of the composition of their cells. Normally, though, we have less difficulty in distinguishing them from men than we have in distinguishing professionals from amateurs. What is far more difficult is the settlement of the question: are women athletes to be viewed as radically and incomparably different from men or as comparable with them, both as amateurs and as professionals?

Whatever difficulty we may have in identifying an individual as a man or a woman, athletic bodies have shown no hesitation in laying down conditions and rules which apply to one and not the other . . .

There is considerable justification for these decisions in the results of tests and studies which have been made on women by themselves and in comparison with men. Women have comparatively less muscular strength and lighter arms, do not use their muscles as rapidly, have a longer reaction time, faster heart rates, and achieve a smaller arm strength in relation to their weight than men do. Their bones ossify sooner, they have a narrower and more flexible shoulder girdle, smaller chest girth, and smaller bones and thighs. They also have wider and more stable knee joints, a heavier and more tilted pelvis, longer index fingers, and a greater finger dexterity. They have shorter thumbs, legs, feet, and arm length, a smaller thoracic cavity, smaller lungs, smaller hearts, lower stroke volumes, a smaller average height, lower blood pressure, fatigue more readily, and are more prone to injury. Their bodies are less dense and contain more fat; they have less bone mass, and throw differently.

Some women are outstanding athletes and have better records than most of the men involved in the sport. Some women have made better records in the Olympic Games than were previously made by men. But it is also true that when women compete in the same years with men, the women's records are not better than the men's. Marjorie Jackson won the 100 meter race in 1952 at eleven and one-half seconds, but the best time made in 1896 by a man was twelve seconds. In 1896 the best time for the men's 100 meter free style swimming race was one minute and twenty-two seconds, but in 1932 Helene Madison made the distance in one minute and six-tenths second. More spectacular advances are reported of Russian women in the shot-put and discus. That these and other women can more than match the records made by men in other years is understandable when we take account of the fact that women begin their athletic careers at an earlier age than they once did, that they are willing to practice for considerable periods, that they are benefiting from improved training methods, that they are using better equipment than they had previously, and that more of them are participating in contests and sports.

Women are unable to compete successfully with the best of men, except in sports which emphasize accuracy, skill, or grace—shooting, fancy skating, diving, and the like. Their bones, contours, musculature, growth rate, size, proportion, and reaction times do not allow them to do as well as men in sports which put a premium on speed or strength.

It is part of our cultural heritage to make an effort to avoid having women maimed, disfigured, or hurt. That is one reason why they do not usually engage in and are not officially allowed to compete in such contact sports as boxing, wrestling, football, and rugby, with inexplicable exceptions being made for karate and lacrosse. In the United States women gymnasts do not compete on the long horse, and since 1957 they do not perform on the flying rings, apparently because they there overstrain and injure themselves. A woman's shoulder girdle is different from a man's.

One way of dealing with these disparities between the athletic promise and achievements of men and women is to view women as truncated males. As such they could be permitted to engage in the same sports that men do (except where these still invite unusual dangers for them), but in foreshortened versions. That approach may have dictated the different rules which men and women follow in basketball, fencing, and field hockey. Where men have five players on a basketball team, women have six, and are not permitted to run up and down the court. Men fence with foils, the target of which is the torso ending with the groin lines, with épées, the target of which is the entire body, and with the sabre the target of which is the region above the waist, including the head and arms, but women fence only with foils and then at a target of which the lower limit is at the hip bones.

Women's field hockey, a most popular team sport, is played in two thirty-minute halves whereas the men play in two thirty-five minute halves.[5] The illustrations can be multiplied. But enough have been given to make the point that in a number of cases the performances of males can be treated as a norm, with the women given handicaps in the shape of smaller and sometimes less dangerous or difficult tasks.

Men and women can be significantly contrasted on the average and on the championship level as stronger and weaker, faster and slower. So far as the excellence of a performance depends mainly on the kind of muscles, bones, size, strength, that one has, women can be dealt with as fractional men. This approach has considerable appeal. It not only allows us to compare men and women, but to acknowledge that some women will be outstanding, and, given their handicaps, surpass the men. But we will then fail to do justice to the fact that there are men who are more like most women in relevant factors than they are like most men, and that there are women who are more like most men in these respects than they are like most women.

Simply scaling women in relation to men in terms only of their physical features and capacities, can lull us into passing over a number of important questions. Are women and men motivated in the same way? Do they have the same objectives? Is the team play of women comparable to that of men's? Negative answers to these questions need not blur the truth that men and women are of the same species, and that what is of the essence of human kind is therefore present in both. If it is of the nature of man to seek to become self-complete, both male and female will express this fact, but not necessarily in the same way. They may still face different problems and go along different routes. The very same prospects may be realized by both of them, but in diverse ways. Their characteristic desires give different expressions to a common drive; similar activities do not have the same import for both of them.

Comparatively few women make athletics a career, even for a short time, and fewer still devote themselves to it to a degree that men do. Many reasons for this fact have been offered. Social custom, until very recently, has not encouraged them to be athletes. Fear of losing their femininity plays some role. Also, the appeal of a social life quickly crowds out a desire to practice and train, particularly where this forces them to be alone and without much hope of being signally successful. Swimmers, champions at thirteen and fourteen, seem bored with competitive swimming as they move toward the twenties. But more important than any of these reasons seems to be the fact that a young woman's body does not challenge her in the way in which a young man's body challenges him. She does not have to

---

[5]On these see Frank G. Menke, *Encyclopedia of Sports* (New York, 1963), and Parke Cummings, ed. *The Dictionary of Sports* (New York, 1949).

face it as something to be conquered, since she has already conquered it in the course of her coming of age. Where a young man spends his time redirecting his mind and disciplining his body, she has only the problem of making it function more gracefully and harmoniously than it natively can and does.

Men are able to live in their bodies only if they are taught and trained to turn their minds into bodily vectors. And they can become excellent in and through their bodies, only if they learn to identify themselves with their bodies and what these do. Normal women do not have this problem, at least not in the acute form that it presents to the men. A woman's biological growth is part of a larger process in which, without training or deliberation, she progressively becomes one with her body. What a man might accomplish through will and practice after he has entered on his last period of biological growth, she achieves through a process of bodily maturation. By the time she passes adolescence she is able to live her body somewhat the way in which a male athlete lives his.

A woman starts with an advantage over the man in that she masters her body more effortlessly and surely than he does his. If he is to be one with his body, he must prevent his mind from continuing to venture according to its bent, and must make it into a director of the body. He, but not she, has to deal with the body as though it were somewhat resistant to a drive toward its own perfection, and needs to be restructured, redirected, and controlled so that it becomes as excellent as it can be. With less effort she becomes better coordinated and more unified than he; she does not have to turn her mind away from its own concerns to make it function on behalf of the body. It never, despite her genuine interest in intellectual matters and her flights of fancy, is long occupied with the impersonal and nonbodily.

A woman is less abstract than a man because her mind is persistently ordered toward bodily problems. Emotions, which are the mind and body interwoven intimately, are easily aroused in her as a consequence. There are times when she will give herself wholeheartedly to intellectual pursuits, and may then distinguish herself in competition with men. But easily, and not too reluctantly, she slips quite soon into a period when her mind functions on behalf of her body in somewhat the way in which a trained athlete's mind functions on behalf of his. A woman, therefore, will typically interest herself in sport only when she sees that it will enable her to polish what she had previously acquired without thought or effort.

The athlete becomes one with his body through practice. Competition in games continues his practice, and in addition offers him a means for measuring his achievements in comparison with those obtained by others, and by himself at previous time. No less than he, a woman wants and deserves to be measured too. By competing in games, she can learn where she stands. There she will discover just what she can bodily do and therefore what she is as a unified being. Usually, though, it is easier for her to judge herself by her attractiveness, and measure this in terms of its social effects. Where a man might be proud of his body, she is proud in her body; where he uses it, she lives it as a lure.

This account raises some hard questions. Why do not more women become athletes? Is it because they find that the advantage that they have in their comparatively easy and satisfying union with their bodies, makes athletic exertion and competition of not much interest? Is that why women athletes are often so young and stop their careers so soon? Why are not men, who have become one with their bodies, content with the result? Why do they go on to use that body, to identify themselves with equipment, to test themselves in contests, and to make themselves into representatives in games? Do they think of their attractiveness as too adventitious and episodic to be able to give them the kind of satisfaction they need? Why is not a good physique enough for all men or even for a good number of those who embark on an athletic career?

An almost opposite set of questions arises when we assume that biologic urge and social pressure tend to make men use an impersonal and women a personal measure of the success they achieve as embodied humans. Why do some men avoid all athletics? Why is it that some women follow an athletic career? It is too easy an answer, and one not apparently supported by the facts, to say that neither is normal. Many a man appears well adjusted, healthy, happy, and admired, despite the fact that he participates in no sport. Many women athletes are attractive; some are married; some have children. We beg our question when we assume that women athletes are men *manqúe*, females without femininity, a fact supposedly evidenced by their devotion to an athletic career; we beg it, too, when we assume that nonathletic men are emasculated males, a fact supposedly evidenced by their unconcern with athletic matters.

If perfection can be achieved through the use of a perfected body, one should expect that women would want to compete with their peers. The fact that most do not, cannot be altogether ascribed to the social demands that are made on their bodies and their time. They are not biologic and social puppets. If they were, must we not also say that men are puppets as well, and that they do not devote themselves, as women do, to the task of making themselves attractive, because this is not a socially respectable goal for them? And what should we say then of those who withstand the pressures? Do they alone have a free will enabling them to counter what the others are driven to do? But a free will is not an adventitious feature, like hair, or bow legs, or a snub nose, resident in only some humans; if some women and men have will enough to withstand natural forces, surely all the others have it too, and might be expected to exercise it.

It is sometimes said that women feel challenged by men and yet know that they are not strong enough to overcome them through force. Their best recourse is to try a different route. This is an old story, told again and again in song, play, and novel, and for that reason alone should give us pause. From this perspective, the woman athlete is seen to be at a disadvantage in comparison with men, and must try to become equal or to prove herself superior to them by deception or flattery, or by disorienting them or taking advantage of their weaknesses. But she can also be taken to suppose that she is suffering from an unfair disadvantage, and must strive first to put herself in the position where her biological and social status is on a footing with his. The first of these alternatives sees women as inescapably inferior beings who compensate through wiles for what they cannot obtain through open competition; the second takes her to be disadvantaged and the disadvantages are to be overcome by discipline and determination. Neither alternative is satisfactory; neither takes adequate account of the joy, the devotion, the dedication, and the independence of spirit exhibited by many women athletes, their concentration on their own game, and their indifference to what the men are doing.

Training and practice can be friendless and boring. A sport such as skiing leaves one much alone. Nevertheless, there are women who train and practice; others ski in competitions with great intensity. While making enormous efforts and sacrifices to become highly skilled, they refuse to obscure the fact that they are women. They emphasize their femininity. It would be obviously wrong to say that they reject their sex or that they are less feminine than non-athletic women. It is no less incorrect to say that they train, practice, and perform only in order to ensnare or to show themselves to be the equal of men.

A woman must train and practice if she is to become an athlete. This demands that she make an effort to stand away from her body. The result she obtained through biological maturation she must for a while defy.

Most women do not make the effort to train or to participate because they are not subject to the tensions that young men suffer—tensions resulting from the discrepancy in the ways in which their minds and bodies tend to be disposed; the women have already achieved a satisfying integration of mind and body. Nevertheless, women can improve the functioning of their bodies. This is best done through exercise. And it can be helped through a vital participation in games.

A woman who wants to be an athlete must, for the time being, stand away from her body in preparation for the achievement of a different kind of union than that which she naturally acquired, and then must work at reaching the stage at which a man normally is. He starts with a separated mind and body; she must produce this before she can enter on an athletic career. She has to make a sacrifice of a natural union before she begins her athletic career, while he must for a while sacrifice only the pursuit of merely intellectual matters.

A man, of course, has achieved some union of mind and body, but it is not as thorough as a woman's normally is; she, of course, has had her intellectual moments and has found them desirable, but they do not last as long nor come as frequently as his do. Embarked on their athletic careers, both must make similar sacrifices of time and interest in other tempting activities. But some of them—security, a family, and a home—appeal to the woman more strongly and at an earlier age than they appeal to the man, and as a consequence she is prone to end her athletic career sooner than he.

Comparatively few women interest themselves in sport, and when they do they rarely exhibit the absorption and concern that is characteristic of large numbers of men. They do not have as strong a need as men to see just what it is that bodies can do, in part because they are more firmly established in their roles as social beings, wives, and mothers, than the men are in their roles as workers, business men, husbands and fathers, or even as thinkers, leaders, and public figures.

The number of people who give themselves wholeheartedly to an athletic career is not large. More men do so than women, but not enough to make the women who do have the shape of aberrational beings who are to be accounted for by means of a distinct set of principles. Both women and men seek to be perfected. But a woman finds that her acceptance of her matured body, promoted by her carrying out biological and social functions, offers a readily available and promising route by which the perfection can be reached.

Team play does not have much of an appeal to most women. The contests women enter are usually those in which they function as individuals alongside one another. Women are evidently more individualistic in temper, more self-contained than men. They live their own bodies while men spend their time and energy on projects, some of which demand team work.

Like men, women inevitably represent something other than themselves, and in the last resort, like men, represent man as such and at his best, given such and such a nature and such and such rules determining how he is to perform. But despite their status as a member of some team, and as a representative of all of us, women do not normally assume a role which is carried out in the light of the way in which others carry out their roles. They do not readily function as teammates.

There are, of course, exceptions. Women make good partners in tennis, and good members of teams in field hockey, basketball, and lacrosse. These exceptions do not belie a general tendency of women to perform as individuals. That tendency is supported by the fact that team sports invite undesirable injuries, and the fact that a woman's acceptance of her body, gradually intensified as she develops, encourages an individualistic outlook. This persists even when she makes a strong effort to abstract from her natural bodily condition and tries to identify herself with her body in the way male athletes identify with theirs.

Considerations such as these make desirable a distinctive approach the problem of how to interest women in athletics. Apparently, they must be made to see that it is good to separate oneself from one's body for a while in order better to unite with it later. One must make evident to them that the later union is a better union but of the same kind as that which they natively acquired. Some young women have been able to see that this is a truth which gymnastics, swimming, diving, skating, and skiing sustain; other sports could be similarly supported.

Once women have decided to engage in athletic activities they must, like men, train and practice; otherwise they cannot hope to do well. Their training follows the same general procedures followed by men, with account, of course, being taken of their difference in musculature, strength, and attitudes toward exhaustion injury, and public display. Since they do differ from men in these regards, there should be sports designed just for them, enabling them to make maximal use of their distinctive bodies. Thought should be given to the woman's lower center of gravity, her greater flexibility in the shoulders, girdle, and fingers, to her greater stability in the knee joints, and to her greater heat resistance, if we are to give her opportunities for attaining a degree of excellence comparable to that attained by men, and this without taking her to be a fractional male. Though basketball was not designed to take advantage of neglected muscles or organs, but merely to provide an opportunity for men to play in summer and winter, with a minimum amount of easily available equipment, etc., it testifies to the truth that a sport can be a fresh creation, made to satisfy definite purposes. Other new sports could be created; some of these should be built around the use of a woman's body. The rules that govern women's games, particularly those involving teams, today often pay attention to what women can do and what they wish to avoid. Still further rules could be introduced which promote the perfecting of women, by making it possible for them to use their distinctive bodies in distinctive ways.

The sports we have today are heterogeneous. They do not explore every side of the human body; they are not grounded in an understanding of the main bodily types. More often than not, they are accidental products of history, slowly modified to take advantage of various innovations and to avoid discovered limitations. It is not likely that they are now in the best possible form for men; foreshortened versions cannot be expected to be altogether appropriate to women.

Apart from softball and what is called women's lacrosse, thinking about women's athletics has tended to emphasize gracefulness, accuracy, and coordination, particularly in those sports where some attempt is made to avoid imitating the men. There is an inclination to treat their sports as developments and extensions of the dance. Part of the reason for this, undoubtedly, is our socially inherited view of women's capacity and function; another part is traceable to the fact that women have come into educational institutions and public activities in only comparatively recent times; a third reason is the firm conviction that women should be graceful rather than strong or swift. It is also true that thinking about women's athletics has been characterized by a singular lack of imagination, inventiveness, and concern.

Little choice has been given to women to do more than dance or to adapt the sports which men pursue. Rarely has there been an attempt made to observe and objectively measure what they do. Even in those educational institutions reserved for them, the needs of women are not given the attention they deserve. Women's high schools and colleges often yield to the temptation to become vocational schools preparing women for an eventual career as homemakers and mothers, as though it were the task of an educational institution to prepare students for the kind of lives previous generations led, or which most of the students will most likely lead. The institutions seem to have forgotten that it is their task to promote the self-discovery, the awakening of interests, the extending of the imagination, the civilizing of students, to set them on the way toward becoming enriched, matured beings.

Calisthenics and gymnastic programs, long ago pushed aside in men's schools, still find a large and sometimes a primary place in the physical education of women. Calisthenics is exercise without equipment; gymnastics is exercise making use of equipment; both have as their objective the promotion of all-round development, and perhaps gracefulness. They are thought to be ideal means for making the body healthy and well-coordinated. Their practitioners sometimes compete with one another in exhibition. In contests and games, calisthenics and gymnastics have at best only a minor, incidental role. They may, of course, be mastered as part of an athletic training course, aimed at the production of a different type of result. But then they are used only to make the body fit to engage in contest or game which is not covered by a calisthenic or gymnastic program.

The gymnastic programs in vogue today are largely combinations of the German, French, and Swedish. The Germanic strain emphasizes strength, the French gracefulness, and the Swedish mechanical precision. Once, each of these was pursued independently, under rigid codes, with set exercises and well-defined steps and stages. Around the turn of the century all were forced to give way to a "natural" gymnastics which concentrated on the development of the entire body. The large place such a program continues to have in women's school confirms the view that women are thought to have a matured and accepted body, and that they need only to polish it.

"Gymnastics" comes from the Greek. Its literal meaning is "engaging in exercise nakedly." The Romans disapproved of the nakedness. We have continued to follow the Romans, but with some appreciation of the French gracefulness and the Swedish precision.

In the end, the very devotion to the cause of making fine bodies defeated the gymnastic programs from remaining in a dominant position in the men's colleges. Once given the chance to train for games, students revolted against doing set exercises as ends in themselves. They found them to be tedious, repetitive, meaningless.

Today, fitness programs are being reintroduced for men. This may lead to a welcome reintroduction of strong gymnastic programs for them, parallel to those now supported in women's colleges. Men will perhaps return to them again, once they see gymnastics as not only making possible a better participation in games, but as enabling them to become splendid incarnated beings.

A game is a sequence of turning points, each of which must be dealt with appropriately if the activity is to terminate successfully. At each moment the player shows what he has mastered and what still remains to be done. Having dedicated himself to the task of doing all he can, he then finds that he must bring to bear all his power and emotional capital to achieve the best results. The participation forces him to make and live through the crucial decisions, and possibly add to his skills. The benefits are not predicated on his sex. Women, too, should be prompted to train, to prepare, to practice, so as to be ready to test themselves in relation to others, and thereby discover how excellent they have made themselves become.

A decent and civilized man controls his body along the lines required by society, a well-mannered man controls his body along the lines of convention, and an intellectual controls his body to enable himself to concentrate on other matters, while an athlete controls his body so as to be able to identify himself with his equipment, and to master the obstacles that confront him. This last opportunity is denied to women when they are not provided with sports that are regulated and programmed to their structures and rhythms.

One of the aims of a good athletic program is the development and intensification of good character. With the growth of professionalism in the schools, it has been cynically remarked that character building is the most that coaches of losing teams can produce. Were that true it would be enough. Character building justifies an emphasis on athletics in the high schools and colleges. And it is no less needed by women than it is by men. They, too, can profitably learn how to meet crises, how to withstand fear, and where to draw the line between self-indulgence and excessive restraint. And they can learn these things effectively, as men now do, in the gymnasium and on the field. Because the building of character is one of the tasks of education, both women and men should be given the opportunity to prepare themselves for vigorous participation in relevant sports.

Character is built by engaging in limited, well-controlled acts. By imitating what had been splendidly done in the large, the young are helped to grow. We then teach them how to make a proper estimate of who they are and what they can do, by promoting their correct assessment of when and where they are to advance and retreat. Like other virtues, assessment is habit; like all habits, it is strengthened through repetition. A game allows for its manifestation and provides additional opportunities to entrench it further.

The adoration of the crowds, of the young, and of girls, can make a male athlete misconstrue just what he has achieved, what he is yet to achieve, who he is, and what he might become. The virtues which he painfully acquired in practice are then muted and sometimes distorted; he begins to lose focus and to misunderstand the nature of sport. Women are fortunate in that few of their games come to the attention of the public; they are thereby enabled to avoid most of the misconstructions which beset male athletes. But it is also true that men have in their games a unique opportunity to show what they can do under well-specified, controlled, yet trying circumstances. Men are normally put to tests much more difficult than women face, and as a consequence are able to attain heights denied to them.

The comparative neglect of team sports by women entails that they have fewer opportunities to see themselves as needing to work on behalf of the rest, to make sacrifices for others with whom they share a common objective, and to function in coordinated roles. Because they have fewer occasions when they can carry out difficult tasks together with other players, they do not have the opportunity to master specialized skills, or to know the kind of bodily mastery which others have achieved and of which they make effective use.

Women need to be disciplined and self-disciplined, trained and self-trained, both as individuals and as members of groups. They should have the right and the privilege of contributing in judgment, skill, and imagination to the making of a distinguished game. They, too, have need for and deserve to be suffused with the pleasure that comes from a game well played. They, too, can gain by belonging to something bigger than themselves, such as a tradition-bound sport.

Even when women have little aptitude or interest, they can profit from athletic activity. Physical fitness and bodily tone are thereby usually improved. The women most likely will become healthier, perhaps more graceful, and gain some sense of the fair play that proper playing demands. They might thereby become better adjusted to themselves and to others.

Maladjustment is a form of illness. He who is inharmonious is not well. The movement from the state of being ill to that of being well is therapy or cure. Athletics, because it enables one to move from a poor to a better state of being, can be viewed as a branch of medicine, but one which fortunately finds room for the expression of spontaneity, ingenuity, and judgment. Sport is, of course, not to be treated as primarily an agency for promoting health—or anything else for that matter—regardless of how important this is. Sport is an end in itself. One can become perfected by engaging in it, but it does not have even that perfection as its aim. Perfection is an inevitable consequence of sport only when this is properly pursued in an enclosed arena where men and women find out what man can bodily be. If health is also achieved, so much the better.

Athletes run the risk of overexerting themselves. They expose themselves to strain and the possibility of injury, with a consequent lessened tolerance to disease. Appetites are developed in training which continue to be insistent later, making an accumulation of fat more likely, and, therefore, shorter breath and conceivably a shorter life expectancy. There is a proneness to accidents, particlarly when challenging and unpredictable situations have to be faced with quick decisions and appropriate action. An error can scar a life, psychologically and emotionally as well as physically. No one likes to see women subjected to these risks. Still, a risk is not yet a failure. Women need to risk more; only if they do, can they hope to gain all that is possible for them.

A well-trained athlete can rightly expect to engage in sport throughout his life, providing that he so alters his interests, intentions, and efforts that he can keep abreast of changes in his age and physical condition. There is no reason why a woman should not be able to continue in a similar way, and maintain a trim, firm body, suffused with a desirable tone, for an indefinite period. If her athletic potentialities are taken with as much seriousness as a man's, it will become more evident than it now is that sport concerns not only males but mankind, and deserves to be viewed as a basic enterprise, devoted to the production of the excellent in and through the body.

General discourse of this sort deals with idealized types of men and women, and is rooted in speculations for which there is little empirical warrant. Its primary justification is that it opens up possibilities for investigation and may help one focus on issues otherwise slurred over. To some degree it rests on the observation that young men's energies overflow to an extent that the energies of women of the same age do not. Young men are restless and exuberant; vigorous action seems natural to them, while women are content to move smoothly, using their energies to improve the union of body and mind that is natural to them.

Sport is a young person's most promising opening into excellence. Unfortunately, no one has a clear and well-substantiated knowledge as to what a career devoted to sport exactly imports for either men or women.

Most of what is claimed for it today is the product of rapid empirical summaries, not a little prejudice and hope, and some limited experiments. We would be on surer ground if we knew how to compare what was done in one sport with what was done in another, and how the various sports were related to one another, for we would then be able to place them all before us and see what they, severally and together, might mean for all, professionals as well as amateurs, women as well as men.

BIBLIOGRAPHY

Suggestions for Further Reading

A growing popular and scholarly literature concerning American sport history exists. This brief list presents selections that provide interesting discussions of developments and issues raised in the primary documents you have been reading.

General

The best survey of American sport history is Benjamin G. Rader, *American Sports: From the Age of Folk Games to the Age of the Spectator* (Englewood Cliffs, N.J.: Prentice-Hall, 1982). Also useful are Betty Spears and Richard A. Swanson, *History of Sport and Physical Activity in the United States* (Dubuque: William C. Brown, 1978) and John A. Lucas and Ronald A. Smith, *Saga of American Sports* (Philadelphia: Lea and Febiger, 1978). Allen Guttman, *From Ritual to Record: The Nature of Modern Sports* (New York: Columbia University Press, 1978) provides an interesting interpretation of the meaning of modern sport.

The Colonial Experience, 1609-1776

Dennis Brailsford, *Sport and Society: Elizabeth to Anne* (London: Routledge and Kegan Paul, 1969) explains English Puritan concerns over participation in sport. Nancy Struna, "Puritans and Sport: The Irretrievable Tide of Change," *Journal of Sport History*, 4 (Spring, 1977) 1-21 continues the story in the American context. Jane Carson, *Colonial Virginians at Play* (Charlottesville: University Press of Virginia, 1965) catalogues the various ways in which Americans participated in physical activity in colonial Virginia. Timothy Breen, "Horses and Gentlemen: The Cultural Significance of Gambling Among the Gentry of Virginia," *William and Mary Quarterly* 34 (April, 1977), 329-47 offers a provocative if not always convincing interpretation of aristocratic Virginians love for horseracing.

The Promise of Sport, 1776-1865

Jennie Holliman, *American Sports, 1785-1835* (Durham, N.C.: Seeman Press, 1931) provides a catalogue of physical activities that nineteenth century Americans engaged in while Peter Levine, "The Promise of Sport in Antebellum America," *Journal of American Culture*, 2 (Winter, 1980), 623-34 offers an explanation of the ways in which middle-class white Americans justified such use of leisure time. Also useful for understanding the reasons why different groups of Americans found both pleasure and purpose in participation in sport are Benjamin Rader, "Quest for Subcommunities and the Rise of American Sport," *American Quarterly*, 29 (Fall, 1977), 355-69, Roberta J. Park, "Embodied Selves:" The Rise and Development of Concern for Physical Education, Active Games and Recreation for American Women, 1776-1865, *Journal of Sport History*, 5 (Summer, 1978), 5-41; and Gerald Redmond, *The Caledonian Games in Nineteenth Century America* (Rutherford, N.J.: Fairleigh Dickinson University Press, 1971). Dale A. Somers, *The Rise of Sports in New Orleans, 1850-1900* (Baton Rouge: Louisiana State University Press, 1972) offers an interesting study of the development of sport in an urban southern setting while Melvin Adelman, *A Sporting Time: New York City and the Rise of Modern Athletics, 1820-1870* (Urbana: University of Illinois Press, 1986) does the same for New York. Elliot Gorn, *The Manly Art: Bare-Knuckle Prize Fighting in America* (Ithaca: Cornell University Press, 1986) is a provocative and exciting book about the significance of boxing for understanding questions of class and gender in nineteenth century America. Harold Seymour, *Baseball: The Early Years* (New York, Oxford University Press, 1960) and David Voigt, *American Baseball: From Gentleman's Sport to the Commissioner System* (Norman: University of Oklahoma Press, 1966) provide the best overall accounts of the early history of baseball down to the twentieth century.

The Emergence of Modern Sport, 1865-1910

Donald Mrozek, *Sport and American Mentality, 1880-1910* (Knoxville: University of Tennessee Press, 1983) offers the most comprehensive understanding of the emergence of modern sport in late nineteenth century America. Similar concern with a particular emphasis on baseball, the middle-class and the role of the entrepreneur can be found in Peter Levine, *A.G. Spalding and the Rise of Baseball: The Promise of American Sport* (New York: Oxford University Press, 1985). Roy Rosenzweig, *Eight Hours For What We Will: Workers and Leisure in an Industrial City, 1870-1920* (London and New York, Cambridge University Press, 1983) and David Nasaw, *Children of the City: At Work and At Play* (New York: Doubleday, 1985) underline the significant contributions of working-class immigrants and their children to the development of modern sport and leisure. Less analytical is Robert A. Smith, *A Social History of the Bicycle: Its Early Life and Times in America* (New York: American Heritage, 1972). Stephen Hardy, *How Boston Played: Sport Recreation and Community, 1865-1915* (Boston: Northeastern University Press, 1982) covers the gamut of sporting experience in one urban setting. Randy Roberts, *Papa Jack: Jack Johnson and the Era of White Hopes* (New York, Free Press, 1983) places the career and personality of this great champion in the context of the racist times in which he lived.

Twentieth Century Sport: The Business of Sport

Benjamin Rader, *In Its Own Image: How Television Has Transformed Sports* (New York: Free Press, 1984) and William O. Johnson, Jr., *The Super Spectator and the Electric Lilliputians* Boston: Little Brown, 1971) both detail the impact of television on the commercialization of sport. Lee Lowenfish and Tony Lupien, *The Imperfect Diamond: The Story of Baseball's Reserve System and the Men Who Fought to Change It* (New York: Stein and Day, 1980) traces the reserve rule and the challenge to it from the 1870s to 1980. Also of interest is Steven A. Riess, *Touching Base: Professional Baseball and American Culture in the Progressive Era* (Westport, Conn.: Greenwood, 1980). Harold Seymour, *Baseball: The Golden Age* (New York: Oxford University Press, 1971) and David Voigt, *American Baseball: From the Commissioners to Continental Expansion* (Norman: University of Oklahoma Press, 1970) both place the story of labor-capital relations in the broader context of baseball's growth as sport and business. David Halberstam, *The Breaks of the Game* (New York: Alfred A. Knopf, 1981) provides comparable analysis for professional basketball by following the Portland Trailblazers for one season. Joseph Durso, *The Sports Factory: An Investigation into College Sports* (New York: Quadrangle/New York Times, 1975) offers an overview of the problems of big-time intercollegiate athletics. David Wolf, *Foul! The Connie Hawkins Story* (New York: Warner Books, 1972) documents the exploitation of a young black Brooklyn basketball player who overcame a number of obstacles in establishing himself as one of the game's best. Stanley Cohen, *The Game They Played* (New York: Farrar, Straus and Giroux, 1977) details the college basketball scandals of 1950-51 with a particular focus on the City College of New York basketball team.

Twentieth Century Sport: Race and Sport

Jack Olsen, *The Black Athlete: A Shameful Story* (New York: Time-Life Books, 1968) focuses on the exploitation of the black college athlete. Robert Peterson, *Only the Ball Was White* (Englewood-Cliffs, N.J.: Prentice-Hall, 1970) tells the story of the

Negro Leagues while Donn Rogosin, *Invisible Men: Life in Baseball's Negro Leagues* (New York: Atheneum, 1983), based extensively on interviews with former ball-players, also provides an engrossing account of black baseball before Jackie Robinson broke the "color line." Roger Kahn, *The Boys of Summer* (New York: Harper and Row, 1971) places Robinson in the context of Brooklyn Dodgers and the city in which he played. Jules Tygiel, *Baseball's Great Experiment: Jackie Robinson and His Legacy* (New York: Oxford University Press, 1983) goes even further in a rich account that assesses Robinson's impact on the Civil Rights Movement of the 1950s and 1960s. Harry Edwards, *The Revolt of the Black Athlete* (New York: The Free Press, 1969) offers an activist's account of black protest and proposals for change. William Baker, *Jesse Owens, An American Life* (New York: The Free Press, 1986) analyzes the career of one of the world's greatest track athletes in engrossing fashion. Bill Russell and Taylor Branch, *Second Wind: Memoirs of an Opinionated Man* (New York: Random House, 1979) and Arthur Ashe and Neil Admur, *Off the Court* (New York: New American Library, 1981) offer insights about the situation of blacks in American society from two outstanding men—the dominant center for the Boston Celtics and one of the world's best tennis players of the last quarter century.

Twentieth Century Sport: The Politics of Sport

John J. MacAloon, *This Great Symbol: Pierre de Coubertin and the Origins of the Modern Olympic Games* (Chicago: The University of Chicago Press, 1981) describes the origins of the modern games while John Lucas, *The Modern Olympic Games* (New York: A.S. Barnes, 1980) and William O. Johnson, Jr., *All That Glitters Is Not Gold: The Olympic Games* (New York: Putnam's, 1972) provide extended historical accounts. Richard Mandell, *The Nazi Olympics* (New York: Macmillan, 1971) clearly demonstrates Hitler's attempts to politicize the Olympics. Richard Espy, *The Politics of the Olympic Games* (Berkeley: University of California Press, 1979) provides an overview of such activity in post World War II Olympics. Serge Groussard, *The Blood of Israel: The Massacre of the Israeli Athletes* (New York: William Morrow, 1975) grimly recounts the murder of the Israeli Olympic team by Palestinian terrorists at the 1972 Munich games. Robert Lipsyte, *Sportsworld: An American Dreamland* (New York: Quadrangle/New York Times, 1975) offers an intelligent and readable discussion of sport and politics. Paul Hoch, *Rip Off the Big Game: The Exploitation of Sports by the Power Elite* (Garden City, N.Y.: Anchor Books, 1972), Jack Scott, *The Athletic Revolution* (New York: The Free Press, 1971), and Richard Lipsky, *How We Play The Game: Why Sports Dominate American Life* (Boston: Beacon Press, 1981) are also of interest. For the connection between sport and the racial politics of apartheid see Richard Lapchick, *The Politics of Race and International Sport* (Westport, Conn.: Greenwood Press, 1972).

Twentieth Century Sport: Women and Sport

Ellen W. Gerber, et al., *The American Woman in Sport* (Reading, Mass.: Addison-Wesley, 1974) and Carol A. Oglesby, ed. *Women and Sport: From Myth to Reality* (Philadelphia: Lea and Febiger, 1978) offer interesting collections of articles on the subject. Especially useful is Stephanie Twin, ed., *Out of the Bleachers: Writings on Women and Sport* (Old Westbury, N.Y.: Feminist Press, 1979) which contains first person accounts of women athletes and an excellent introductory historical essay by the author. Babe Didrickson Zaharias, *This Life I've Led* (New York: A.S. Barnes, 1955) and William Oscar Johnson and Nancy P. Williamson, *"Whatta-Gal": The Babe Didrickson Story* (Boston: Little, Brown, 1977) recount the story of this extraordinary woman.

In addition to the sources listed on page ii, the following are gratefully acknowledged:

"NFL TV Pact $2 Billion" is Copyright © 1982 by The New York Times Company. Reprinted by permission.

"The Legacy of Curt Flood" is reprinted by permission of © *Sport Magazine*, 1977 and Stu Black.

"The Student Athlete" is Copyright © 1979 by The New York Times Company. Reprinted by permission.

Excerpts from *I Know Why the Caged Bird Sings*, by Maya Angelou is Copyright © 1969 by Maya Angelou. Reprinted by permission of Random House, Inc.

"Talk About Doctors Instead of Athletes" is Copyright © 1977 by The New York Times Company. Reprinted by permission.

"I Never Had It Made" is reprinted by permission of Mrs. Jackie Robinson and Mr. Al Duckett.

"The Olympic Project for Human Rights: An Assessment Ten Years Later" is reprinted by permission of *The Black Scholar*.

"Five Ways to Reform the Olympics" is Copyright © 1976 by The New York Times Company. Reprinted by permission.

"The Varsity Syndrome" is reprinted from *Varsity Syndrome* by Robert Lipsyte in volume no. 445 (Sept. 1979) of The Annals of The American Academy of Political and Social Science.

Excerpt from BILLIE JEAN by Billie Jean King. Copyright © 1974 by Billie Jean King. Reprinted by permission of Harper & Row Publishers, Inc.

"What College Must Do To Avoid Sex Bias In Sports" is reprinted by permission of *The Chronicle of Higher Education*.

"Sport: A Philosophical Inquiry, by Paul Weiss. Copyright © 1969 by Southern Illinois University Press. Reprinted by permission of the publisher.

INDEX